Struggles for Liberation in Abya Yala

Edited by

Luis Rubén Díaz Cepeda

and

Ernesto Rosen Velásquez

WILEY Blackwell

Library of Congress Cataloging-in-Publication Data applied for:
Paperback ISBN: 9781394181230

Cover Design: Wiley
Cover Images: Courtesy of Mara I Ayala

Set in 10/12.5pt Photina by Straive, Pondicherry, India

SKY10070666_032424

Contents

Notes on Contributors   v

Introduction   1
Ernesto Rosen Velásquez and Luis Rubén Díaz Cepeda

Section I   Theoretical Approaches   9

1   Liberation Philosophy and the Search for Combative Decoloniality:
A Fanonian Approach   11
Nelson Maldonado-Torres

2   Decolonizing Understanding: A Utopian Reading of Aníbal Quijano's
Coloniality of Power and Knowledge   29
Alejandro Vallega

3   Transmodernity as a Postulate: First Eurocentrism, Prejudice, and Critique   43
Enrique Téllez Fabiani

Section II   Gender   59

4   Reflections on the Erotics of Liberation: A Contemporary, Feminist Latin American
Perspective   61
AFyL Women Collective

5   Sylvia Wynter's Gender and Genre for a Queer and Trans-inclusive Politics   73
Elisabeth Paquette

Section III   Education   85

6   Struggles to Make Black Lives Matter   87
Ernesto Rosen Velásquez

7   In the Trap of Critique: Making Decolonization Metaphor   105
Stephanie Rivera Berruz

8   Education in Latin America: Decolonization as an Ethical–Political Urgency   116
Nadia Heredia

9   Philosophy of Liberation Praxis in Mexico City   127
Gabriel Herrera Salazar

Section IV   Social Movements   **139**

10   Experiences of Weaving: The Chilean Social Revolt as an Esthetic Proposal   141
Paloma Griffero

11   Migration Justice in Times of Pandemics in the Borderland of Ciudad Juárez/El Paso   161
Luis Rubén Díaz Cepeda

12   Latin American Animal Ethics   173
Iván Sandoval-Cervantes and Amy Reed-Sandoval

13   Zapata Revisited: Views on the Zapatista National Liberation Army   182
Ernesto Castañeda

14   Decolonizing Peyote Politics in Mexico and Southwest U.S.   197
Osiris Sinuhé González Romero

Index   211

Notes on Contributors

AFyL Women Collective is a group of *compañeras* from diverse territories and disciplines throughout Latin America who are part of the Philosophy of Liberation school of thought. Their objective has been to trace the contributions and categories that are fundamental to produce theory and politics from their own experience and testimony as Latin American feminist women. They also seek to walk together as they move toward the production of a feminist perspective in the philosophy of liberation.

Ernesto Castañeda is director of the Immigration Lab, and the Center for Latin American and Latino Studies at American University in Washington, DC. Among other books, he is the author of Building Walls: Excluding Latin People in the United States (Lexington Books 2019), Social Movements 1768–2018 with Charles Tilly and Lesley Wood (Routledge 2020), and co-editor with Cathy L. Schneider of Collective Violence, Contentious Politics, and Social Change: A Charles Tilly Reader (Routledge 2017/UNAM 2022).

Osiris Sinuhé González Romero earned his PhD at Leiden University, in the Faculty of Archaeology—Heritage of Indigenous Peoples. In 2015, he was awarded the Coimbra Group Scholarship for Young Professors and Researchers from Latin American Universities. González Romero taught undergraduate courses in the Faculty of Philosophy at UNAM. He is a postdoctoral fellow on cognitive liberty and the psychedelic humanities at the University of Saskatchewan. His research interests include philosophy of psychedelics, history of medicine, indigenous knowledge, heritage studies, decolonial theory, political philosophy.

Paloma Griffero (Research Center for Latin American Aesthetics, CIELA, Chile) is a teacher, mother, poet, cultural manager, and activist. She has served as National spokeswoman for Cultures of Social Unity and has participated in the creation of the area of Cultures, Arts and Heritage of the Government Program of President Gabriel Boric. She has promoted processes of children's and collective creation, through support for the management of books, music albums by migrant children, and short films by Mapuche children.

Nadia Heredia (National University of Comahue, Argentina) is an associate professor at the National University of Comahue; member of the coordinating team of AFyL Argentina and academic coordinator of the program in Philosophy of Liberation. She is a teacher by choice and she has a love of the world and its people. She is a human rights activist and works on disability issues.

Her research focuses on the Philosophy of Liberation. Specifically, she focuses on the works of Enrique Dussel and its ethical-pedagogical derivations, from a Latin American perspective.

Gabriel Herrera Salazar (Metropolitan Autonomous University-Iztapalapa, UAM-I, México) is currently doing postdoctoral research at Metropolitan Autonomous University-Iztapalapa, UAM-I in Mexico. He has specialized in the fields of ethics, political philosophy, and liberation philosophy. He is the author of the following books: *Vida Humana, Muerte y Sobrevivencia* (2015), *Ensayos Heréticos* (2016), *Metodología de la Liberación Para las Ciencias Sociales* (2018), and *Buscando Fondo en el Vacío y Otros Cuentos* (2019). He has been a member of the Association of Philosophy and Liberation (AFyL) since 2010.

Nelson Maldonado-Torres, PhD (Rutgers University) is professor of Latino and Caribbean Studies and chair of the Program in Comparative Literature at Rutgers University, New Brunswick. He is also director of the Rutgers Advanced Institute for Critical Caribbean Studies, professor Extraordinarius at the University of South Africa, and honorary professor at the University of KwaZulu-Natal in Durban, South Africa. He is a former president of the Caribbean Philosophical Association (2008–2013) and co-chairs the Fondation Frantz Fanon with Mireille Fanon Mendés France. His publications include dozens of articles and book chapters on decoloniality, and several monographs and edited books, including *Against War: Views from the Underside of Modernity* (Duke UP 2008) and *La Descolonización y El Giro Des-colonial* (Universidad de la Tierra, 2011).

Elisabeth Paquette is an assistant professor of Philosophy and Women and Gender Studies at University of North Carolina Charlotte. She works in political philosophy, decolonial theory, feminist theory, critical race theory, queer theory, and continental philosophy. Her publications can be found in *philoSOPHIA*, *Philosophy Compass*, *Radical Philosophy Review*, *Hypatia*, *Philosophy Today*, and *Badious Studies*. She is author of *Universal Emancipation: Race Beyond Badiou* (University of Minnesota Press, 2020).

Stephanie Rivera Berruz is an associate professor of philosophy and co-director of the Center for Race, Ethnic, and Indigenous Studies at Marquette University. She received her PhD in Philosophy from SUNY Buffalo in 2014. She is the recipient of the Woodrow Wilson Career Enhancement Fellowship (2017–2018) and The Way Klinger Young Scholar Award (2021) for her work on Latinx feminisms, Caribbean, and Latin American Philosophy. Her research is inherently interdisciplinary and explores historiography, social identity, current political issues. She published a co-edited anthology: *Comparative Studies in Asian and Latin American Philosophies* (2018), and her work has been featured in *The Stanford Encyclopedia of Philosophy*, *Genealogy*, *Hypatia*, *Inter-American Journal of Philosophy*, and *Essays on Philosophy*. She is also an avid salsa dancer, a lover of travel, and fervent activist in her local community.

Ernesto Rosen Velásquez is an associate professor of Philosophy at University of Dayton. He specializes in decolonial thought, Latinx and Latin American philosophy, critical philosophy of race and political philosophy. He is editor and contributor to a collection put together with Ramón Grosfoguel and Roberto D. Hernández, *Decolonizing the Westernized University: Interventions in Philosophy of Education* (Lexington Press, 2016). Some of his publications are "Jorge J.E. Gracia's Contributions to Latina/X/o Philosophy and His Engagement with Philosophy of Liberation" in *The Philosophical Legacy of Jorge J.E. Gracia* eds. Robert Delfino, William Irwin, and J.J. Sanford (Rowman Littlefield, 2022); "Criminalization and Undocumented *Migrante* Laborers in the Zone of Nonbeing,"

Critical Philosophy of Race, 7(1): (2019); and "Dussel's Metaphysics of Alterity and the Aesthetics of Liberation," *Inter-American Journal of Philosophy* 8 (2) (2017).He is preparing a manuscript titled *Problem People* with SUNY Press.

Luis Rubén Díaz Cepeda is a philosopher and a sociologist. He is an assistant professor in the Humanities Department at the Autonomous University of Ciudad Juárez in Mexico. His research focuses on ethics, borders, social movements, decolonial theory, and philosophy of liberation. Having published a number of book chapters and journal articles in Mexico, Argentina, Colombia, and the United States, his most recent works include *Latin American Philosophy and Social Movements: From Ciudad Juárez to Ayotzinapa* (Lexington Books, 2020) and he is co-editor with Amy Reed Sandoval of *Latin American Immigration Ethics* (AUP, 2021).

Amy Reed-Sandoval (UNLV, USA) is an assistant professor of Philosophy at the University of Nevada, Las Vegas. She works in the areas of political philosophy, with a special interest in issues of migration, Latin American and Latinx philosophies, bioethics, and feminist philosophy. She is the author of *Socially Undocumented: Identity and Immigration Justice* (Oxford University Press, 2020). She is the founding director of the Philosophy for Children in the Borderlands program in El Paso, Texas and Ciudad Juárez, Mexico.

Iván Sandoval-Cervantes (UNLV, USA) is an assistant professor of Anthropology at the University of Nevada, Las Vegas. He works on the anthropology of migration, particularly the analysis of internal and transnational migrations, gender (masculinity and femininity), indigeneity, kinship, and care. He also does work on multi-species ethnography, legal anthropology, and the anthropology of social movements, particularly through the study of activism and animal rights in the Mexico-US borderlands. He is the author of *Oaxaca in Motion: An Ethnography of Internal, Transnational, and Return Migration* (University of Texas Press, 2022).

Enrique Téllez-Fabiani (Iberoamerican University, México) has been a professor at several universities for over 20 years. He is the author, co-author, and editor of several books on literature, history, and philosophy. For several years, he has organized international academic events as a member of the Association of Philosophy and Liberation (AFyL) and the Philosophical Association of Mexico (AFM).

Alejandro Vallega (University of Oregon) works in Continental Philosophy and Decolonial Thought. He is the author of *Tiempo y Liberacion* (AKAL, 2020), *Latin American Philosophy: From Identity to Radical Exteriority* (Indiana University Press, 2014), and *Hiedegger and the Issue of Space: Thinking on Exilic Grounds* (Penn State University Press, 2003). He is also faculty at the Center of Study and Investigation for Decolonial Dialogues, Barcelona Spain.

Introduction

ERNESTO ROSEN VELÁSQUEZ AND LUIS RUBÉN DÍAZ CEPEDA

It is obscene and paradoxical how human beings can use the power of imagination—often touted as making us special and superior to other animals—in ways that has and continues to produce the legalized institutionalization of death that could in the future ultimately make human beings extinct. Some people have and continue to face immediate existential threats through the prison industrial complex, anti-black police violence, immigrant detention centers, ongoing wars and other forms of state sanctioned violence that target racialized/sexualized people. Nuclear war, pandemics, environmental catastrophe, intelligent racist AI robots, any one or combination of these human inventions could destroy all human life and perhaps all life on earth as we know it. If we end up annihilating our species what would mother earth say? Imagine mother nature waiting to exhale at some point takes a deep breath again and says "finally my gang rapist abusers invested in fracking, pollute my veins-waters, air, engage in thoughtless deforestation in the name of profits and collectively chant 'drill baby drill' can leave me alone. But I will miss the land defenders who struggled at the Dakota access pipeline, those who fought against environmental racism/sexism and countless others around the world throughout history who fought on the frontlines and everywhere else for my care and well-being."

It is also incredible how human beings can use their imagination to come together to feed other bodies and souls; to lean on each other in trying times; to forge deep emotional connections; to cry, laugh and learn together; to collectively create beautiful meanings that inspire us and bring out the best in us that is waiting to blossom. This collection you hold in your hand dear reader not only aims to clearly lay out and understand some of the various intermingled catastrophes people face but also what folks occupying different positionalities do to try to resist these life-threatening conditions and through such collective processes of struggle make new meanings, create new forms of relationality and subjectivity that transform the organization of space and time. Struggling is an important notion in the title of this book because struggles for liberation are linked with ongoing histories of resistance, direct collective action, youth movements, community organizing, and protest. We cannot simply think and write our way out of this totally avoidable and unnecessary hell on earth that has been generated, persists, and tries to continue to persist in the future. We cannot choose to avoid getting our hands dirty, rubbing shoulder to shoulder, being arm in arm with, and alongside social movements that protest against injustice.

Neither can we disregard the importance of reconceptualization. We need to change our attitudes and ways of thinking, speaking, and doing if we want to change the world. To think transformation can happen only through mass protest is also not straightforward. In the face of cross-racial mass protests emerging in the United States and around the world when Black Lives Matter clearly expressed a demand to defund the police, what is the response by the US state at federal and local levels? Using taxpayer funds to develop cop city in Atlanta Georgia or spot-shooter technology in Dayton Ohio or investment in Boston Dynamic's police robots in New York city or president Biden's solution to the problem of anti-black police violence: increase the police budget and "train them to shoot them in the leg instead of the heart." These and other collective actions of citizen mobilization (after months of peaceful protest think of the people's occupation of president Rajapaksa's mansion in Sri Lanka that called for his resignation) show us that protest by itself is not enough. We also need to take power in the sense of occupying governmental positions at all levels because utterly incompetent, self-interested, greedy, wildly ignorant, malevolent individuals occupy positions of power that pass legislation that effects the people and environment in harmful ways and blocks the creation of more participatory democratic governmental procedures. We need all of this and more if we want to fundamentally change the world.

Since people are participating in constant struggles for liberation around the world pushing for another better future, this collection focuses on some of these sites of contestation. While the perspectives in this collection are operating primarily within the context of the United States, Latin America, and the Caribbean, we do not identify the location of the struggles within America or América. This is because America is the term European cartographers chose in honor of the Italian navigator, merchant, explorer Amerigo Vespucci who understood that the continents Columbus landed on were not India but new continents unknown to European Spanish explorers. Thus, while the term "America" initially referred to the two continents—North America and South America—and then later was appropriated by the English 13 colonies and given an exclusive reference to the United States, we reject the parochial use of America. While we are aware that it has been said that Anglo control of northern Mexico's territory is an occupation of a part of the American hemisphere this does not imply, we adopt the broader earlier use deployed by European cartographers in the sixteenth century. The latter choice of spatiotemporal reference tracks sixteenth century European cartography and opens up a way of connecting with continental uses of América by Caribbean and Latin American philosophers such as José Marti, Roberto Fernández Retamar, Simón Bolivar, and Edmundo O'Gorman. However, it is limited. It assumes acceptance of European colonizer's naming and "discovery" of indigenous people who dwelled in these regions for millennia prior to the voyages of Columbus. In order to shift the emphasis away from this European and Spanish mestizo centered spatiotemporal cartography, it is perhaps more appropriate to shift the geography of reason and use the name *Abya Yala* deployed by indigenous peoples to refer to these lands as a way of trying to avoid the occlusion of their experiences, life-worlds, histories of oppression, and struggles for liberation. This is why we chose to name the book *Struggles for Liberation in Abya Yala*. But what does it mean for us to acknowledge indigenous lands in the title of this book?

We do not intend this land acknowledgment to be merely rhetorical. We do not intend it to be akin to what Lorgia García Peña identifies as the relatively recent practice of faculty and administrators automatically and non-reflectively reading land acknowledgements prior to any university event in North America.[1] She astutely observes how this practice does not take seriously that the westernized university "sits on stolen land built by enslaved labor to support and justify the project of colonizing exclusion."[2] To avoid this kind of performance of ornamental multiculturalism, we need to struggle to get the land back, fight for reparations, stand in solidarity with, and abolish dispossession. As we write this people of color still live in a state of emergency. What do people do in these catastrophic conditions in which the planet's sacred elements of water, air, earth, plants, animals, humans, and all life in water and on land are being destroyed and polluted in order to gain financial profits and hold onto the levers of power in the federal, state and local political machinery? They protest. But what often happens when people protest and call attention to structural problems and they articulate clear demands? The prevailing order kills, silences, criminalizes, imprisons or diminishes the thrust of the original demand and offers a minor reform that does not fundamentally address the problem. Although the range of contributors may not always necessarily share the same view, method, or liberation praxis, each of them in some form declare another world is possible. Such is the scream that comes from the underside of modernity; from the people that have chosen to rebel and act in solidarity against the system that oppresses them. These voices have been listened to and amplified first by philosophy of liberation and later by the decolonial turn, which has grown to be a fruitful philosophical tradition with influence in Africana philosophy, feminism, critical race theory, ethics, and political philosophy. It is in the latter area where we focus in *Struggles for Liberation in Abya Yala* by reflecting on the theoretical reach of the decolonial turn, as well as its implications in education and social movements in search of liberation in the United States, México, Argentina, Chile, and the Caribbean.

As it is known, the decolonial turn implies the recognition and undoing of the hierarchical structures promoted and constitutive of capitalism and Western modernity. Maldonado-Torres explains that it has three important moments. The first one is the early 1900s with the independence movements in America. Having origins in the Haitian revolution, the first begins with the problems of emancipated peoples of the African diaspora at the end of the nineteenth century and the beginning of the twentieth century. A second moment emerges with the disenchantment with Europe as a result of a series of wars, the Jewish Holocaust, and liberation movements that took place in Asia, Africa, and the Caribbean, propelled by Césaire and Fanon's writings on colonialism. The third and current moment started with the fall of the Soviet Empire and the 500-year anniversary of the conquest of America. Also, in the early 1990s, Anibal Quijano coined the notion of coloniality of power to describe the continuation of oppressive colonial relations fired up by European modernity. As Mignolo and Walsh claim, this brought intellectual and social movements that have spread all over the world in connection with social organizations.

Both philosophy of liberation and the decolonial turn have drawn wide attention to capitalism and colonial relationships that facilitate the exploitation of a large segment of the population. In response to these conditions, their members think with the *people* and have developed forms of resistance. In this book, we give continuity to this *praxis* of merging theoretical work and in-field struggles beyond what was known as the progressive governments in Latin America. We do so by presenting present day social struggles in search of liberation and freedom in the Americas from the perspective of scholars who take part in them. Thus, we aim to show and advance both the explanatory and normative power of philosophy of liberation and the decolonial turn. In a few words, *Struggles for Liberation in Abya Yala* is a collective book about a hands-in theoretical analysis of current social changes among all the American continents made by a combination of both well-established and rising scholars who are committed to radical social transformations that support victims of the system. It is divided into three sections: the first deals with a comprehensive analysis of the decolonial turn, philosophy of liberation, and the meaning of thinking from a liberatory feminism. The second section is devoted to education. Here, through the analysis of case-studies in the United States, México City, and Argentina, the authors encourage readers to promote social mobilization through education and to decolonize the Westernized university and educational practices. The final section addresses different struggles for social justice in México and Latin America as a whole. The authors reflect on challenging issues such as the relationship between social movements and political parties as well as the relationship between migrants, social organization and the state in México, the emancipatory capacity of art in Chile, the potentiality of farmers in Brazil, and animal rights movements in Latin America.

Outline of the Chapters

The first chapter opens with a piece called, "Searching for Combative Decoloniality" by Nelson Maldonado-Torres. As decolonial thought begins to impact various fields and becomes institutionalized in an academic way with little to no engagement with social movements, he unpacks a concept gleaned from Fanon's life and his writings on various stages of a colonized intellectual's formation that bears attention: the notion of combative decoloniality. To illustrate the complexities with noncombative, anti-combative, and combative modes of operating, this piece does bridge-building work that shows the impact of how Fanon is taken up in the philosophical conversations between Salazar Bondy and Leopoldo Zea and connections are made to the contemporary movement efforts of La Colectiva Feminista en Construcción in Puerto Rico and Decolonize This Place in New York City. The second chapter, "Decolonizing Understanding: A Utopian Reading of Anibal Quijano's Coloniality of Power and Knowledge" by Alejandro Vallega argues for a hermeneutic reading of Quijano. In contrast to a scientific reading that focuses on an analysis of the modern/colonial world system and victims resistance to this order, Vallega sketches another way of understanding decolonial reason. It is one that departs from the concrete lived esthetic senses that are outside of the oppressive grip of those being colonized. The third chapter, "Transmodernity as Postulate: First Eurocentrism, Prejudice, Critique" by Enrique Téllez-Fabiani explains that the dominant historical narrative of modernity is made up of several components tied up in a single knot, making single categories difficult to discern. Cultural-historical concepts (colonialism, imperialism, modernity, globalization, etc.) intersect with historical economic systems (mercantilism, capitalism, socialism, neoliberalism, etc.) and historical political systems (liberalism, fascism, communism, etc.). Because of this intersection, their limits are not entirely clear and often seem to disappear. Additionally, because this intersection is taken as the totality, it then seems that a single cultural unit—western globalization—is the only standard to which other cultures should be thought. Thus began, for Dussel, a long-term philosophical project in which he tries to explain and overcome this disturbing idea. Dussel asks, then, how to place Latin America in world history. In order to answer this question, Tellez offers a broad argument, so as not to lose sight of some indicative aspects of the meaning of modernity, and Dussel's counterproposal: trans-modernity.

The book then enriches the discussions by focusing on the role that gender plays in how we understand oppressive structures and philosophy of liberation. Chapter 4 thinks of the strengths and limits of philosophy of liberation when gender is taken into account. It is a piece called, "Reflection on the Erotics of Liberation: A Contemporary Feminist Latin American Perspective" by AFyL/Women. This text is intentionally a collective creation made by a group of *compañeras* from diverse territories and disciplines throughout Latin America who are part of the Liberation Philosophy school of thought. They follow an ethical and political commitment that seeks to decenter the *ego cogito* of the hegemonic academy to position themselves from a feminist epistemology that is devoted to building more horizontal spaces where they can speak from their affections, feelings, bodies, to produce and create collectively and collaboratively between women. In this chapter, they analyze Dussels' works: *Liberation of Women and Latin American Erotics* and its subsequent edition-correction *For a Latin American Erotics* with the objective to trace those contributions and categories that are fundamental to continue producing theoretically and politically from their own experience and testimony as Latin American feminist women. They recognize in the philosophy of liberation the ethical and political commitment against the oppression of women but also the limits and biases that make it impossible to understand the alterity of women and the critical power of their horizon of liberation. In Chapter 5 "Sylvia Wynter's Gender and Genre for a Queer and Trans-Inclusive Politics", Elisabeth Paquette fleshes out the distinctions between gender and genre in the Afro-Caribbean philosopher Sylvia Wynter's thought. Paquette takes the time to carefully unpack the expansiveness of Wynter's project and the value that it has for thinking through and alongside queer, and trans forms of resistance.

The book then turns to education issues and opens Chapter 6 with the article, "Struggles to Make Black Lives Matter" by Ernesto Rosen Velásquez. Here, he reflects on black death and the events leading up to the attacks on the capitol as a way of contextualizing philosophy departments in the United States. He reflects on some of the internal challenges token Latinx philosophers in departments face when attempting to make substantive change within Westernized universities. The author fleshes out the philosophical significance of the youth movement-led initiative that declared Breonna Taylor Day. As a way of challenging tokenization, he thinks through the collective process of meaning-making that can emerge when doing community-based initiatives. He considers the potential to create other kinds of practices with a different temporality that does not fit neatly within the framework of national holidays, university academic calendars of black history month or anniversaries as people work to decolonize the Westernized university from within and without. Chapter 7 "In the Trap of Critique: Making Decolonization Metaphor" by Stephanie Rivera-Berruz asks what critical race scholars owe to the political realities they draw from for the livelihood of their scholarship. Berruz notes, the truth of our world is one that is, in the words of Sylvia Rivera Cuscicanqui, a "world upside down," a traumatic turn, set in motion by the construction of modernity through colonization. In this world, the murder of George Floyd is not aberrational and the crystallization of inequality during a global pandemic is not circumstantial. This essay is as a meditation on the paradoxes of being a scholar whose livelihoods feeds from political moments for inspiration. The author argues that if we are truly committed to the intimacies that philosophy of race and other liberatory philosophical areas (e.g., decolonial philosophies), then we really need to contend with our positionality as knowledge producers that extends beyond alignment with ideological trends that absolve of failures to act.

Chapter 8, "Education in Latin America: Decolonization as an Ethical-Political Urgency" by Nadia Heredia tells us that reflecting on education in Latin America implies placing it in the historical context of permanent economic, political, and cultural tensions that cross it. From the founding dichotomy of the educational discourses of modernity—civilization or barbarism—Latin America has been the testing ground of the Global North in terms of educational policies. The center-periphery tension planted in Argentina in the 1970s and 1980s remains intact in its hardest core. Heredia asks then, what interests support the fact that education is considered as the privilege of a few? What links can be established between the discourses that underlie current educational exclusions and the discourses sustained by colonial modernity? In this chapter, she intends to deepen these questions from the Dusselian Philosophy of Liberation, as a way to contribute to the educational epistemological resistance that looks to raise its voice in favor of life in the middle of this civilizational crisis. In Chapter 9, "Philosophy of Liberation Praxis in Mexico City," Gabriel Herrera Salazar offers an excellent discussion of how a critical social science can be developed. He develops the thesis that Dussel's ethics of liberation has human life as both his material content and necessary principle to layout the foundations of critical social sciences. From this perspective, research methodologies should surpass the notion of "object of study" and give more emphasis to the inter-subjective communities as groups of human beings, who are non-objectifiable. The intention is to humanize, to make conscious, to liberate, and to decolonize in the development of dialogue and the cultural exchange. By doing so, we can learn from the wisdom of the other person, and together achieve a common objective with the intention of achieving justice for the oppressed, the victims or in other words those excluded.

The book then weaves in and elaborates on themes of social movements. For instance, Chapter 10 "Experiences of Weaving: The Chilean Social Revolt as an Esthetic Proposal" by Paloma Griffero attends to the significance of esthetics as it relates to resistance movements in Chile. In December 2021, Gabriel Boric, a former student leader and Congressperson of the Republic, was elected President in Chile. Pedemonte analyzes his rise in esthetic terms. She claims that Boric's presidential campaign was consolidated fundamentally from "memes" that rose from all corners of the country, as if inhabitants in each territory felt as personal the responsibility of supporting the campaign from their own esthetic expressions and cultural identities. Humor and creativity were used as a tool for the manifestation of the *people*. This form of pluriversal expression began to develop since the Social Revolt of 2019, a spontaneous and disruptive movement, which demonstrates the need for esthetic identification and symbolic connotation in the places of protest, where cultural and generational heterogeneity is revealed. In this chapter, the author analyzes, from decoloniality and the esthetics of liberation, the emancipatory capacity of the cultural manifestations of the Chilean people in the Social Revolt and subsequent elaboration of a new Constitution and the election of the leftist candidate, Gabriel Boric.

Chapter 11 then shifts to Luis Rubén Díaz Cepeda's discussion of the roles of immigration social movements. His contribution, "Migration Justice in Times of Pandemics in the Borderland of Ciudad Juárez/El Paso" shows how migration is an inherent human activity that has allowed us to explore and inhabit new territories. Its patterns depend on natural, personal, and sociopolitical circumstances. In this text, Díaz Cepeda reflects on the relationship between migrants and the institutions pursuing migrant rights/justice. He situates his study in the Ciudad Juárez-El Paso borderland, focusing specifically on the last three years when caravans of national and international migrants arrived. He observes how for the most part, migrants have been welcomed and have received the support of locals, primarily in the form of donations (and services) from social, religious groups, as well as a handful of international organizations—even maquiladora owners have advocated for working visas out of a sudden corporate empathy. While this support network is certainly welcomed and needed, the author asks: Does this equate to immigrant justice? Or, what would justice for migrants look like? From the perspective of the coloniality of being, Díaz Cepeda argues that any actions taken to assist migrants, social justice entities must recognize moral autonomy and agency. Only through this recognition and migrants' full and active participation that true immigration justice can be achieved. Chapter 12 "Latin American Animal Ethics" by Iván Sandoval Cervantes and Amy Reed-Sandoval attends to how the animal rights/welfare movement in Latin America has frequently engaged the central questions proposed by animal rights ethicists from the United Kingdom and the United States. Importantly, however, it has also responded to the particular situation of the subcontinent. In Latin America, within the so-called *animalista* movement (an umbrella term that encompasses people interested in animal rights and wellbeing), different activist groups have connected their struggles directly to their territories and, thus, to violent conflicts that have shaped human/non-human relationships. In this chapter, the authors argue that acknowledging that animals are part of a particular territory, as many Latin American animalistas have done, productively problematizes debates around the rights of non-human animals, which are all-too-often de-territorialized. They also explore how comprehending non-human animals as situated within violent social conflicts allows for new ways of thinking about liberation and animal rights within specific contexts. Finally, in this chapter they seek to ground important features of the Latin American animalista movement within the theoretical frameworks of Latin American liberational philosophy and decolonial theory. They do this with a view toward challenging the widespread idea that animal ethics and animal welfare-based social movements are mere "impositions" on Latin American from the so-called Global North.

Chapter 13 shifts to Ernesto Castañeda's analysis of the social historical context from which the Zapatista movement emerges. In "Zapata Revisited: Views on the Zapatista National Liberation Army" he presents a historical synopsis of the evolution of the Ejército Zapatista de Liberación Nacional (EZLN) while discussing its challenges to the liberal paradigm through its rejection of the definition of Mexico as a homogenous monocultural capitalist liberal democracy. He then proceeds to analyze how different observers and media have covered and reported on the movement through the years. Castañeda ends with an analysis of Marcos and the many challenges that he and the EZLN pose to the neoliberal paradigm. The last chapter by Osiris Gonzalez is "Decolonizing Peyote Politics in Mexico and Southwest USA." He explains three significant moments in colonial history that have influenced drug policies in Latin America. The first occurred during colonization in the sixteenth century, when the trade of endemic plants like cacao and tobacco became globalized. This prevailing Puritanism persisted for around four centuries. The second turning point emerged in the mid-twentieth century after the discovery of Mescaline, LSD, and the spreading of knowledge about ceremonies with psilocybin mushrooms in Mexico. This sparked international interest in studying and potentially using psychoactive substances for therapeutic, commercial, or military purposes. The counterculture and social movements against the Vietnam War resulted in implementation of the "War on Drugs." The third point of emergence occurred in the second decade of the twenty-first century, known as the Psychedelic Renaissance. Scientific research resumed after several decades of interruption due to the therapeutic efficacy of certain psychedelic substances against mental illnesses and the emergence of a new and broad market.

Notes

1 Lorgia García Peña (2022).
2 Ibid., 29.

Reference

Peña, L.G. (2022). *Community as Rebellion*, 29. Haymarket Press.

Section I

Theoretical Approaches

1

Liberation Philosophy and the Search for Combative Decoloniality: A Fanonian Approach

NELSON MALDONADO-TORRES

The impact of the discourse on decoloniality over the past decade has been palpable in a great number of areas of study, including professional fields in colleges and disciplines within the liberal arts and sciences; yet, the decolonial turn cannot fully take place within the globalized modern Western liberal university. The reason for this is that at the core of the decolonial turn there is a dimension that must be contained, delimited, and ideally removed in liberal and neoliberal settings: its combative character. The deactivation of combativity in academic discourses of decolonization and liberation is not new. It has already been long at work in philosophies and theologies of liberation, among other forms of thinking that were originally grounded on or that obtained inspiration from collective movements that challenged the basis of the modern/colonial world.

Gradually, as they entered the halls of the liberal university and theology seminars, liberation discourses were taken to be less the expression of reason emerging in combat, and more a body of perspectives, approaches, and critical theories to be for the most part studied and deployed in academic settings, publications, and debates. In this context, liberation philosophies and theologies largely became areas of expertise represented by middle-class academics with little to no engagement in collective movements for liberation, while combativity tended to be confused with and collapse into the critique of Eurocentrism and other forms of domination, all within the purview and horizon of the liberal arts and sciences. In this way, the structure of the white academic field (Maldonado-Torres 2020) and the ethos of *modern/western homo academicus* (Radebe and Maldonado-Torres forthcoming) largely remained untouched, even as the topics changed.

The deactivation of combativity in liberation philosophy and in decolonial theories, however, is not only a result of their integration within certain circles of the liberal academy. There are also internal contradictions and ambiguities in certain expressions of these areas that make them complicit with this deactivation. More than six decades ago, the Afro Caribbean philosopher, psychiatrist, and militant Frantz Fanon outlined important general contours of the problem. In his classic decolonial treatise, *The Wretched of the Earth* (2004), Fanon identified three stages in the works of intellectuals from colonial contexts: a first, assimilation stage, when the works of the "native" or local intellectual "correspond point by point with those of his metropolitan counterparts" a second, precombat stage, when "the colonized writer has his convictions shaken and decides to cast his mind back", and a third, combat stage, that comes into being when the intellectual is part of the struggle and when writing is no longer the unique domain of the intellectual, both because intellectuals do not only contribute to the combat by writing and because many other writers emerge.[1]

Today, decades after the revolutionary process that inspired Fanon, it would be important to make explicit two additional modalities of intellectual work among colonized and racialized populations. These two modalities combine with the precombat stage to constitute three possibilities between assimilation and combativity. In that intermediate position, in addition to the precombat stage, one finds noncombativity as a firm and more or less set and permanent stage and anticombativity as the explicit or implicit opposition, denial, or blockage of combative decoloniality. The differences between these modalities is not so clear since it could be difficult to ascertain when precombativity morphes into a more permanent noncombative posture. To this challenge, one must also consider that noncombativity and even pre-combativity can easily work in function of anticombativity when they remain solely or for the most part inside the academy, since the function of the academy is to instill non- or anti-combative liberal values.

This Fanonian typology is particularly useful today when philosophies of liberation reappear under the banner of decolonial philosophy, and when references to decoloniality spread in the academy. For, overwhelmingly, it is arguably non-, pre-, and anti-combative intellectual activities and literature that are understood in the academy as modalities of the decolonial. The confusion is not difficult to explain since these forms of literature represent a challenge to the more clearly colonial, assimilation stage. Different from assimilation, non-, pre-, and anti-combative activity can include drawing up lists "of the bad old ways characteristic of the colonial world" as well as offering descriptions and analyses of the pervasiveness of death in the colonial context. Sometimes this literature can take on more optimistic tones and recall "the goodness of the people," who are depicted as "the guardians of truth".[2] Despite the appearance of radicality and declarations of allegiance to one or another form of non-western culture or thought, however, non-, pre-, and anti-combative intellectuals tend to see themselves and/or behave primarily as individuals and maintain an "outsider's relationship" with struggles in combat zones of decolonial activity.[3]

Fanon's critique of colonized intellectuals and his appreciation of combative decolonial activity played an important role in the formation of liberation philosophies since the mid-to-late 1960s, yet, overwhelmingly, liberation philosophy also arguably lost track of Fanon's insights. This chapter seeks to illustrate this by focusing on the early formation of Latin American liberation philosophy. Latin American philosophers had long been concerned with the question about the existence of philosophy in Latin America and about its degree of authenticity. Early liberation philosophers, such as the Peruvian Augusto Salazar Bondy and the Mexican, Leopoldo Zea, combined the existing concerns among professional philosophers in the region—such as the question about the existence of philosophy and its authenticity—with the analyses and challenges that were emerging among combative intellectuals in the Third World. Fanon's work became perhaps the most usual reference in this context. However, while the liberation philosophers received inspiration from Fanon's combative approach to philosophy and intellectual labor at large, the questions about the existence of philosophy and about its authenticity squarely fit within the pre-combative framework and project that Fanon described.

That the question about the existence of philosophy in certain regions of the world is problematic has been made perhaps most explicit by African philosophers, such as Moboge Ramose (2002) and Kwasi Wiredu (2004). They argue that the question about whether there is philosophy in Africa is one that mainly non-Africans ask, and one that is ultimately a racist question, since it presupposes the possibility that Africans cannot think philosophically. This claim raises the question as to why Latin American mestizos and Spanish philosophers exiled in Latin America found the question about the existence of Latin American philosophy to be so important for them. Where Latin American and African philosophers seem to agree is in the concern with the question about the authenticity of philosophy in their respective regions: it is one thing to know that there is philosophy in Latin America, Africa, or Asia, and another to differentiate between an authentic philosophy in the region and other philosophical expressions that may exist there, particularly in places like Africa, where prejudiced Europeans first started to write explicitly about African philosophy. From a Fanonian point of view, though, the question about the authenticity of a continental philosophy (e.g., Latin American and African), while not racist, is fundamentally a noncombative or at most a pre-combative one that put a limit to those who ask it. In this chapter, I expand a call for post-continental philosophy (Maldonado-Torres 2006a, 2006b, 2011c, 2022) in a combative decolonial direction.

The main argument in this chapter is that the early Latin American philosophy of liberation recognized in Fanon's work a new "philosophical attitude," a combative one that animated the call for liberation. However, while Fanon's combative decolonial attitude led him to challenge the traditional role of the scholar and the philosopher, readers of his account of combativity often reproduced noncombative questions and concerns. This chapter offers but one example of the ways in which academic knowledge formations reframe and mistranslate combative decolonial epistemologies and *saberes*. The problems do not stop there, for commodified versions of the critical, liberation, and the decolonial generate a field of their own and a sphere of relatively subordinated knowledge/power that keep combative decolonial thinking/pedagogy/praxis at bay—often used to obscure, mistranslate, silence, and/or discipline combative formations— while affirming the problematic approaches to coloniality and racism (via policies of diversity, inclusion, and the appreciation of difference) within the liberal academy across the North and the South.

Toward a Combative Decolonial Critique of the Philosophy of Liberation

From a Fanonian point of view, the decolonial turn in philosophy involves a questioning of the definition of philosophy, both as a professional discipline, on the one hand, and as *weltanschauung* or world view, on the other. These two approaches to philosophy became central in the context of the formation of the modern Western research university in the nineteenth century. As a discipline, philosophy is taught in universities and approached as a form of study and reflection on the basis of established canons. As a *weltanschauung* or world view, philosophy is considered a conglomerate of ideas through which nations and collectives make sense of the world.

The Argentinean philosopher Mario Casalla brings up the distinction between philosophy as discipline and as *weltanschauung* in a dialogue among Latin American intellectuals who explored the meaning and significance of a Latin American liberation philosophy (Salazar Bondy 1995b). The dialogue included the presence of the Peruvian philosopher Augusto Salazar Bondy and the Mexican philosopher Leopoldo Zea, whose intellectual exchanges in the late 1960s had set the terms of the debate about authentic philosophy and liberation philosophy in Latin America (Salazar Bondy 1969; Zea 1996).

In the dialogue, Salazar Bondy makes clear that when he writes about philosophy, he means mainly a "systematic body of conceptual elaborations that in one way or another demand the work of a specific group of people who are 'specialists'".[4] In that sense, Salazar Bondy makes clear that when he refers to the defect and decadence of philosophy in Latin America (1969), he is mainly referring to philosophy as it is taught in universities. However, this does not mean that the philosophy of nations or collectives (*weltanschauung*) is necessarily in a better position for him, since alienation and dependency are not exclusive to professionals or elites.

Salazar Bondy's double critique of philosophy as discipline and as *weltanschauung* was anticipated in Fanon's work, a figure who had already become a major reference to Latin American liberation philosophers. Fanon engages disciplinary philosophy critically since his first book, *Black Skin, White Masks* (2008), where he took a decolonial transdisciplinary approach to study what he took to be the multidimensional problematic of understanding blackness (Maldonado-Torres 2015). By decolonial transdisciplinarity, I mean not only the use of multiple disciplines, but, most importantly, the critical interrogation of disciplines on the basis of the problems, questions, aspirations, and lived experiences of those who Fanon later referred to as the condemned of the earth (Fanon 2004), particularly within contexts and projects of decolonial collective formation and mobilization (Maldonado-Torres 2019b).

Fanon's critique of philosophy as a discipline is also implicit in his analysis of the work of colonized intellectuals in *The Wretched of the Earth* (2004). Fanon comments that the colonized intellectual takes on the role of a "sentinel on duty guarding the Greco-Roman pedestal" (2004, p. 11). At stake here is not only the reproduction of certain concepts and methods but also a mode of teaching, cultivating, and producing ideas even when they turn out to be critical of Western imperialism. Among these ideas, Fanon emphasizes the devastating character of individualism, the modern Western bourgeois notion of "a society of individuals where each is locked in his subjectivity, where wealth lies in thought".[5] Intellectuals who are driven by individualism have yet to complete a decolonial turn since, locked in their individualistic liberal ethos, their behavior reflects, in Fanon's words, a certain "egoism, arrogant recrimination, and the idiotic, childish need to have the last word".[6]

Fanon also identified the limits of philosophy as *weltanschauung* or world view when he asserted that "In the weltanschauung of a colonized people, there is an impurity or a flaw that prohibits any ontological explanation".[7] The flaw in question is the result of modern European colonization, which involves the systematic devaluing, commodification, and selective eradication of native customs, concepts, and values, along with the institutions that sustain them, while it also imposes a foreign idea and a project of civilization. Therefore, any notion of "the people," the other, or the colonized subject for that matter, as the site of a pure pool of symbols, concepts, practices, and ideas is hopelessly mistaken.

Fanon approaches modern European colonization/civilization as a global catastrophe: a project to undo and redo the world according to a Manichean logic that remains in place even after juridico-political colonization has ended.[8] At the heart of this Manichean logic is anti-indigeneity, antiblackness, and the coloniality of gender (Lugones 2010a, 2010b, 2022; Wynter 1984, 1991, 2003). Fanon makes it clear that the goal or telos of global modern/colonial catastrophe is the complete eradication or domestication of the ideas, symbols, practices, and institutions that are fundamentally different from or that challenge the idea of modern Western civilization. In that sense, the catastrophe is still in the making and it continues to generate, not so much contact zones between the colonizer and the colonized, but combat zones where coloniality is not only resisted but also countered and defied.

Fanon's account of philosophy and of decolonization are highly informed by his view of colonization as global catastrophe. From a Fanonian point of view, decolonial philosophy refers to the forms of thinking that emerge out of combative decolonial attitudes, which are at once practical and theoretical, in the combat zones of the modern/colonial world. If the modern/colonial catastrophe is both systematic and global, then decolonial philosophy is not just one area among others within the discipline of philosophy, but the condition of possibility for avoiding the "defect" and "decadence" that Salazar Bondy identifies in academic philosophy. Salazar Bondy himself goes in this direction when he refers to the need for liberation philosophy to identify the sectors that are undergoing the most brutal forms of domination and that are "en la lucha" (in the struggle or combat) to then "plug" with them.[9] Salazar Bondy remarks that without this "plugging" philosophy would remain an "accomplice to domination".[10] This is what Salazar Bondy describes as the methodology of the philosophy of liberation.

Salazar Bondy's notion of "plugging" with collective movements for liberation was inspired in the work of intellectuals like Fanon and Che Guevara. Fanon's and Guevara's models of intellectual activity went beyond "plugging," though: they joined the movements of liberation and wrote as part of larger collectives. Fanon went as far as resigning from his position as Director of a psychiatric hospital to join the Algerian National Liberation Front. Fanon's combative decolonial conception of intellectual work promotes resignation as part of collective combative praxis/thinking/being. From a Fanonian point of view, decolonial resignation is an attitude and an action that prioritizes the collective struggle for decoloniality and the active engagement in rehumanization. Decolonial resignation is one aspect of the decolonial turn: a denaturalization of the roles for individuals in the modern/colonial world and a reorientation that prioritizes the needs of the ongoing struggle for decoloniality.

Salazar Bondy delinks from Western philosophy, but he does not resign from professional philosophy.[11] For that reason, he can only conceptualize the work of the liberation philosopher in terms of analyzing and "plugging." What Salazar Bondy misses, partly because of his own residual investment in philosophy as a discipline, is the extent to which the start of liberation or decolonial philosophy is found, not among professional philosophers who seek to "plug" themselves to people in various struggles, but among the organized decolonial collectives themselves. The task of "liberating philosophy" demands the decolonization of continental liberation philosophies, which, from a Fanonian point of view, might be best pursued in rethinking the philosophy of liberation in terms of combative decoloniality.[12] This is a lesson that we obtain from Fanon's work, who writes *The Wretched of the Earth* (2004), *A Dying Colonialism* (1965), and most parts of *Towards the African Revolution: Political Essays* (1988), which included collective writings published under Fanon's name, as an active participant and as a member of the Algerian Liberation Front in the combat zone of the struggle for Algerian independence. The similarities and differences between Fanonian combative decoloniality and Salazar Bondy's liberation philosophy will become clearer in the next section, which examines the references to Fanon in texts by Salazar Bondy and Leopoldo Zea.

Encountering and Missing Fanon

That Fanon's work was a fundamental reference to the emerging Latin American philosophy of liberation was evident in Salazar Bondy's and Zea's writings of the late 1960s and early 1970s. Zea's classic *La filosofía americana como filosofía sin más* (1996) makes evident the shift that was taking place in the philosophical scene in Latin America at the time. The text is dedicated to the memory of José Gaos, a Spanish philosopher who was forced to leave Spain during the Spanish Civil War. Gaos was part of a generation of Spanish philosophers who, like other European philosophers at that moment, had become increasingly skeptical of the dominant forms of universalism in European philosophy. Their philosophical point of view and attitude reflected an increasingly generalized crisis of the idea that European thought was universal.

In this context, the rejection of abstract universality was coupled with a return to the concrete, the particular, specific contexts, and to lived experience. Phenomenology, vitalism, and existentialism reflected and further contributed to the exploration of these concerns. Attention to the philosophical relevance of context and experience found enthusiastic readers and contributors in peripheral locations like Spain and Mexico, among other sites, which now could more freely engage in their exploration of their own national, cultural, and/or regional philosophies. Zea sums it well: "Western philosophy discovers itself as a philosophy among other philosophies at the same time that, in Latin America, one encounters the capacity of Latin Americans to philosophize, pure and simply as a concrete expression of any and all philosophizing" (translation mine).[13] In short, the very question about the possibility and authenticity of Latin American philosophy is now fueled by changes in Western philosophy itself.

In *La filosofía americana* (1996), Zea credits Gaos for an extraordinary display of the emerging philosophical attitude, which Zea describes as an "increasing concern for the search of philosophical universality starting from a specific situation or circumstance".[14] Central to this philosophical attitude in Latin America is the question of the authenticity of Latin American philosophy, a question that becomes central in Salazar Bondy's 1968 *Existe una filosofía de nuestra América?* (1969).

Like Zea, Salazar Bondy had been a student of José Gaos. Salazar Bondy discusses Gaos's view of the possibility and originality of Hispanic-American philosophy in the text and thanks Gaos for his comments on the book manuscript. Salazar Bondy also discusses Zea's work, which sought to build on Gaos's contributions to the understanding of philosophy in Mexico and Latin America.

Zea's *La filosofía americana* (1996), published a year after Salazar Bondy's text, sought to respond to Salazar Bondy's challenges regarding the possibility or impossibility of having an authentic Latin American philosophy. Most notable in Zea's response is that he characterizes Salazar Bondy's approach to the question of the authenticity of Latin American philosophy as yet "a new philosophical attitude", different from the previous generation—including Gaos's work. For Zea, this new philosophical attitude makes a connection between the question of authenticity and the problem of domination.[15]

The new philosophical attitude that Zea identifies is at the heart of what came to be called liberation philosophy: a view of philosophy as a way of thinking that seeks not only to "make us aware of our condition of subordination, but also of how to overcome this condition".[16] Zea argues that while this attitude seems new in the context of Latin American philosophy, that it has been already manifested in a number of existing works, first among which he cites the work of Frantz Fanon.

The presence of Fanon's work is central in Zea's *La filosofía americana* (1996). Consider that the first chapter's epigraph is a quote from Jean-Paul Sartre's preface to Fanon's *The Wretched of the Earth* (2004) and that the epigraph of its last chapter, entitled "Of Authenticity in Philosophy," comes from *The Wretched of the Earth* itself. The long epigraph in the sixth and final chapter of *La filosofía americana* is taken from the first chapter and the conclusion of *The Wretched of the Earth*, and it starts with a direct reference to decolonization. In the chapter, Zea comments that "Jean Paul-Sartre is surprised about a philosophy like that of Fanon because it expresses the most authentic expression of the *decolonization of consciousness*" (translation and emphasis mine).[17]

Zea's discussion of Fanon's philosophy makes evident how the decolonial turn impacted what came to be named Latin American liberation philosophy.[18] While Salazar Bondy does not cite Fanon in *Existe una filosofía*, he credits Fanon, along with Leopold Senghor and Ernesto "Che" Guevara in a crucial moment in a dialogue on philosophy of domination and philosophy of liberation that took place in 1973 (Salazar Bondy 1995b). Fanon, Senghor, and "Che" are for him representatives of what he refers to as "the message of the Third World".[19] This is the post-World War II message—a crucial part of the second major of the decolonial turn (Maldonado-Torres 2018)—that generated the new philosophical attitude to which Zea refers, an attitude that is different from the previous generation, represented in the work of José Gaos and Mexican philosophers like Samuel Ramos. For Salazar Bondy, the new philosophical attitude is reflected in the "methodology" of the emerging philosophy of liberation, with its attention to struggles of liberation and the act of "plugging" that was critically analyzed in the previous section.

That Fanon's work and his philosophical perspective were crucial for Salazar Bondy, and that Salazar Bondy considered Fanon a central figure in liberation philosophy, is made even clearer in his *Bartolomé o de la dominación* (Salazar Bondy 1974a, 1995a), a portion of which also appeared with the title "Diálogos indianos entre Bartolomé de las Casas, Frantz Fanon, el cacique Hatuey y Ginés de Sepúlveda" (Salazar Bondy 1974b). This text, published in 1974, shortly after Salazar Bondy passed away that year, is a work of fiction in dialogical form in which Salazar Bondy gives voice to the philosophical positions and attitudes that are generated out of the "discovery" and conquest of the New World.

Fanon in Salazar Bondy's "Dialogues"

Salazar Bondy's "Bartolomé o de la dominación" (1995a) is undoubtedly inspired in the debates between Bartolomé de las Casas, who "defended" the Indians, and Ginés de Sepúlveda, who believed that indigenous peoples were natural slaves and that they could be conquered and enslaved. The debate between las Casas and Sepúlveda took place in the mid-sixteenth century and has come to represent not simply a chapter in the history of modern Western colonialism, but also a staging of some of the most fundamental questions and terms about the meaning of the human in the context of Western modernity.

In addition to Las Casas and Sepúlveda, the short version of the debate includes two more characters. One of them is the Taíno cacique Hatuey, based on the historical figure with the same name who sought to organize Taínos, and some say also enslaved Africans, in their struggle against the Spaniards in Hispaniola and Cuba. The historical Las Casas documented some of Hatuey's actions and sayings, including a report of an exchange with a priest when he was about to be burnt alive. When the priest told Hatuey about heaven and hell, he said that he would prefer going to hell, where he thought he would not find people as cruel as Christians.[20] Hatuey demonstrates a similar attitude toward Las Casas in the dialogue.

The other character in the short version of the dialogue is a Black man named Frantz, who is identified in the title of the text as Frantz Fanon. Frantz appears in the long version of the dialogue as Frans. The other characters in the long version of the dialogue are Don Diego, surely based on Cristobal Colon's first son Diego, who served as governor of the island of Hispaniola, and Micaela, based on the eighteenth century figure Micaela Bastidas, who led a revolt against the Spaniards with her husband Tupac Amaru II in what later came to be known as Perú. Among Bastidas's roles in the rebellion, she helped persuade male and female indigenous leaders to join. Some of this is reflected in the dialogue, where Micaela corrects Hatuey's impression that his indigenous combatants are men. "Hay más de una decidida a combatir" [more than one woman has chosen to engage in combat], asserts Micaela, before offering a list of names of indigenous women leaders through the centuries.[21] Micaela does not participate in the dialogue for too long because she leaves the discussion to gather revolutionary forces. For this reason, it is not credible that, when Micaela returns to the scene, she is afraid of Hatuey's dismissal of Christianity and sides with Bartolomé's theological approach.[22] This is remarkably different from what happened with the historical Micaela Bastidas, who died as a combatant and was tortured and killed by the Spaniards. This gap between the fictional and the historical figure of Micaela might be the most problematic part of the dialogue, one that reflects a view of combative women as never completely dependable or consistent.

In the full dialogue, after Micaela's initial departure, Bartolomé notices an emerging figure whom he believes is a "cimarrón en fuga".[23] The man asserts that he comes to join Hatuey, identifies himself as Frans Oblitas, and asserts that he is a man "from Africa and America".[24] While it would seem that Africa and blackness first come into the scene with Frans, they were already there in some way through the reference to Micaela Bastidas, who was known as a *zamba* because she was the daughter of an Afro-descendent man and an indigenous woman. The dialogue does not make reference to this aspect of Bastidas's biography.

There is of course no doubt in the long dialogue that Frans Oblitas makes reference to Frantz Fanon, who is identified as such in the short version. Oblitas is a familiar last name in Perú and its etymology is connected to the Greek name "hoplites," which refers to foot soldiers in ancient Greece. Hoplites were also characterized by being armed with spears and shields, meaning that they were ready for combat. The hoplites' function "was to fight in close formation," becoming a "massed hoplite phalanx breaking through enemy ranks" (Britannica 2023). This approach to military combat differed quite sharply with an individualistic model that predominated before the appearance of the hoplites in the late eighth century BCE, one that depended on the "individual brilliance of aristocratic champions" (Britannica 2023). That Salazar Bondy uses the last name Oblitas in the reference to Frans/Frantz therefore suggests that he was aware of Fanon's critique of individualism and of the value of collective combat in Fanon's conception of liberation/decoloniality.

In the long version of the dialogue, Frans introduces himself as an executioner of slave merchants and scourge of magistrates and encomenderos (translation mine).[25] He also declares that he is "preparing the great combat of the condemned of the earth ... who are the only ones with the capacity to build true freedom to every human being" (translation mine).[26] Frans points out that he was claiming his own freedom when he gave himself the name Frans Oblitas, which indicates that he had been enslaved. Upon seeing him and listening to his introduction, Ginés de Sepulveda remarks cynically: "Hi! We have a Black philosopher. It is always time to learn ..." (translation mine).[27] Frans does not hesitate in replying in a statement that reflects Salazar Bondy's views of the methodology of liberation philosophy: "We will definitely unmask the Gineses who justify our slavery with poor reasons and we will cancel domination from its historical roots" (translation mine).[28]

The full dialogue is too long to consider in depth here, but one notable part that appears in both the short and the long version is an exchange between Bartolomé, Hatuey, and Frans/Frantz, where Frans/Frantz intervenes to denounce the limits of Bartolomé's humanism and to alert Hatuey of a "fundamental difference" between Bartolomé's consciousness and theirs.[29] Frans/Frantz identifies two problems in Bartolomé's posture: first, that he questions the war upon Indians, but justifies the right of the Spanish to govern them, and, second, that Bartolomé defends the Indians and other non-European groups, but only to the extent that they can be integrated to or included in the West.[30]

Whether Frans/Frantz's critiques of Bartolomé properly recognize the complexity of the position of the historical Las Casas is not the point here since the dialogue is reflecting the views of a fictional Bartolomé who seems to simultaneously stand for certain views found among liberal elites, mainstream Western humanists, and liberation theologians.[31] For Frans/Frantz, Bartolomé is at "the edge of true science, even though he is unable to advance by idols of his spirit that he ignores in good faith".[32] Salazar Bondy puts in Frans/Frantz's voice an argument about the willful ignorance of the colonizer and about the colonial dimension of his apparent benevolence.

Frans/Frantz also becomes the purveyor of the argument for liberation/decolonization in the dialogue: "And the struggle for liberation, the war of the oppressed, is based on this rejection and in the evidence that ... all the nations of the earth are human beings. Only that, for us, the complete truth of this beautiful formula is this: all the peoples of the earth, with their own forms of being, are human beings, and the human being is those ways of being".[33] Hatuey goes along and affirms Frans/Frantz reasoning. When Frans/Frantz recognizes the gravity of social, economic, and political alienation (alienación "del poder") and describes the alienation of "basic personality" as the "most profound," Hatuey remarks: "They go together, Oblitas, which is why they must be combatted at the same time, with the mind and with the fist" ("hay que combatirlas al mismo tiempo").[34] To this, Frans/Frantz replies: "I agree; it won't be me who stops the combat" ("no seré yo quien frene el combate").[35] Here it is important to indicate that earlier in the dialogue, Bartolomé explains that when Hatuey gets baptized, his new name will be Ernesto, a "beautiful name that means 'decisive combatant' (combatiente decidido)".[36] The connection with Ernesto "Che" Guevara should be clear, especially since Salazar Bondy had identified Fanon and Che as two major figures who carried the message of liberation.

Through the dialogue, Frans/Frantz voices ideas that one can find in the first chapter and in the conclusion of *The Wretched of the Earth*. In one moment of the discussion in the long version of the dialogue, Bartolomé asserts that Frans/Frantz advances the notion that war among human beings is a natural state, to which Frans responds: "We aspire to the end of combat when humanity is fulfilled. In the meantime, combat is a fact".[37] There is also another important moment in the long dialogue when Bartolomé tells Hatuey that there has always been domination, including within his own people. Frans puts a stop to Bartolomé's efforts to undermine the basis of decolonial combat by telling Hatuey that he "very well knows when and how, in our concrete case, war starts, since [he is] an actor in it".[38] Hatuey confirms it: "For us it started the same day that Europeans touched on our lands; there is no doubt".[39] Having no doubt that one lives in conditions of war and that the war in question started with European "discovery" and colonization is a major feature of combative decoloniality. This idea anticipates the thesis that modernity/coloniality can be understood as a paradigm of war (Maldonado-Torres 2008) and that decoloniality is, first and foremost, a combative activity (Fanon Mendès France and Maldonado-Torres 2021).

In addition to Frantz/Frans's interventions, Salazar Bondy mobilizes the voice of Hatuey in the critique of Bartolomé. Some time after Frantz/Frans had already left the dialogue, Hatuey refers to God as the "Gran Dominador" and depicts references to divine transcendence as counter-revolutionary.[40] This is a view that Salazar Bondy himself had raised against liberation theology.[41] This perspective was surely also in tension with forms of liberation philosophy that had emerged in Argentina, which had a closer relationship with liberation theology than either Salazar Bondy's or Zea's work.[42] A brief comparison with the work of the then Argentinean (and later Argentinean-Mexican) philosopher Enrique Dussel demonstrates some of the most important differences as well as a key similarity: the role of mestizo-filia, a narrow definition of philosophy, and the search for authenticity in a view of liberation that fails to reach the level of combative decoloniality.[43]

The Philosophy of Liberation Under the Shadow of Mestizaje

Throughout his entire philosophical oeuvre, Dussel has characterized Las Casas as one of the most important figures in the formation of liberation philosophy. Consider that the first volume of his *Para una ética de la liberación latinoamericana*, published in 1973, starts with an epigraph from Bartolomé de Las Casas's *Brevísima relación de la destrucción de las Indias* (Bartolomé de Las Casas 1992) and that Dussel identifies Las Casas as the earliest precursor of liberation philosophy in his *Filosofía de la liberación* of 1977.[44] Like Zea, Dussel considers Fanon an important figure in the history of the struggle for liberation, but unlike Zea, Dussel did not consider Fanon strictly a philosopher.[45] Instead of Fanon, Dussel takes Emmanuel Lévinas as the central figure of his early work, which is reflected in that the second epigraph of *Para una ética de la liberación latinoamericana* (Dussel 1973) is taken from Levinas's *Totality and Infinity* (Levinas 1969).[46]

While Salazar Bondy's dialogue places Hatuey and Fanon, against Las Casas, at the forefront of liberation philosophy, Dussel takes Las Casas and Levinas as the most important figures. Later on, in the context of massive indigenous opposition to the 500th anniversary of the "discovery" of the Americas in around 1992—yet another crucial moment in the genealogy of the decolonial turn; Maldonado-Torres 2018—Dussel (1995) seems to go in Salazar Bondy's direction when he selects Bartolomé de Las Casas and Moctezuma as those who expressed the highest forms of critical consciousness regarding the evils of the emerging Western modernity. Dussel would return to the topic in his "Anti-Cartesian Meditations" of 2008, where he presents Las Casas's work as representing "the first philosophical anti-discourse of *early* Modernity", and Felipe Guamán Poma de Ayala as an example of a critique of Modernity from "radical exteriority".[47] That the categories of otherness and radical exteriority were part of Dussel's interpretive framework made clear that Levinas's thought remained very much central to Dussel.

Salazar Bondy's fictive dialogue anticipated Dussel's explorations of the forms of consciousness that were generated out of the "discovery" of the Americas, and the globalization of the institutions and modes of thinking that emerged or were solidified in that context. There are several notable differences between the approaches, in addition to the style and genre. One of them is that Salazar Bondy's references to Hatuey, Fanon, and Diego indicate what could be interpreted as a higher appreciation of the dynamics that took place in the Caribbean for understanding the formation of modern/colonial and decolonial consciousness than Dussel, who focused on continental figures from what became Mexico (Moctezuma) and Peru (Poma de Ayala). Mexico and Peru had been major sites of urban indigenous life prior to the arrival of the Spaniards and were made into pivotal centers of the empire. The Caribbean went through a massive destruction of indigenous life to the point of near extinction in some areas, which led it to become the first site of enslaved African population.

Salazar Bondy's dialogues evoke these connections between indigeneity and blackness in the Caribbean by placing Hatuey and Fanon in dialogue. The connection between blackness and indigeneity is also manifest in the selection of Micaela as the third major critical voice in the dialogue, since, as it was pointed out earlier, the historical Micaela Bastidas was referred to as *zamba*—of mixed African and indigenous descent. Dussel considers indigenous people and enslaved Africans the first two "visages" or historical groups among the colonized in the Americas, but he reserves a special place for mestizos. In *The Invention of the Americas*, Dussel approaches mestizos as the only *new* population group in the Americas after the "discovery," and as the one that "represents what is unique, positively or negatively, to Latin American culture".[48] The mestizo, Dussel adds, "is responsible for building Latin America, Luso-Hispanic America, Hispano America, Ibero-America as a cultural block beyond mere geography (South America, Central America, North America, and the Caribbean)".[49] The original text in Spanish makes reference to "la cultura propiamente latinoamericana" (properly Latin American culture), which echoes concerns with cultural authenticity, and to the idea that this culture will continue to be built "en torno al mestizo" (around the mestizo).[50] Dussel reproduces here a mestizo-centric perspective, even as he is aware of the contradictions and tensions within mestizo society and culture. His view on mestizos and their historical protagonism has implications for the roles that non-mestizos should expect to have in "Latin" America, which contradicts the views of a great many Black and indigenous organizations through Abya Yala.

Dussel's view of mestizos and about the contemporary relevance of indigenous political movements may have started to change after the Zapatista revolt of 1994. In his "Sentido ético de la rebellion maya de 1994 en Chiapas," he refers to it as a "profound ethical interpellation" that will provoke "much to reflect, mature, analyze, and conclude in the years ahead" (translation mine).[51] He concludes his essay, written shortly after the revolt, with the assertation that "we, whites and mestizos" as well as "award winning poets and so many university intellectuals" are yet to learn "much culture, beauty and poetry to be at the level of the 'eldest among the elders' of the Chiapas mountains. May history forgive us for our ignorance and arrogance!".[52]

Challenges to mestizaje are by no means new or recent, and it is crucial here to note that one of the strongest expressions of the critique of mestizaje in "Latin" America is contemporary to the early philosophy of liberation: the Indianism-Katarism of the Bolivian thinker Fausto Reinaga. Reinaga, who considered "Indianism" the "ideological and political instrument of the Third World

Revolution" (translation mine), wrote his *La Revolución india* (1969) and the *Manifesto del Partido Indio de Bolivia* (1970).[53] Bolivian Indianism is a political, cultural, and intellectual revolution that aimed to counter the coloniality of mestizaje and to overcome the limits and violence of Western civilization and culture. For Reinaga, mestizo intellectuals were largely responsible for instituting the "reign of colonization" in Latin America (Reinaga 1978, p. 102, translation mine). They have been a "destructive rage" for Indians (Manifesto 59) and "*the pest* for peoples of the New World" (translation mine).[54]

Reinaga was aware of Latin American philosophy, which he considered a mestizo philosophy that went, from liberal in the nineteenth century, to revolutionary "che-guevarista" in his time.[55] In his critique, Reinaga explicitly targets some of the principal figures in Latin American liberation philosophy, including Zea and Salazar Bondy, which indicates that Dussel is by no means the only figure who struggles with mestizo-centrism and mestizo filia among liberation philosophers.[56] Mestizaje runs large through discourses that seek to identify authentic expressions of philosophizing in *Latin* America, and it has been a crucial part of the coloniality of Latin American thought, including the philosophy of liberation.

Reinaga's critique of Latin American philosophy as a mestizo philosophy raises numerous questions and challenges for the Latin American philosophy of liberation. I will limit myself here to note the irony that, while Salazar Bondy was writing a dialogue where the voices of the Caribbean Hatuey and Fanon are depicted as the most revolutionary, Reinaga had been drawing from Indian revolutionary struggles and from Fanon's work in his formulation of the Indian revolution just a few years prior to the publication of Salazar Bondy's fictional philosophical work (Ticona Alejo 2010a, 2010b, 2012; Zapata and Oliva 2016). This gap reflects not only limits of mestizo intellectual activity, but it is also a testament to the difference between noncombative and combative philosophical expressions that I have outlined earlier. The obsession with the question about the authenticity of Latin American philosophy remains within the orbit of mestizo intellectuality. This search for authenticity, along with the fundamental presuppositions of the mestizo worldview, put limits to the kind of "plugging"—and, beyond that, of combative decoloniality—that the philosopher would aim to do.

Concluding Thoughts

Perhaps the main virtue of Salazar Bondy's dialogue is that it gestures toward an understanding of the difference between noncombative and combative consciousness. For both, Micaela and Fanon leave the dialogue to join other combatants in their respective combat zones. Particularly illuminating on this point are Frans's last words in the dialogue: "I leave from where I came; I should continue preparing the great struggle, but I will always be with you until we find ourselves in a decisive tomorrow. With regards to today's combat, I leave you in the best shape, ready to continue advancing toward liberation".[57] The passage points to the difference between the fictive semi-academic zone where individual characters engage in a debate and the combat zone where the intellectual is no longer solely an intellectual and fully participates within a comprehensive struggle.

Salazar Bondy points to the difference between the sphere of academic debate and that of decolonial struggle, but he does not thematize the extent to which the combat zone itself is a zone of philosophizing—indeed, the zone of decolonial thinking *par excellence*. Instead, Salazar Bondy has

Frans become the voice that validates, without challenging, the pre-combative space of dialogue, where Las Casas's voice is dominant and where he keeps referring to Hatuey as Ernesto. What the dialogue does not convey is that if Frans/Frantz was anything like the historical Frantz Fanon, then (i) his philosophizing would not have stopped in the dialogical engagement with the various figures that he engages—in fact, the opposite of this would be true, and (ii) he would not have been completely satisfied with philosophical elaborations that took place outside combat.

From a Fanonian perspective, there is no philosophy of liberation without the transformations of consciousness that take place while participating concretely body-to-body with others in the struggle for liberation. For Fanon, the decolonization of the mind could not take place without the decolonization of the body schema, and this can only happen within collective movements for decolonization. The reason for this is that decolonial collectives constitute anticipations of and engines for "the world of *you*", even as their work is by no means free from limits and contradictions. Collective work by the *damnés* in the combat zones of decolonial struggle offers the possibility of intellectual, existential, and political resignations from mestizaje.[58]

In Fanon's work, the philosopher is combatant and the combatant philosopher. This is what takes place at the combative level of intellectual activity and decolonial struggle. In the combat zones, philosophy becomes a collective activity of and for actual liberation, rather than a professional exploration of authenticity and inauthenticity.

From the outset, Fanon is critical of the search for authenticity and approaches liberation as rehumanization. This is reflected in his view that, for the most part, Black people are unable to "take advantage" of a descent to a zone of nonbeing "from which a genuine [authentic] new departure can emerge" (Fanon 2008, Maldonado-Torres 2016).[59] A new departure can only take place by the adoption of decolonial attitudes, which include self-critique, the questioning of coloniality, and the concrete solidarity (beyond North–South or South–South "dialogues," which can easily reproduce the noncombative and anti-combative attitudes identified here) with the condemned of the earth. As organizations like the Soweto-based Blackhouse Kollective (Radebe and Maldonado-Torres forthcoming), Decolonize This Place (n.d.) (New York City, USA), and La Colectiva Feminista en Construcción (Puerto Rico; Colectiva Feminista en Construcción 2018) continue teaching us today, it is in the process of collective combative struggle itself that consciousness can be decolonized, a new subjectivity emerge, and combative decolonial thinking/praxis/creation unfold.

Notes

1   Fanon (2004, p. 159).
2   Ibid., p. 158.
3   To the distinction between rewesternization, dewesternization, and decoloniality (Mignolo 2011), it is thus important to add the differentiation between noncombative, pre-combative, and anti-combative, on the one hand, and between decoloniality at large and combative decoloniality, on the other. These additional differentiations can help us better understand the uniqueness of the theoretical, creative, and strategic work that emerge from the activities of social movements and collective struggles.
4   Bondy (1995b, p. 160).
5   Fanon (2004, p. 11).
6   Ibid., p. 11.
7   Fanon (2008, pp. 89–90).

8 For an account of coloniality as catastrophe, see Maldonado-Torres (2016, 2017, 2019a).
9 Bondy, p. 168.
10 Ibid., p. 169.
11 Decolonial resignation is related but is different from what Walter Mignolo, following Anibal Quijano, has referred to and elaborated as delinking and epistemic disobedience (Mignolo 2007a, 2007b). Delinking and epistemic disobedience are undoubtedly important activities in the process of decolonization, yet they could remain noncombative in character. That is, delinking helps explain the transition from the stage of assimilation to the stage of noncombative or pre-combative "decoloniality," but it does not necessarily entail or involve the combative stage. For, delinking does not need to involve combativity in the ways that Fanon envisioned, and there are a myriad ways of disobeying the dominant episteme, not all decolonial or combative. While Mignolo is clear that delinking and epistemic disobedience are only two aspects of decoloniality, there has arguably been a tendency in the academy to collapse the decolonial into activities like delinking and epistemic disobedience, which can be used to preserve the traditional role of the intellectual and scholar. How much Mignolo's own conception of these concepts and of "the politics of decolonial investigations" (Mignolo 2021) remain close to or challenge these tendencies is an open question. My sense is that Fanon's work poses hard questions like these to anyone and everyone whose primary function is teaching and/or doing research in the academy, particularly if they maintain or express ideas that seek to advance decoloniality and liberation. The analysis of the differences between the noncombative, the pre-combative, and the combative remains key.
12 Ramose (2002, pp. 6–7).
13 Zea (1996, p. 69).
14 Ibid., p. 68.
15 Zea (1996, p. 118).
16 Ibid., p. 118.
17 Zea (1996, p. 100).
18 While explicit references to coloniality and decoloniality started in the early 1990s, I have mapped out prior moments of the decolonial turn (Maldonado-Torres 2011a, 2011b, 2011c, 2018).
19 Bondy (1995b, p. 161).
20 Las Casas (1992, p. 27).
21 Bondy (1995b, p. 216).
22 Ibid., pp. 262–263.
23 Ibid., p. 216.
24 Ibid., p. 216.
25 Ibid., p. 216.
26 Ibid., p. 216.
27 Ibid., p. 216.
28 Ibid., p. 216.
29 Ibid., p. 223.
30 Ibid., pp. 223–225.
31 For an exposition of Salazar Bondy's critiques of liberation theology, see Orvig and Sobrevilla (1995, pp. 42–44) and Marangoni (1974, pp. 215–216).
32 Ibid., p. 225.
33 Ibid., p. 226.
34 Ibid., p. 226.
35 Ibid., p. 226.
36 Ibid., p. 191.
37 Ibid., p. 227.
38 Ibid., p. 227.

39   Ibid., p. 227.

40   Ibid., p. 262.

41   Ibid., p. 216.

42   It is generally agreed that the philosophy of liberation emerges in 1971 in Argentina. Salazar Bondy and Zea were both major precursors and contributors. For an analysis of Salazar Bondy's place in the early history of the philosophy of liberation, see Orvig and Sobrevilla (1995, pp. 56–63). Orvig and Sobrevilla outline some important differences between Salazar Bondy's approach and that of the Argentinean liberation philosophers, including the influence of Heidegger and Levinas in the work of the Argentinean philosophy of liberation (p. 62). Zea explicitly engages the philosophy of liberation and includes both Salazar Bondy and Fanon, along with Enrique Dussel, as part of it in a paper entitled "La filosofía latinoamericana como filosofía de la liberación" presented in a conference on dependency and cultural creation that took place in Buenos Aires in 1973 (Zea 1974).

43   Dussel draws significantly from Salazar Bondy's diagnosis of philosophy in Latin America and from his appreciation of the importance of liberation (Orvig and Sobrevilla 1995, pp. 60–61), while Salazar Bondy appreciated what he took to be Dussel's reformulation of traditional philosophical issues (Salazar Bondy 1973, p. 397). Salazar Bondy's passing in early 1974 eliminated the possibility of what could have been a deeper engagement between the figures and the elaboration of their respective liberation philosophies.

44   Dussel (1977, p. 21).

45   Ibid., p. 94.

46   For an expansion of this argument and an exploration of philosophical work at the intersection of Levinas, Fanon, and Dussel, see Maldonado-Torres (2008).

47   Dussel (2014, p. 27 & 36).

48   Dussel (1995, p. 125).

49   Ibid., p. 125.

50   Dussel (1994, p. 190).

51   Dussel (2007, p. 412).

52   Ibid., p. 413.

53   Reinaga (1970, p. 16).

54   Reinaga (1978, p. 102).

55   Ibid., 99.

56   Ibid., 99.

57   Bondy (1995a, p. 240).

58   Fanon (2008, p. 91 & 206).

59   Ibid., p. xii.

References

Bartolomé de Las Casas (1992). *A Short Account of the Destruction of the Indies*. Translated by Nigel Griffin. London: Penguin Classics.

Britannica, T. Editors of Encyclopedia(2023). hoplite. In: *Encyclopedia Britannica*. January 23. https://www.britannica.com/topic/hoplite.

Colectiva Feminista en Construcción (2018). The Anti-Racist Manifesto of Colectiva Feminista en Construcción. *Latino Rebels* June 7.

Decolonize This Place. https://decolonizethisplace.org.

Dussel, E. (1973). *Para una ética de la liberación latinoamericana*, vol. vol. 1. Buenos Aires: Siglo XXI.

Dussel, E. (1994). *El encubrimiento del otro: hacia el origen del mito de la modernidad*, third ed. Quito: Editorial Abya Yala.

Dussel, E. (1995). *The Invention of the Americas: Eclipse of "the Other" and the Myth of Modernity*. Translated by Michael D. Barber. New York: Continuum.

Dussel, E. (1977 [1996]). *Filosofía de la liberación*, fourth ed., 1977. Bogotá, Colombia: Nueva América.

Dussel, E. (2007 [1994]). Sentido ético de la rebelión maya de 1994 en Chiapas. In: *La economía social desde la periferia: contribuciones latinoamericanas* (ed. J.L. Coraggio), 397–413. Buenos Aires: Editorial Altamira.

Dussel, E. (2014 [2008]). Anti-Cartesian meditations: On the origins of the philosophical anti-discourse of modernity." Trans. George Ciccariello-Maher. *Journal for Cultural and Religious Theory* 13 (1): 11–52.

Fanon, F. (1965). *A Dying Colonialism*. Translated by Haakon Chevalier. New York: Grove Press.

Fanon, F. (1988). *Toward the African Revolution: Political Essays*. Translated by Haakon Chevalier. New York: Grove Press.

Fanon, F. (2004). *The Wretched of the Earth*. Translated by Richard Philcox. New York: Grove Press.

Fanon, F. (2008). *Black Skin, White Masks*. Translated by Richard Philcox. New York: Grove Press.

Fanon Mendès France Mireille, and Nelson Maldonado-Torres. 2021. "For a Combative Decoloniality Sixty Years After Fanon's Death: An Invitation From the Frantz Fanon Foundation." Last Modified November 30, 2021. Accessed March 17. https://fondation-frantzfanon.com/for-a-combative-decoloniality-sixty-years-after-fanons-death-an-invitation-from-the-frantz-fanon-foundation/.

Levinas, E. (1969). *Totality and Infinity: An Essay on Exteriority*. Translated by Alphonso Lingis. Pittsburgh: Duquesne University Press.

Lugones, M. (2010a). The Coloniality of Gender. In: *Globalization and the Decolonial Option* (ed. W.D. Mignolo and A. Escobar), 369–390. London: Routledge.

Lugones, M. (2010b). Toward a decolonial feminism. *Hypatia* 25 (4): 742–759.

Lugones, M. (2022). Gender and universality in colonial methodology. In: *Decolonial Feminism in Abya Yala: Caribbean, Meso, and South American Contributions and Challenges* (ed. Y. Espinosa-Miñoso, M. Lugones, and N. Maldonado-Torres), 1–22. Lanham: Rowman & Littlefield.

Maldonado-Torres, N. (2006a). Post-continental philosophy: Its definition, contours, and fundamental sources. *Worlds and Knowledges Otherwise* 1 (3): 1–29.

Maldonado-Torres, N. (2006b). Toward a critique of continental reason: Africana studies and the decolonization of imperial cartographies in the Americas. In: *Not Only the Master's Tools: Theoretical Explorations in African-American Studies* (ed. L. Gordon and J.A. Gordon), 51–84. Boulder, CO: Paradigm Press.

Maldonado-Torres, N. (2008). *Against War: Views from the Underside of Modernity*. Durham: Duke University Press.

Maldonado-Torres, N. (2011a). Enrique Dussel's liberation thought in the decolonial turn. *Transmodernity: Journal of Peripheral Cultural Production of the Luso-Hispanic World* 1 (1): 1–30.

Maldonado-Torres, N. (2011b). El pensamiento filosófico del 'giro descolonizador'. In: *El pensamiento filosófico latinoamericano, del Caribe, y "Latino" (1300–2000)* (ed. E. Dussel, E. Mendieta, and C. Bohórquez), 683–697. Mexico D.F.: Siglo Veintiuno Editores.

Maldonado-Torres, N. (2011c). Thinking through the decolonial turn: Post-continental interventions in theory, philosophy, and critique – An introduction. *Transmodernity: Journal of Peripheral Cultural Production of the Luso-Hispanic World* 1 (2): 1–15.

Maldonado-Torres, N. (2015). Transdisciplinariedad y decolonialidad. *Quaderna* 3: http://quaderna.org/?p=418.

Maldonado-Torres, N. (2016). *Outline of Ten Theses on Coloniality and Decoloniality*. Frantz Fanon Foundation Last Modified October 2016. Accessed April 5, 2019. http://fondation-frantzfanon.com/outline-of-ten-theses-on-coloniality-and-decoloniality/.

Maldonado-Torres, N. (2017). On metaphysical catastrophe, post-continental thought, and the decolonial turn. In: *Relational Undercurrents: Contemporary Art of the Caribbean Archipelago* (ed. T. Flores and M.A. Stephens), 247–259. Los Angeles: Museum of Latin American Art.

Maldonado-Torres, N. (2018). The decolonial turn. In: *New Approaches to Latin American Studies: Culture and Power* (ed. J. Poblete), 111–127. London: Routledge.

Maldonado-Torres, N. (2019a). Afterword: Critique and decoloniality in the face of crisis, disaster, and catastrophe. In: *Aftershocks of Disaster: Puerto Rico Before and After María*, 332–342. Chicago: Haymarket Books.

Maldonado-Torres, N. (2019b). Ethnic studies as decolonial transdisciplinarity. *Ethnic Studies Review* 42 (2): 232–244.

Maldonado-Torres, N. (2020). *Interrogating Systemic Racism and the White Academic Field*. Frantz Fanon Foundation Last Modified June 16, 2020. Accessed March 20, 2022. https://fondation-frantzfanon.com/interrogating-systemic-racism-and-the-white-academic-field/.

Maldonado-Torres, N. (2022). El giro decolonial, el Caribe y la posibilidad de una filosofía poscontinental. *Transmodernity: Journal of Peripheral Cultural Production of the Luso-Hispanic World* 9 (8): 1–27. https://escholarship.org/uc/item/3w33x7bm.

Marangoni, V. (1974). Crónica de la discusión. *Stromata* 30 (1–2): 193–224.

Mignolo, W. (2007a). Delinking: The rhetoric of modernity, the logic of coloniality and the grammar of de-coloniality. *Cultural Studies* 21 (2–3): 449–514.

Mignolo, W. (2007b). Epistemic disobedience: The de-colonial option and the meaning of identity in politics. *Niterói* 22: 11–41.

Mignolo, W. (2011). *The Darker Side of Western Modernity: Global Futures, Decolonial Options*. Durham: Duke University Press.

Mignolo, W. (2021). *The Politics of Decolonial Investigations*. Durham: Duke University Press.

Orvig, H. and Sobrevilla, D. (1995). Introducción: Los escritos de Augusto Salazar Bondy sobre dominación y liberación. In: *Dominación y liberación: escritos 1966–1974* (ed. A.S. Bondy), 15–64. Lima: Fondo Editorial de la Facultad de Letras UNMSM.

Radebe, Z. and Maldonado-Torres, N. (forthcoming). Combative decoloniality and the BlackHouse paradigm. In: *Knowing/Unknowing: African Studies at the Crossroads* (ed. S. Ndlovu-Gatsheni and K. Schramm).

Ramose, M.B. (2002). The struggle for reason in Africa. In: *Philosophy from Africa: A Text with Readings* (ed. P.H. Coetzee), 1–8. Oxford: Oxford University Press.

Reinaga, F. (1969). *La revolución india*. Partido Indio de Bolivia: La Paz: Ediciones PIB.

Reinaga, F. (1970). *Manifiesto del Partido Indio de Bolivia*. Partido Indio de Bolivia: Ediciones PIB.

Reinaga, F. (1978). *El pensamiento amáutico*. Partido Indio de Bolivia: Ediciones PIB.

Salazar Bondy, A. (1969). *¿Existe una filosofía de nuestra América?* Mexico, D.F.: Siglo Veintiuno Editores.

Salazar Bondy, A. (1973). Filosofía de la dominación y filosofía de la liberación. *Stromata* 29 (4): 393–397.

Salazar Bondy, A. (1974a). *Bartolomé o de la dominación*. Buenos Aires: Ciencia Nueva.

Salazar Bondy, A. (1974b). Diálogos indianos entre Bartolomé de las Casas, Frantz Fanon, el cacique Hatuey y Ginés de Sepúlveda. *Crisis* 12: 37–39.

Salazar Bondy, A. (1995a). Bartolomé o de la dominación. In: *Dominación y liberación: escritos 1966–1974*, 191–264. Lima: Fondo Editorial de la Facultad de Letras UNMSM.

Salazar Bondy, A. (1995b). Diálogo sobre dominación y liberación. In: *Dominación y liberación: escritos 1966–1974*, 159–177. Lima: Fondo Editorial de la Facultad de Letras UNMSM.

Ticona Alejo, E. (2010a). La producción del conocimiento descolonizador en contextos del colonialismo interno: el caso de Fausto Reinaga en Quallasuyu-Bolivia. *Integra Educativa* 3 (1): 37–48.

Ticona Alejo, E. (2010b). s. *Saberes, conocimientos y prácticas anticoloniales del pueblo aymara-quechua en Bolivia*. La Paz: Agruco, Plural Editores.

Ticona Alejo, E. (2012). Frantz Fanon y el compromiso político de los intelectuales: Homenaje a los 50 años de su muerte (1961–2011). *La Migraña: Revista de análisis político* 4: 62–71.

Wiredu, K. (2004). Introduction: African philosophy in our time. In: *A Companion to African Philosophy* (ed. K. Wiredu), 1–27. Malden, MA: Blackwell Publishing.

Wynter, S. (1984). The ceremony must be found: After humanism. *Boundary 2* 12 (3): 19–65.

Wynter, S. (1991). Columbus and the poetics of the propter nos. *Annals of Scholarship* 8 (2): 251–286.

Wynter, S. (2003). Unsettling the coloniality of being/power/truth/freedom: Towards the human, after man, its overrepresentation – An argument. *The New Centennial Review* 3 (3): 257–337.

Zapata, C. and Oliva, E. (2016). Frantz Fanon en el pensamiento de Fausto Reinaga: cultura, revolución y nuevo humanismo. *Alpha* 42: 177–196.

Zea, L. (1974). La filosofía latinoamericana como filosofía de la liberación. In: *Dependencia y liberación en la cultura latinoamericana*, 32–47. Mexico City: Editorial Joaquín Mortiz.

Zea, L. (1996). *La filosofía americana como filosofía sin más*, 16th ed. Mexico, D.F.: Siglo Veintiuno Editores.

2

Decolonizing Understanding: A Utopian Reading of Aníbal Quijano's Coloniality of Power and Knowledge

ALEJANDRO VALLEGA

> *La vida esta hecha de la misma madera que los sueños.*
> *Life is made of the same material as dreams.*
> Aníbal Quijano

> *... utopian philosophy and its sensibilities situate themselves in the transgression of the fixity of cultural determinations, opening up a field of liberation in the present that suspends the values of continuous cultural projections ..."*
> Omar Rivera

In the following pages, I present a double reading of Aníbal Quijano's analysis of the coloniality of power and knowledge. The reading came about as a result of teaching Quijano's work in two contexts outside academic philosophy. One was a group of psychotherapists and graduate students working on depth psychology at the Pacifica Graduate Institute in Santa Barbara, California, in the decolonial psychology specialization. The other is the group of students that gather each year at the Summer decolonial school in Barcelona. What is significant about these students is that they are open to and presented modalities of thinking and understanding outside the traditional limits of philosophical analysis. The context works as an acoustic box in which new tones and possibilities come forth as we read and discussed his work. Thinking out of the kinds of attunements and sensibilities I find in such dialogues, and looking closely at specific seminal texts in Quijano's work, one finds in his work utopian openings for thinking beyond the sociological, political, economic, historical analysis that marks the Peruvian sociologist's work. Another way to say this is that in what follows I wish to mark a shift from a scientific reading to a hermeneutical reading, that is, as the engagement with coloniality of knowledge moves from the analysis of the system of power in its functioning to the question of how one may begin to understand and affirm the senses of being found in engaging the living concrete understanding of those being colonized. While in the first way of thinking one may ask about various methodologies that may be used in order to describe and critique the power system in its arising, functioning, and perpetuation, the latter question refers to understanding and meaning, the meaning and understanding figured by concrete lives under oppression and in transformative resistance in their happenings. I should note that I speak of "those being colonized" rather than of the "colonized" past tense, in order to indicate that full colonization has never happened, and that to speak of the "colonizer" over against the "colonized" places the latter in a *fait accompli*, in a situation already decided before any possible active affirmation beyond a dependent resistance to the colonizer, leaving those active resisting lives to be recognizable only as victims or reactive types, as peoples and lineages fated to be the *damne*. Again, my aim is to shift the discourse to the affirmation of distinctness in the living happening of those lives and ways of being not determined by coloniality of power and knowledge.

In "*Estética de la Utopía*" (Aesthetics of the Utopian), Quijano (2014) writes, "It is persistently proven that the transformation of the world happens first as an esthetic transfiguration."[1] As Quijano goes on to state, all utopias must have an esthetic dimension. What brings together the utopian and the esthetic is a shared drive for subversion. For Quijano at the heart of decolonial thought appears the need for the subversion of the colonized "imaginaries" that have been shaped and captured by the coloniality of power and knowledge.[2] It is through such a process that may come about "the constituting of a new rationality, of a new historical sense of social existence, be it individual or collective."[3] That this new sense of historical being and of existence requires the subversion of imaginaries refers decolonial thought to living's embodied, felt, memorial, and most ephemeral happenings, to pre-reflexive being in meaningful ways, in short to the aesthetic dimensions that would figure a fundamental point of engagement for a decolonial turning. This suggests that decolonial thinking cannot take its direction and form only in terms of the analysis of normative configurations, in terms of the world available to rational critique, to sociological and historical analysis, to the economic, political, and economic configurations of power on which much of Quijano's work focuses. In what follows I find openings toward incarnate, lived liberatory thinking, not through a critical reading of Quijano but by attending to dimensions in Quijano's work that increase or augment the questions and challenges found in seeking a decolonial turning. I should also note that, as the second citation above indicates, this work continues my dialogue with the Peruvian philosopher Omar Rivera (2019).[4]

Other Beginning: Modernity and Coloniality of Power and Knowledge as "*El Nuevo Patrón de poder*"

Aníbal Quijano's work is one of the foundations of decolonial thought.[5] In his seminal work, "Coloniality of Power, Eurocentrism and Latin America" he offers a socio-political historical analysis and critique of the coloniality of power and knowledge.[6] As he shows in the first section of the essay (titled, "America and the New Model of Global Power"), at the heart of modernity is a matrix of domination and violence, a racist and economic hegemonical system, a new world power that dominates and transforms the very sense of human existence. In speaking of this new system of power, Quijano uses the expression *"un nuevo patrón de poder."* The sense of *"patrón"* is important here, since it indicates a "model" or "form" of power, a kind of directive of power.[7] This power finds its form and directionality in the relation of race and capital. The two are the basic pillars of the coloniality of power. Race is a mental construction, a naturalized (hence eventually justified) hierarchical system, a hierarchical differential applied to populations worldwide. The second axis is the development of world capitalism around a single market system for all of world economies. That is, capitalism works through the control of all forms of labor, resources, and production.

At the beginning of Quijano's essay, it becomes clear that the work is not a mere socio-political and economic analysis of some historical event among others. In his essay, Quijano offers an account of the beginning of modernity, specifically its hidden origins. While the historical facts and Quijano's line of thinking in this account are well known, what passes almost undetected is precisely this: that Quijano is offering an account of the beginning of modernity. This is an account of the origin of the world in which we live. In the first section of the essay Quijano writes, "America was constituted as the first space/time of a new model of power of global vocation, and both in this way and by it became the first identity of modernity."[8] We are speaking of the "first space/time" of modernity, of the formation and manifestation of the coloniality of power and knowledge, the new *patrón de poder*. America appears as "the first identity of modernity." The full weight of the claim becomes clear when one considers that what results from the configuration of the patrón de poder is "a new temporal perspective of history."[9] Just like a mythical or a cosmological account, Quijano's account bespeaks the coming into being of a world order, its distinct time-space. In this case, the new understanding of time is created by a mental operation that leaves the other of Western consciousness in the past by creating a double temporality, a temporality that manifests in the binary distinctions such as, "primitive-civilized, magic-mythical-scientific, irrational-rational, traditional-modern."[10] In short, Quijano's essay begins with an account of the coming into being of the world in which we live and the logic which orders it.

With this account, Modernity is displaced in its supposed European beginning and recalled into its happening through another, distinct beginning. The origin of modernity is no longer situated by the cartesian ego cogito, as Hegel would situate it. At issue is the inceptive encounter and long process of the Atlantic exchange through which identities become under the patrón de poder. The central theme of the essay, as Quijano explains is "the implications of coloniality of power regarding the history of Latin America." This does not mean that Latin America appears as the subject of the coloniality of power and of modernity. Rather, Latin American existence figures the unfolding of modernity, from the outset, as the first identity—a figuration that, as we will see, makes evident that which ultimately cannot be circumscribed or thought in terms of European identity and rationality alone. In Quijano's analysis in its relation in/with/through coloniality of power or the patrón de poder, Latin American existence figures the other or invisible inceptive beginning of modernity. America bears a distinctness that the rationalist calculative project of progress that organizes around and justifies coloniality of power, conceals, ignores, subjugates, and continuously works to destroy. As such, this other beginning, in decentering the place of rationalism and historical modern understanding, would also necessarily put into question the concept of history and critique operative in the very unfolding of Quijano's socio-political and economical historical analysis. At issue here is not the refutation or a critique of Quijano's analysis, nor for that matter the need for the exclusion of European thought: the point is that in being attentive to Quijano's analysis, one finds an increase, a deepening and broadening, of the very question of modernity and the very task of thinking in light of this broadening. This deformative turn is already indicated at the beginning of Quijano's analysis. As we have seen there he gives an account (all be it in terms of sociology, history, etc.) of a new beginning of world order and of the categorization of humanity, a new way of being of the human, and in as much, an account that resonates with mythical accounts in that he is presenting the beginning and operative arche (patrón de poder) of modernity. With such a gesture, Quijano's very analysis has already set itself off beyond the limits of objective rational analysis and critique. His historical account in its mythical resonance and lineages, in its departure sets itself at a limit that will have no return, all be it through a socio-political and economic historical analysis.

Re-identification

The founding of this new world order happens through the global incorporation of world populations and regions into a single hegemonic order, ultimately through an historical "re-identification." People's identities, and this means the cultures and histories that serve to constitute their identities, are also violently appropriated, translated, and ultimately often destroyed. This amounts to the determination of "new geocultural identities."[11] The historical reidentification of peoples is fundamental in the unfolding of the patrón de poder or coloniality of power and knowledge, hence, to modernity.[12] Quijano discusses reidentification in his essays (Coloniality of Power, Eurocentrism, and Latin America), in the section titled, "The New Model of World Power and the New World Intersubjectivity." Following Quijano's discussion in this part of his essay the socio-political and economic historical approach in his analysis becomes explicit and also meets a marked limit.

As Quijano explains, the re-identification happens in a manner similar to the way capitalism comes to work. The diverse and heterogeneous cultural histories are subsumed into one world, into one homogeneous sense of cultural and intellectual meaningful existence, ending up under one cultural global order. The elements Quijano identifies that are affected under this homogenizing appropriation are "all of the experience, the histories, resources and cultural production."[13] Then he adds, other elements, "the control of subjectivity, culture, and specially of knowledge (*conocimiento*) and the production of knowledge."[14] Thus far in the analysis, the possibility for a critical engagement and critical destruction of the very power that organizes the world system we call modernity lies on the critique of the two axes (race and capitalism), in terms of economy, geopolitics, and sociological stratification. Ultimately, we are speaking of an analysis grounded on an objective critical position toward historical development.

Quijano goes on then to outline some of the main ways the appropriation happens.[15] The first aspect Quijano takes up is the appropriative expropriation of knowledge that is most convenient to the project of progress operative in the coloniality of power and knowledge and the development of this patrón de poder. Here, appropriation figures the infinite expansion of coloniality of power. The second aspect is the repression of the culture of the colonized: Quijano explains that this occurs through the destruction of their forms of production of knowledge, their models (patrónes) of production of sense, their symbolic universe, their forms of expression and of objectification of subjectivity. The third aspect happens with the re-education of those being colonized into the dominant cultural formations. The destruction of culture goes hand in hand with forced re-education that serves the furthering of domination and of the strengthening of the patrón de poder. Under the rubrics of education appear, "the field of technology and material activity or subjectivity, especially Judeo-Christian religiosity."[16] Then Quijano concludes, "All of those turbulent processes involved a long period of the colonization of cognitive perspectives, modes of producing and giving meaning, the results of material existence, the imaginary, the universe of intersubjective relations with the world: in short, the culture."[17] The forced education that accompanies the coloniality of power's unfolding ends up resulting in the colonization of cognitive perspectives, modes of production and giving meaning, in the colonization of material experience, but also in the colonization of "imaginaries" and "the universe of intersubjective meanings." Quijano concludes by gathering all of these dimensions of coloniality under one general category, "culture." But here, with the introduction of imaginaries something else has happened that slips from Quijano's sociopolitical and economic analysis and critique. While imaginaries seem to fit Quijano's analysis when placed under culture, something different happens when one considers the senses of imaginary in their lived happenings.

Imaginaries

Imaginaries are not mere productions of images that copy material reality. They are not mere fixed general images that accompany political projects and ideologies. Imaginaries are complex dynamic configurations of meaning. We are speaking of conscious as well as pre-reflexive articulations, which have basic aesthetic dimensions. By aesthetic I mean pre-reflexive embodied, memorial, emotional, and affective modalities of being, which bear meaning always in individual as well as communal horizons. We are speaking of meanings that increase the sense of being of individual and community. It is through the play of imago, of image making, that power takes form and becomes history, fact, and the object of critical consciousness. Such is the play of imaginaries. Imaginaries are not copies of rational structures of power but they are the way such structures take shape as they appear (*imago*). The patrón de poder, its dynamic force, gathers and becomes an arche through the imaginaries produced. Such is the taking place of imaginaries.

In the awareness of such dynamics in imaginary happenings becomes evident that one is not referring to static delimitations, identities, binary dialectics, but to processes that flow enacting figurations of power, dynamics that cannot be engaged in terms of static cultural ideologies.[18] This is a play of incarnate simulacra without a conceptual or teleological direction in their originary movement or happening, no-thing, no concept, no logical necessity, no necessary binary as their other, rather a dynamic movement with no ontological valance beyond its configuring of power. "Fanciful, visionary, fantastic, chimerical, quixotic," to be sure, the synonyms of imaginary make clear that this is not primarily associated with rationality, logic, and scientific or be it historical scientific fact. Omar Rivera captures this unbridled sense of imaginaries well in *Delimitations of Latin American Philosophy* when speaking precisely of Quijano's sense of imaginary, he writes: "The former means the web of intersubjective relations, both material and symbolic relations, that is grasped not through reason's analytic, atomistic conceptual, and instrumental form, but through intuition, feeling, and imagination—that is aesthetically."[19] Rivera goes on to make clear that such imaginaries have sense and how sense happens. "The latter (sense) means the way in which this web [the density of imaginaries] is given and grasped, both meaning and actual, and as in process of determination."[20] Imaginary happenings are aesthetic and dynamic, and this means they are lived, incarnate pre-reflexive configurations of understanding in the processes of configurating as they come to stand and appear.

Imaginaries happen in performative ways, they happen as they are lived. That is, they take form through enactments at various levels of understanding. They happen at pre-reflexive levels as well as in the way they come to be sedimented into rationalities and logics of present worlds, in practices and institutions, private and public. Indeed, imaginaries function not within or outside reason and already operative conceptual and ideological configurations. In their configuring happenings, they violate the difference between the rational and the irrational, the present and the invisible, and carry us into a latent time-space invested not only with reason's operations but into the entanglement, porosity, and permeability of configuring consciousness.[21] Neither inside nor outside the rational, neither subjectively/internally inhabited nor externally/objectively situated, imaginaries happen through embodying, affective, memorial experiences.[22] I should add that given the dynamics of imaginary happenings, and regardless of their duration, they happen "beyond the restrictions of the real."[23]

Thinking with Imaginaries in Mind

The centrality of the imaginary in Quijano's analysis of coloniality of power and knowledge is only more emphatically stated in other texts. In "Colonialidad y Modernidad/Racionalidad" Quijano writes:

> This is not only the subordination of other cultures with respect to Europe, in an exterior relation. It is about the colonization of other cultures, although without doubt with different intensity and depth according to each case. It consists, first of all, in a colonization of the imaginary of the dominated. That is to say, it operates in the interiority of that imaginary. To a certain extent it [*the patrón of domination*] is part of it.[24]

Coloniality of power, the patrón de poder, works within the imaginary, but not only does the patrón affect the imaginaries in the reidentification, or invention of peoples' identities. The patrón is at work "within" imaginaries. But how does one understand "within"? One can follow Quijano's path. Here a differentiation and relation are established. The partrón would seem to be outside, other than the imaginaries. Power affects imaginaries and inserts itself in the imaginaries. This can be understood through the three of moments of appropriation: coloniality of power destroys, appropriates, and re-educates. The material history takes hold and ultimately recreates the peoples' imaginaries. But this ignores the dense happening of imaginaries, which are not simply images and ideas of present material reality. As noted above, the imaginaries perform the imago, they give form and sustain power in its configurations. Therefore, a more accurate and incisive way of seeing imaginaries would be to invert the relation and ask how the imaginaries themselves operate, and specifically to what extent their happening remains beyond and yet fundamental to the configuration of political material projects, and how they may be essential to the appropriating and reconfiguring of material reality, and to the transformation of culture. We are speaking here of the mental images that orient consciousness, of mythical and symbolic levels that precede and yet orient rational thought in its historical and critical approaches, in the configuring of concepts, and in the projecting of ideas and even possible knowledge, even in the encountering of experience considered worthy as knowledge, i.e., in the orientation that affords the configuring of values. Here we find not only the level of production of knowledge, but the realm of imaginaries, and with it the projections, desires, fears, loss, the oniric (*oneiros, dream*) levels of understanding and knowledge making that do not correspond or are subsumed under rationality, at least as traditionally understood (and separated from body and affectivity).[25] This plunges us into the (un)consciousness of those under siege, under the active threat of colonization ... and almost unnoticed, it puts the question of coloniality of power and knowledge beyond rational objective judgement and the categories that would sustain such sense of history and critique. The issue is that once the imaginaries appear as dimensions of coloniality, reason and socio-economic and political historical conditions are no longer sufficient for understanding the coloniality of power, nor can an historical analysis and critiques that follow Quijano's line of analysis be taken as sufficient to engage the padrón de poder in its happening.[26]

From Being Colonized to Gerundive Incarnate Resistance

In "*Estética de la Utopía*" (Esthetics of the Utopian) Quijano writes: "What the dominant culture dishonors, blocks or hides, above all in cultures with a colonial origin ... is, most of the time, what the oppressed speaks, dreams, loves; their ways of relating to forms, colors, to sounds, to their bodies and words; everything that they do or omit in order to satisfy or realize themselves without permission or the resources of the oppressor ..."[27] We find here the aesthetic dimensions we have associated with the happening of imaginaries. Here the emphasis is not on social–political or economic dimensions of coloniality, and the issues that appears could hardly be contained by a historical analysis such as the one we found in the other texts in discussion. Speaking (not writing), dreams, and love, the ways of relating to forms, colors, and sounds become the target of the padrón de poder on the way to reidentification. But the esthetic here is not understood as that which has been dominated and entirely transformed. Rather, at this esthetic level, "What is indigenous and what is black lead to the recreation of all forms, all rhythms, all the veins of relation with the universe, they lead to their own reception of what comes from globalization and all the world news."[28] The padrón de poder figures in its hegemonic movement its own failure, as in the attempt to create a single world it brings together lineages, histories, simultaneous temporalities, ways of being, imaginaries that lead beyond it.[29] Rather than the reduction of lives and ways of being and *conocimiento*, one finds here, as Quijano turns to esthetics and utopia, a radical liberatory movement, a radical interiority operative within and yet beyond the padrón de poder. At this level the decolonial question is not about the conquered, the ontologically damned in a past tense, as a static form of identity. The struggle is ongoing: the being of the oppressed figures a time-space of ongoing struggle and resistance.[30] Indeed, as Rivera shows in *Andean Aesthetics and Anticolonial Resistance*, at the level of imaginaries and aesthetic living one finds dynamic thresholds, a time-space of incarnate resistance and transformative happenings. Under such struggle, Quijano writes, "The presence of the dominated in their reconstituting of the universe of intersubjectivity in Latin America" becomes "more alive and stronger."[31] While in this essay Quijano puts forth the continuous transformative struggle and potential decolonial turns at the level of esthetics, he ultimately phrases the very liberatory movement back into history as a question separate and above the imaginaries. Quijano concludes, "And it is the birth of this new history, that may lead to the liberation of the imaginaries of the dominated and to world subversion ..."[32] Here we find that a new history figures the movement that will liberate the imaginary. However, as we saw above in our discussion, the relation between material history and imaginaries cannot be understood in such limited terms, but as an incarnate movement of imaginaries, of the imago, a movement that remains beyond historical or sociological analysis alone. How may we begin to understand history in light of such living, incarnate happenings?[33] With their pre-reflexive dynamics? What dimensions of experience are in question here? What is the phenomena that may introduce us to a decolonial liberatory imaginary movement beyond Quijano's sociopolitical and economic historical analysis?

Anti-Phenomena

We can begin to respond to these questions by listening to another voice concerning the reidentification under the patrón de poder and the potential for resistance and transformation within it and beyond it. In "Toward a Decolonial Feminism," Maria Lugones (2010) writes,

> The civilizing transformation justified the colonization of memory, and thus of people's senses of self, of intersubjective relation, of their relation to the spirit world, to land, to the very fabric of their conception of reality, identity, and social, ecological, and cosmological organization. Thus, as Christianity became the most powerful instrument in the mission of transformation, the normativity that connected gender and civilization became intent on erasing community, ecological practices, knowledge of planting, of weaving, of the cosmos, and not only on changing and controlling reproductive and sexual practice.[34]

Before considering the various levels of phenomena this passage opens for us, I should note that in her essay Lugones adds another dimension to the issue of coloniality of power and knowledge. In it she shows the coloniality of gender that happens in the draft and as an elemental in the *patrón de poder*.[35] At the same time, she also notices that Quijano's approach implicitly allows for the impression that there was nothing in the Américas prior to the inceptive quickening of modernity. The emphasis in the creation of new peoples and ways of being in the unfolding and under de patrón gives the impression of a prior emptiness. Lugones writes,

> The global, capitalist, colonial, system of power that Anibal Quijano characterizes as beginning sixteenth century in the Americas and enduring until today met not a world to be formed, a world of empty minds and evolving animals ... Rather, it encountered complex cultural, political, economic, and religious beings: selves in complex relations to the cosmos, to other selves, to the earth, to living beings, to the inorganic, in production; erotic, aesthetic, and linguistic expressivity, whose knowledges, longings, practices, institutions, and forms of government were replaced but met, understood, and entered into in tense, violent, and dialogues and negotiations that never happened.[36]

As Lugones points out, the Américas were fully inhabited by peoples, by ways of being and thinking, by modalities of understanding and knowing that are simply ignored, at times lost, subjugated, and certainly missed with the inception. These are precisely the dimensions that in our attentive reading have begun to appear at the edge of Quijano's analysis, insights beyond the objective rationalist analysis of coloniality of power and knowledge.

In light of Maria Lugones' words, let us consider now for a moment the various level that appear as one begins to think about what is being destroyed and disallowed: living practices, habits, traditions; and behind these, images, projections, affective experiences, memory (voluntary and involuntary), desires, dreams, fears, embodied existence in the carrying of lineages, ways of being, senses of the world around, relationality between people/s, family, nutrition (what/who we eat or do not eat), sexuality, the elements, earth and sky ... the time-space for the configuration of identities, of concepts and of ways of interpreting experience and giving it its value through senses of relation and through knowledge configurations ... directionality (past, present-future, their position with regards to one's consciousness, and the placement of one's consciousness in light of how the three terms are related: mythical, seasonal, historical, clock time) ... the projective time-space of the becoming of consciousness and in which movements one's subjectivity and common sense are constituted; the time-space affective and embodied in which delimitations, limits, and possibilities occur. Imagination, consciousness, and existence are inseparable here, and always in relation to a limit that is not determined solely by a rational subject's desires, calculative projections, and cogitation.

Rituals, myth, imaginaries, cosmologies, the embodied originary ways of engaging existence in its movement, such ecological rather than egological being (*estar-siendo*),[37] the originary encounter with the nonhuman, with the uncanny—these ways of being in the world, with their depth, this is what is not allowed. If what is expropriated is what is useful to the calculative and instrumental rationalism that aims to conquer all existence, what is forbidden and excluded is what impedes, deviates, and remains beyond the grasp of modern rationalism. Ultimately, what those being colonized must unlearn are the mythical, imaginary, and the sacred—the basic ways in which even prereflexively one finds a place and world through the originary engagement with existence beyond subjective rationalism, instrumental calculative reasoning, and most importantly, beyond the knowledge produced by historical analysis and critique. Under coloniality of power, the living cosmos must become resource and matter, the native, the mestizo, the negro must become bodies that labor, not vessels and thresholds of embodied knowledge; their ways of connecting with existence in the movement of being (*estar-siendo*)[38] beyond domination, control, manipulation, their ways of being in the world through ritual must be forbidden, or at least they must be rendered epistemically obsolete. Knowledge that is beyond the rationalist productive desire of the capitalist economic and technological world system would negate the ordering of the conqueror and therefore must be erased.

With the introduction of imaginaries and the sacred Quijano's discourse goes beyond its limit, but in doing so, it also performatively exposes concealed, submerged, obscured, and subjugated dimensions of modernity, that which in the absence of a dialogue in the inceptive happening keeps missing, subjugating it, covering over it, dismissing it, or destroying it. Here we are touching not only on the excluded socioeconomically, but that which cannot be said, that which is not of the rational, and also not of the psychoanalytic (if the latter is understood as a way to reincorporate the subject into the "rational" modern world). This displacement occurs as modern consciousness appears inseparably from the imaginary, the symbolic–mythic, inseparably from the excluded ritual. Here what was once the other of rationality appears on its own, as a kind of anti-phenomena, neither wholly determined by reidentification, nor as the other of such determinations, that is, it appears as nothing, meaningless.

Indirectly, the symbolic ritual, the imaginary, those elements of consciousness in its taking flight in the inceptive movement in configurations of new meaning do appear in the third moment of appropriation in Quijano's account. Quijano's third point, as I have already pointed out is that the dominated must learn another consciousness, they must learn a new mythical symbolic system. This is why Quijano says that in Latin American re-education, indoctrination happens primarily in terms of the connection to "Judeo-Christian religions."[39] To say it in another way that underscores a point of convergence between the capitalist racism that secures the world system of exploitation and the exclusive appropriative element of mythic–symbolic re-education: What those being colonized must learn is the separation between body and mind/spirit, the division that is articulated from Descartes on in modern philosophy, and which as Quijano notes in his discussion of European thought, only indicates the fact of the new world-order operative under Eurocentric instrumental/utilitarian modernity. And yet, those being oppressed, exiled, excluded, carry in their ways of being meaning, sense, depth, constellations of being: precisely in their/our distinct living they/we (*nosotros*) appear as living anti-phenomena.[40] This living anti-phenomena in its radical happenings bears the full force of openings to fecund understanding.[41]

Decolonizing Understanding

The ways of being and understanding made evident through the present reading are acknowledged by Quijano in his analysis and are dramatically made explicit by two moments. In Quijano's (1993) "Modernity, Identity, and Utopia in Latin America,"[42] speaking of the distinct sense of Latin American consciousness, he writes:

> For many of us, this was the most genuine meaning of our searches and confusion during the period of the agitated debates over dependency theory. It is also true, however, that we were able to get at the question of our identity only intermittently. It was no accident that it was not a sociologist but a novelist, Gabriel Garcia Marquez who, by good fortune or coincidence, found the road to this revelation, for which he won the Nobel Prize. For by what mode, if not the aesthetic–mythic, can an account be given of this simultaneity of all historical times in the same time? And what but mythic time can be this time of all times? Paradoxically, this strange way of revealing the untransferable identity of a history proves to be a kind of rationality, which makes the specificity of that universe intelligible.[43]

Here Quijano refers to what he finds to be the key to Latin American consciousness and identity, namely simultaneous temporality.[44] I should underscore that it is this simultaneity that is understood historically above, when in "Estética de la utopía," Quijano speaks of the indigenous and black reception of globalization in their own way, in a new formation of history. The ground for that new history is the living force of imaginaries composed of various temporalities, various relational and simultaneous asymmetrical values, epistemic expectations, ways of making and encountering meaning, and of undergoing lived understanding. Briefly, forms of material production that would be considered in the past of capitalist progress, viewed as left behind in the infinite horizontal movement of modernity, in Latin America are operative and in a vertical relation configure present consciousness. We are speaking of relational gatherings into consciousness and senses of border identities and shifting presents outside the Western myth of historical progress, homogeneous subjective rational objectivity, beyond the analytical rationality that grounds Quijano's historical analysis.[45]

To return to the text above, Quijano's reflection on Marquez and esthetic-mythic thought can only make sense if one considers that Quijano, in and through his own analysis, is brought to phase existence beyond the rational historical paradigm behind his sociopolitical and economic historical critique. Quijano's engagement of the esthetic–mythical marks not a dismissal of history but brings forth a question, the question of the sense of history that remains to be rethought. Reading closely Quijano's work, one must at least take pause in encountering a sense of history that cannot be simply incorporated to modern rationalism. A displacement has occurred. The displacement is marked in that while Quijano situates his thinking within the social sciences and logical material-ism, he must turn to Garcia-Marquez who is able to engage Latin American reality in its broad sense. It is that writing beyond the logic of Quijano's analysis that opens thought to the happening of existing in Latin America. This writing refers to a kind of "rationality" says Quijano ... but what does "rationality" mean once it begins to call for engaging the imaginary and aesthetic dimensions of understanding and meaning? The issue cannot be solved by remaining with the difference between the rational vs. the mythical religious.

This displacement is not a move away from concrete situations, rather, in its attentiveness to the concrete dynamic situation it would become a movement of thought fitting to the coloniality of power's blind side, to the anti-phenomena, in its circumstance and in the overturning of the patron de poder or coloniality of power and knowledge. The overturning can only happen in the draft, fac-ing the force of the patrón de poder, going through it. But the overturning is precisely in the increase, in the way the thinking and praxis do not repeat or remain with the same rational positionality of Quijano's analysis. More specifically, the decolonial movement of history happens, and decolonial thinking with it, only if analytic objectivity gives way to living concreteness, and this means aban-doning a position of judgment from a rational point zero, or from an objectivity subjectivity that returns to reason's historically assigned judging place in response to concreteness. Following atten-tively Quijano, beginning in displacement, thought figures a dynamic transformative force, a draft beyond the patrón. This is why speaking of political change and utopia, Quijano states a few pages later in "Modernity, Identity, and Utopia in Latin America":

> The fact that such a project was first lodged in the aesthetic or symbolic expressive sphere does nothing other than indicate, as always, that it is within that sphere that the possible transformations of the his-toric totality are prefigured. Is this not what was at issue in the debates of our European counterparts Lukacs, Adorno, Benjamin, and Brecht before the Second World War? Was not aesthetic liberation seen as, in effect, the antechamber of a possible social liberation?[46]

At issue now appear the dimensions of being that slip from Quijano's analysis. Indeed, following Quijano's words as a clue, the questions that appear in making explicit the complexity added to the reading of Quijano when one considers the imaginary now would invite a rereading of Lukacs, Adorno, Benjamin ... this would be a rethinking of modernity but from a concrete incarnate Latin American thinking and experience without suspending the workings of imaginaries from philo-sophical thought.

The double reading of Quijano's work opens and increases the registers and force of it. Its dimen-sion beyond historical analysis and critique appear only more striking when one considers that, if Latin American consciousness is constituted with, in, and as the relational movement of asym-metrical simultaneous temporality then, then the mythical, cosmological, memorial, affective, embodying dimensions of that consciousness would be operative in the very happening of under-standing. At issue is not the mythical, cosmological over against the analytical historical, but a simul-taneous anachronic gathering of distinct ways of thinking, living, and being, configurations that in that simultaneity augment the sense of being that may be found in a binary thinking in terms of either history and reason *or* the mythical, or in the dialectic tension between the two. The challenge is thinking in/with/through the irreconcilable distinctness that is the happening of the colonial difference, a thinking that happens in standing in, embodying, letting go, in loss and transfiguration, i.e., in departure with the present concepts of history as scientific fact, of critique, and in departure with the colonial difference.[47] This is a necessary opening I find already figured by the Peruvian historian Alberto Flores Galindo, when referring to the round table in which Quijano and other sociologist in 1965 engaged critically and negatively the work of the Peruvian writer and scholar José Maria Arguedas, he writes, "Concepts and categories insulated sociologists from reality. Arguedas, on the contrary, confused his own life with those debates: 'I feel terror at the same time as great hope.'"[48]

Notes

1   EU, p. 733.
2   EU, p. 734.
3   EU, p. 735.
4   In this case, this is specifically a dialogue with, Omar Rivera (2019).
5   I offer a detailed reading of Quijano's work in chapter five of *Latin American Philosophy, from Identity to radical Exteriority* (Alejandro Vallega, 2014–2015).
6   Aníbal Quijano (2000).
7   Patrón comes from the Latin "pater" "father."
8   CP, p. 533.
9   CP, p. 542.
10   CP, p. 542.
11   CP, p. 540.
12   CP, p. 540.
13   CP, p. 540.
14   CP, p. 540.
15   CP, pp. 540–541.
16   CP, p. 541.
17   CP, p. 541.
18   This is a crucial point that Rivera makes in his discussion of decolonial dynamics in *Delimitations of Latin America Philosophy, Beyond Redemption*. DLAP, p. 178.
19   DLAP, p. 164.
20   DLAP, p. 164.
21   Thinking beyond the binary reason and subconscious is concretely possibla, as is the case in Gloria Anzaldúas work, and as Omar Rivera (2024).
22   In chapter three of *Indigenous and Popular Thinking in América*, Rodolfo Kusch offers a rethinking of this dichotomy between inside and outside forms of understanding, as a double simultaneous movement in understanding, in which intellect (outward understanding) and emotion and affect (inward movement) happen together (Rodolfo Kusch 2010).
23   Here Rivera is speaking specifically of community, indigenous thought, and in reference to the surrealist aesthetic discipline found in Mariátegui, as well as in such events as the festival. DLAP, p. 166.

24 CMR, p. 12.

25 Vide foot note 23.

26 Evidence of this is found in that the very happening of coloniality of power in its material history is not based on a rational moment but in a relation of unfathomable violence that establishes the originary nexus of power, the differential of domination is the difference between conqueror and conquered first, before becoming rationalized, evangelized, naturalized, and institutionalized. As we already noted, power is not something that someone has, it does not have any ontological valance. Power is relation, material relation, but in light of the fundamental operation of imaginaries, that materiality in a sociopolitical and economic historical sense cannot be identified as the origin of power in its dynamic happening. The issue is that with the engagement with imaginaries, one must wonder if there is not more to power than material historical relations and that which rational critique and historical sociopolitical and economic analysis can reveal.

27 EU, p. 740.

28 EU, p. 740.

29 This internal undoing of coloniality of power is well articulated by Glissant in his discussion of the plantation and the origins of jazz in "Close Place, Open Word" in *Poetics of Relation* (Édouard Glissant 2010). "Lieu clos, parole ouvert" (Édouard Glissant 1990).

30 To use Omar Rivera's term in *Andean Aesthetics and Anticolonial Resistance: A Cosmology of Unsociable Bodies*.

31 EU, p. 740.

32 EU, p. 740.

33 This is not the place to develop a thesis about this, but I should note that I am thinking of the way the sense of history may be rethought in light of Alberto Flores Galindo's (2010) work. Alberto Flores Galindo (1993). This question beings to open when one reads Rivera's analysis of Quijano's in contrast to José Carlos Mariátegui and Alberto Flores Galindo in chapter six of *Delimitations*, titled, "Aesthetic Disciplines." DLAP, pp. 141–170.

34 María Lugones (2010, p. 745).

35 "I use the term coloniality following Anibal Quijano's analysis of the capitalist world system of power in terms of "coloniality of power" and of modernity, two inseparable axes in the workings of this system of power. Quijano's analysis provides us with a historical understanding of the inseparability of racialization and capitalist exploitation as constitutive of the capitalist system of power as anchored in the colonization of the Americas. In thinking of the coloniality of gender, I complicate his understanding of the capitalist global system of power..." TDF, p. 745.

36 TDF, p. 747.

37 "*Estar-siendo*" is a term meant to indicate a dynamic sense of being, dynamic in the sense that being is understood as an incarnate gerundive happening, not oriented by egological consciousness but as partaking in ecological being.

38 See note 37.

39 CP, p. 541.

40 This is for example behind the sense of the "nepantleras" and of "*conocimiento*" in Gloria Anzaldúa. Regarding the nepantleras, Anzaldúa writes, "We're not quite at home here but also not quite at home over there. Like queer and bisexual people who must live in both straight and gay worlds, or like rural people living in cities—stuck between the cracks of home and other culture—we experience dislocation, disorientation .... Dwelling in liminalities, in-between states or nepantlas, las nepantleras cannot be forced to stay in one place, locked into one perspective or perception of things or one picture of reality.... Nepantleras are not constrained by one culture or world but experience multiple realities" (Gloria Anzaldúa 2015).

41 This is shown for example in Gloria Anzaldúa's sense of "conocimiento," "la facultad," and of the "nepantlera" consciousness in Luz en *Light in the Dark / Luz en lo Oscuro*. Ibid.

42 From here on MIU followed by the page number. In this section I am engaging Quijano's later writing, which, as Rivera shows, should be differentiated from his earlier works (such as Quijano 1979).

43 MIU, p. 150.

44 I have treated the question of simultaneous temporality and Latin American time consciousness in *Latin American Philosophy: from Identity to Radical Exteriority*, ch. 6. LAP, pp. 120–136. On the question of temporality, also see Alejandro Arturo Vallega (2021).

45 MIU, p. 150

46 MIU, p. 153.

47 EU, p. 733.

48 ISI, 205. "*Los conceptos y las categorías preservaban a los sociólogos de la realidad; Arguedas, en cambio, confundía su vida misma con estos debates: "Siento algún terror al mismo tiempo que una gran esperanza.*" BI, 358. Original text by Arguedas in *¿He vivido en vano? Mesa Redonda sobre Todas las Sangres, 23 de junio de 1965* (Lima, Perú: IEP ediciones, Instituto de Estudios Peruanos, 1985), p. 68.

References

Anzaldúa, G. (2015). *Light in the Dark/Luz en lo Oscuro*, 81–82. London: Duke University Press.

Galindo, A.F. (1993). *Buscando un Inca*. México: Editorial Grijalbo.

Galindo, A.F. (2010). *In Search of an Inca*. Tr. Carlos Aguirre, Charles F. Walker, and Willie Hiatt. Cambridge University Press.

Glissant, É. (1990). *Poétique de la Relation*, 77–99. Paris: Gallimard.

Glissant, É. (2010). *Poetics of Relation*. Tr. Betsy Wing, 63–75. University of Michigan Press.

Kusch, R. (2010). *Indigenous and Popular Thinking in América*. Tr. María Lugones and Joshua M. Price, 21–22. Duke University Press.

Lugones, M. (2010). Toward a decolonial feminism. *Hypatia* 25 (4): 742–759.

Quijano, A. (1979). *Encuentro y debate: Una untroducción a Mariátegui*. Lima: Mosca Azul.

Aníbal Quijano (1993). "Modernity, identity, and Utopia in Latin America," boundary 2, 20 (3), *The Postmodern Debate in Latin America*, Autumn, 140–155.

Quijano, A. (2000). Coloniality of power, eurocentrism and Latin America. *Nepantla: Views from South* 1 (3): 533–580.

Quijano, A. (2014). "*Estética de la Utopía*," Cuestiones y Horizontes. *Ontología Esencial: De la dependencia histórica-estructural a la colonialidad/descolonialidad del poder* (ed. D.A. Climaco), 733–741. Buenos Aires: Clacso.

Rivera, O. (2019). *Delimitations of Latin American Philosophy, Beyond Redemption*. Bloomington, IN: Indiana University Press.

Rivera, O. (2024). *Andean Aesthetics and Anticolonial Resistance: A Cosmology of Unsociable Bodies*, 183–185. London: Bloomsbury Press.

Vallega, A. (2014–2015). *Latin American Philosophy, from Identity to radical Exteriority*, 99–119. Bloomington: Indiana University Press.

Vallega, A.A. (2021). *Tiempo y Liberación: Exordio a pensamientos liberatorio, vivenciales y dcoloniales*. Mexico: AKAL/Inter-pares.

3

Transmodernity as a Postulate: First Eurocentrism, Prejudice, and Critique

The historical narrative dealing with modernity comprises several entangled concepts that are difficult to identify. Indeed, it blends a variety of cultural concepts (Modernity, Empire, Globalization, Coloniality, and Renaissance, among others) with economic ones (for example, Mercantilism, Capitalism, Socialism, and Neoliberalism) as well as political ones (such as Liberalism, Fascism, Republicanism, and Parliamentarism), blurring or often entirely fading their boundaries. In abstract terms, all these historical systems are confused with a single Totality from which they are thought to emerge. This cultural whole is conveniently called Globalization and is regarded as a single trunk from which minor cultural differences arise. How can we *locate* Latin America in world history without having it deny itself as a ramification of this modernity or as a millenary geopolitical autonomy? To answer the question, it is necessary to offer a broad argument, with some indicative aspects of the meaning of modernity and what it has left aside, which defines what will from here on be referred to as *transmodernity*. The argumentative reconstruction is not easy; yet, this work will attempt to address general aspects, and although doing so entails the risk of losing details, it will also enable the reader to obtain a fuller panorama.

The False Dilemma: Assimilation or Extinction

There is an implicit perception of belonging to a single cultural unit in which any culture is a branch that is only recognized as compared to the European trunk. Any cultural aspect is only measurable in relation to the Christian culture of northwestern Europe, which is the only point of reference for a culture to acquire a sense of its own, even if it is found in a remote place on the planet. From this

Struggles for Liberation in Abya Yala, First Edition. Edited by Luis Rubén Díaz Cepeda and Ernesto Rosen Velásquez.
© 2024 John Wiley & Sons, Inc. Published 2024 by John Wiley & Sons, Inc.

Eurocentric perspective, the entire world is unevenly incorporated, relegating other cultural forms to lesser significance or insignificance. The incorporation of the Americas to the European world was carried out through explicit acts of political-military conquest marked by violence. This caused the absolutization of the Iberian culture (Hispanics and Lusitanians) and the simultaneous annihilation of the multiple and innumerable people of the Americas.

Nevertheless, from the early Latin American perspective, such an abrupt change in the cultural world meant the disappearance, albeit partially, of three millennia of geopolitical continuity in an enormous space running from the Artic Circle to Patagonia. In any case, that rupture restricted their cultural practices to acts of resistance and placed them on the edge of survival. It is perhaps the most critical event in world history as it is the first occupation by a cultural block (minute in number to some extent) of an entire continent, and its consequences are worldwide and very long term, an issue sometimes not seen in all its breadth and depth.

The military triumph of the Conquest was the material condition that determined the cultural implantation in the Americas, resulting in a structurally violent cultural synthesis. It is not a culture featuring violent aspects that are parts of a more peaceful whole, but a culture defined by violence. It is a material culture whose form is violence itself. The simple territorial occupation took place together with the excessive depletion of nature and the enslaving exploitation of human labor. The geopolitics of domination marks a temporary turning point in human history. In addition, it creates a structural inequality as a matrix of violence that represents the starting point of any possible interpretation. Before any cultural representation, there was the cataclysm of mass murder by an unexpected, undeclared, and irrational war. Before the symbolic death of culture, there was material death marking the end of politics and the beginning of war.

This war culminated in the seizing of the urban centers in both Tenochtitlan and Cuzco. The European way of being was then imposed until it became the natural way in the following decades. It is an ambiguous process full of contradictions, without precise planning, and whose expansion encounters all forms of resistance. However, this does not mean that the war is over. On the contrary, the process of occupation and human subordination is so long that "pacification" is still spoken of to this day, under new denominations and euphemisms. Such (political-military) pacification first sought moral authority over the "conquered"; then, it proceeded with cultural events such as patron saint festivities, the replacement of images, and the teaching of Spanish to mitigate explicit violence. Finally, Christendom sought to endorse it in an effort to legitimize its unequal presence. Since then, culture has been a form of violence, yet mitigated; that is, it is a continuation of the war through other means. While politics operates primarily within urban centers, outside them, direct armed confrontations persist against ancestral cultures that are geographically marginalized and culturally oppressed.

The cultural reference for a young, middle-class Latin American in an urban environment is his/her proximity or remoteness to the Western culture (European or North American, mainly), while a young Latin American from lower down on the social scale or in a rural environment has other cultural references such as belonging to a *pueblo originario*[1] (which she/he can accept or reject, but which will always disturbingly accompany her/him). It is genuinely exceptional that the first group peeps into the culture of the other to the point of being suspicious of strangers who inevitably share the same neighborhood. There is an implicit conflict in this situation. The former can easily accept Western culture while prioritizing their lifestyle, while the latter will perceive this stance as morally contradictory. They view such cultural adoption as a betrayal of their origins, as the very rejection that originally caused their cultural eclipse. Consequently, their communities and families have dissolved, leaving them stranded in a cultural limbo where they have not assimilated the foreign culture but have already lost their own. This is where the dilemma arises.

Nowadays, individuals who deeply study the cultures close to their own, whether for geographical, linguistic, symbolic, or religious reasons, may deem the recovery of ancestral traditions as useless. Thus, without much questioning, they simply carry on in their "Western" tradition, whether it would be in the most privileged part of New York or in a marginal neighborhood in Quito. Only in exceptional cases will they go back to the different cultures or some of their aspects to explain to them their world. When defining their position, or "consciousness," some perspective can be raised about their interpretation of the "Modernity" experienced. It is an uncritical, lively but no less valid interpretation; yet, even critical interpretations revolve around the same "zero point" of the "universalized" culture: Modernity. Therefore, an activist using an umbrella in Taiwan can defend freedom of expression with the same idea of liberal democracy as a Moroccan citizen can against the Monarchy. In these cases and many others, recovering "non-Western" traditions would be considered useless or "non-modern," or simply those left aside as marginal, subterranean, or subaltern. Furthermore, in many cases, it is an instinctive reaction against cultural hegemony. Thus, Lady Gaga (the one that is, the one that is worthy, the significant one) can dress in diamonds, and a follower (the one that is not, the invalid, the insignificant) in some marginal neighborhood in Mexico or Bamako will be dressed simply in plastic.

Different expressions revolve around a cultural system that subsumes everything—a system that swallows what comes its way and makes it part of itself. This process is a culturalist fallacy in which what is excluded or marginal can never be like what it constitutes. It is a fallacy because the aspirant's condition of possibility is subject to the object of the aspiration, whose ideal is simply unattainable, and it is, for the same reason, fetishized. Furthermore, this level of irrationality promotes cultural dynamism at all other levels, however critical they may be. The "post-moderns" thought that these expressions had surpassed modernity; however, they have not distinguished between being a part and a totality in the planetary cultural pluriverse.[2] Mistaking particularity for the totality is part of the problem, for example believing that their "rule of law" is universal and not a set of "usages and customs" imposed through the colonization war.

The dilemma around cultural consciousness emerges again: it is either accepted or rejected. The "Western" is either assimilated, even under the appearance of affordability, or extinguished in its isolation, in a gesture of collective suicide. It does not seem trivial that most of the *pueblos originarios* in Latin America feel relatively autonomous. However, there is an isolation that rather marginalizes and excludes them from the possibilities afforded to the national states to which they belong. Paradoxically, this cultural feature of countries also expresses different possibilities in the face of "modernity." In this sense, the *Kuna* in the San Blas region (Comarca) enjoy the most significant autonomy. However, their isolation is like that of the *Mapuche* or *Rarámuri* peoples, who could be easily exterminated due to the oblivion of the society around them.

Furthermore, in very exceptional cases, such as the Bolivian State in recent years, the dilemma takes on a radically different meaning from what was expected before Evo Morales' government, with its expected contradictions or conflicts about political feasibility. This case is precisely one of those that reveal the falsehood of the dilemma: it is not the resignation to accept nor the instinctive impulse to reject; it is cultural affirmation. It is impossible to assimilate everything uncritically or to tacitly accept extermination, as posed by the most aggressive version of modernity. The need arises to enter a committed relationship in a frank dialogue with modernity. The problem is not the acceptance/rejection dyad as a single future solution but the way to establish another link in all marginalized cultures' relationship with modernity, with a clear global angle. This new paradigm must be considered fallible but not negligible in the claim of cultural affirmation of marginalized and excluded peoples. It is not, therefore, an all-or-nothing bet. In the face of the political contrast of the different ways of solving local problems, it becomes necessary to identify aspects of daily life for each person's ecological achievement and cultural recreation.

Such cultural traits are part of a scattered and discontinuous set that modernity does not subsume. Cultures are despised and, therefore, find themselves in a strange ambiguity: they are devalued but not annihilated. Although they are considered victims of this rejection, and despite their apparent insignificance, the indifference of "the West" gives them a future possibility. It is in this sense that one can understand why it is a "project," still absent empirically:

> This is why I call the attempt to start from the generating nucleus of new cultural developments, from the living tradition of different cultures of modern Identity in dialogue with Modernity, a 'transmodern' program. The future project would not be a single, homogeneous universal culture; but rather a *differentiated pluriverse*, creation of the indicated dialogue between the tradition excluded from the great cultures (and even the less universal and secondary ones) of the postcolonial periphery with Western Modernity (one of the existing cultures today, the dominant one and the one that by its own tendency attempts to *destroy* all other cultures, even through its global market, in which the goods of transnational capital are equally material carriers of spiritual culture).[3]

In light of the above, everything not subsumed in Western culture is a source of possibility; that is, what is insignificant for modernity becomes a source of future possibility. The meaning of the insignificant is full significance in the future. Moreover, transmodernity also states that it is not one or the other in this false dilemma. Cultural homogeneity supposes the elimination of the ancestral. It eliminates the possibility of dialogue with the millennial cultural diversity represented by the *pueblos originarios* of the planet. Both components, in a situation of inequality and on a worldwide level, make up a pluriverse as a result of "the positive sense of the politics of liberation."[4]

First Eurocentrism: Prejudice and Critique

Hegel's historical linearity is common to us, and in general terms, it is accepted to this day by most of the academy. Even without knowing the details, it is a scheme inoculated from the height of the Enlightenment. It is not difficult to think that his starting point was a subjective belief that the point of arrival of "world" history was precisely the center of Europe. The prejudice of accepting the cultural superiority of some people, of the European people, runs through all historical appreciation from the Greeks, Romans, Middle Ages, and finally the Central Europeans Enlightened. Hegel makes the analogy between culture and the sun. Somewhere far away, Asia appears as the "rise" of culture, and after passing the "zenith" of the Greek culture, the "sunset" reaches the German world. Such historical linearity was conceived under the prejudice of regarding Europe as the entire cultural unit of the world. As suggested by Amin, the idea of Eurocentrism then arises with a mutant character according to historical circumstances. This is because (1) it obscures the domination of Europe over the invaded territories but illuminates the reproduction of European societies, covering up the inequality between the different strata and (2) it builds the story of the miracle of material abundance in the interior of Europe through the invention of capitalism that supports it. However, it covers up the plunder of the peripheries from which the raw materials were extracted. Finally, (3) Western and Christian Europe will be established in history as an achievement, leaving the responsibility for its failures to the plundered nations. Therefore, "it [eurocentrism] is rather a prejudice that distorts social theories. It draws from its storehouse of components, retaining one or rejecting another according to the ideological needs of the moment."[5]

This prejudice is defined by its profound ambiguity, always manifested in a bipolarity that is difficult to perceive. Indeed, every culture is ethnocentric. However, Eurocentrism proclaims itself as the first ethnocentrism on a world scale, with long-term consequences that are still unsuspected. Additionally, it is the first Christendom outside the space of its own development. As a prejudice, it is an ideology whose function is that of exalting European cultural emancipation to the detriment of the non-European, establishing itself as the first *Metropolis* (Europe as the center) while simultaneously constituting its *Province* (early Latin America as the periphery). That is how the center-periphery relationship on a worldwide scale is born. However, it is not born peacefully: it is born within the framework of the conquest's explicit violence and with expansion as the object of its entire cultural world. In this misrepresentation, and for the first time, Europe gives itself a story consistent with its three-century-long hegemony and is transformed from a geographical region to a geopolitical concept.

Eurocentrism is also an implicit ideology that enhances the ideological function of historical systems such as liberalism, democracy, capitalism, and socialism. As a prejudice, it confuses the *act of thinking* with the *object of what is thought* and assumes that its cultural particularities are universal. A geopolitical critique of this misrepresentation must relativize what is considered universally valid. In other words, the critique must *discover* what was *hidden* by the Empire. Therefore, Modernity is a two-edged movement. On the one hand, within the narrow borders of European geography—the Christian and Western part—cultural emancipation is resolved (sometimes being called "Renaissance," others, "Reform"). On the other hand, abroad, a cultural "unfolding," often violent, changed the daily life of almost everyone, directly or indirectly, simultaneously or eventually. Thus, *Empire* (as a geopolitical category), *Eurocentrism* (as an ideological category), and *Modernity* (as a cultural category) begin to make sense in a single historical argument. This argument considers that the first empirical global Empire was born with the circumnavigation of the world, moving from Spain and across the Americas to arrive in Asia. It is with this journey that Modernity acquires its most profound meaning because it changes the entire understanding of the world. It is important to note that Portugal did not achieve the same level of undertaking despite having shipping enclaves prior to this moment in Southeast Asia. All this has caused most interpretations to have the year 1492 as a reference, so there are already five centuries of modernity, with various stages of a mutant Empire, and of Eurocentrism as the most dominant and influential ideology on the planet.

Eurocentrism is an ideology that starts from an entirely subjective self-perception. It is related to the organicist paradigm, which views the "Enlightenment" as a significant contrast to the "Dark Ages," limiting it to an exclusively intra-European historical category. According to Eurocentrism, the "Enlightenment" was achieved by Europe's "coming of age" and growing to intellectual maturity, making the *State* the most successful institution in history. By then, three centuries of colonialism had passed, the significance of which had gradually faded (partly due to the supposed "black legend" attributed to Las Casas,[6] partly because of the internal regionalism between northern

Europe and the Mediterranean) from the experience of a more dynamic and geographically diversified economy. Indeed, capitalism had succeeded in spreading (from production to consumption) across nearly the entire planet, with its neural center at the so-called English Industrial Revolution. However, it relied on colonialism in the early Latin American peripheries as a condition of possibility. So, by this historical moment, around 1800, there was no question of the linearity between the fact of the American invasion and the "superiority" of capitalist production, with their respective political independence and new economic subjugation. Linearity was then extrapolated into the future: just as Hegel, Weber argued that superiority came from antiquity, and under their influence, the first half of the twentieth century gave continuity to the five-century-long "classical" Eurocentrism, promoting the idea of natural superiority for centuries.

It is impossible to consider only one of the cultural phenomena (modernity, coloniality, etc.) because the articulation that gave a sense of unity to them all is now lost. Modernity is a cultural phenomenon that unfolded toward the Atlantic, "linking" itself to the Americas and becoming "disconnected" from the Mediterranean Renaissance. For the first time, Western Europe, that ancient network of intra-European empires, locked in seclusion for at least seven centuries (since the first Muslim invasions around the year 711 in southern Spain, an intercontinental gateway through the Maghreb and Andalusia), broke the fence imposed from the westernmost part of Morocco to the easternmost part of the Indonesian archipelago and became the "center" of world history, constituting itself as the managing Empire of coloniality and imposing cultural forms such as "usages and customs," which it universalized in daily practice. "Postmodernity" does not question this centrality; it is uncritical of the crudest Eurocentrism. The pivotal point centers on relativizing this centrality in terms of cultural superiority, as seen below.

Such criticism features several stages. However, it is necessary to point out that the problematic horizon is the location of Latin America in the World. The conflict results from the consideration that America was the last to join the "single cultural trunk" and was, therefore, the most unknown. The notion of "location" recovers more than the mere cartographic idea of adherence to the region in the Hegelian linearity (diffusionist model). It also poses an understanding of the world from the search for the geopolitical zero point and the simultaneous relativization of the ideologies that challenge world politics today (pluriversalist model). This clear and precise idea of modernity makes it now possible to establish a project that surpasses it, incorporating it to promote the cultural growth of marginalized peoples in recent centuries.

The first critical stage involves recognizing the Greek and German milestones as linked and as a sort of starting point of the classical Eurocentric narrative. Thus, Hellenocentrism is the first ideological battlefront to relativize. In *Black Athena*, Bernal questions this issue posing that, in a way, the Germanic world of the nineteenth century built the Greek world of antiquity:

> During the 19th and 20th centuries the German cult of, and identification with, the Dorians and Lakonians continued to rise until it reached its climax in the Third Reich. By the end of the 19th century some *völkische* (populist, nationalist) writers saw the Dorians as pureblooded Aryans from the north, possibly even from Germany, and they were certainly seen as very close to the Germans in their Aryan blood and character.[7]

The "ancient model" that focused on the Phoenicians and Egyptians was eliminated at the proposal of several of the "transition" intellectuals. It was not until the first third of the twentieth century that the "Aryan model" entered the scene, with dire consequences. This event entails the reconstruction of the very base of the concealing myth of modernity because, in this story, the Hellenic contribution is not more significant than the Semitic one. Therefore, in more cultural terms, the Greco-Roman tradition goes hand in hand with the Judeo-Christian tradition, and part of the complex sixteenth century is that the intolerance of Carlos V, in command of the kingdoms that today converge in Spain and Portugal, is not explicit because religious traditions, Jews and Muslims, were annihilated under Catholicism. By preserving the religious "purity" of Spain, it remained isolated. It soon fell into oblivion while the money-mercantile dynamism (prior to industrial capitalism) gradually moved from Seville to Antwerp and Rotterdam. At the same time, the Caribbean began to succumb to pirates, this constituting "primitive accumulation" paradigm that would give birth to capitalism. At this time, the Germanic world took on a particular intra-European centrality.

The second critical stage came with the idea of *Orientalism*. Being geographically located in the West means that the rest of the continents remains in the East; thus, there is a "near" (more culturally akin) East and a "far" one (alien and more unknown). Moreover, geographic space and cultural affinity go hand in hand: the more significant the cultural distance, the greater the prejudice. Said makes a sharp distinction between the Orient, as a cultural geography, and *Orientalism*, as a Western attitude that frames the Orient in a specific, often academicist way, which built an insurmountable cultural frontier:

> My contention is that *Orientalism* is fundamentally a *political doctrine* willed over the Orient because the Orient was weaker than the West, which elided the Orient's difference with its weakness [...]. In the classical and often temporally remote form in which it was reconstructed by the Orientalist, in the precisely actual form in which the modern Orient was lived in, studied, or imagined, the geographical space of the Orient was penetrated, worked over, taken hold of. The cumulative effect of decades of so sovereign a Western handling turned the Orient from alien into colonial space. What was important in the latter nineteenth century was not whether the West had penetrated and possessed the Orient, but rather *how* the British and French felt that they had done it.[8]

Culturally, the Orient was rather a product of prejudices that distorted the idea of Oriental culture that one has today. Nowadays, this has opened the door to exacerbated Islamophobia. And the absence of understanding brings about an excess of confusion. What history could not solve for the people that remained on the margins was invented by literature. Even in colonial India, two paradigms coexisted unequally for centuries: the Hegelian story and the itihāsa story, which is a combination of tradition and succession. These coexisted "as the European 'story' and the Indian *itihāsa*, until the former, in its role of World-history, assimilated the latter ... In the event, the battle of paradigms was won for the West. Experience triumphed over wonder; World-history overcame *itihāsa*."[9]

At least in a restricted area, India was assimilated to the Hegelian linearity where, as the title says, History is written at the limit of the grand Western narrative. However, the Eurocentric narrative is fictitiously inscribed as a prejudice that gradually becomes truth and establishes itself as History. Thus, Indian tradition runs parallel to the Eurocentric narration, on the margin but without disappearing from the Indians' collective imagination. It is in this interstice that the friction between literature and History occurs. Such is the case of Rushdie and his criticism: although it is far from being a criticism that his fellow citizens acclaim and for which he is fully welcomed in the West, he is interpreted as a non-Christian writer with more Indian than British traits. He was recently the victim of a stabbing in New York after many years of declaring the Fatwa.

On a third stage, the magnificent work by Needham,[10] to mention a single work, would suffice to account for what is ignored about China. The work addresses historical facts and shows empirical data with which a theory is challenged. This is what Menzies does as he represents an ordered, systematically studied series articulated to cartographic, astronomical, maritime, and other types of evidence which contrast what is historically truthful, yet fallible. If the interpretation obtained from the evidence found by Menzies is true, the voyages of Chinese navigators would be a new milestone in world history, allowing it to be entirely rewritten. Indeed,

> Now at the conclusion of my journey, I returned, believing that I had found the evidence to overturn the long-accepted history of the Western world. I had found a wealth of evidence that the Chinese fleets commanded by Admirals Zheng He, Yang Qing, Zhou Man, Hong Bao and Zhou Wen on that epic sixth expedition had surveyed every continent in the world. They had sailed through sixty-two island archipelagos comprising more than seventeen thousand islands and charted tens of thousands of miles of coastline. Admiral Zheng He's claim to have visited three thousand countries large and small appeared to be true. The Chinese fleets had voyaged across the Indian Ocean to East Africa, around the Cape of Good Hope to the Cape Verde Islands, through the Caribbean to North America and the Artic, down to Cape Horn, the Antarctic, Australia, New Zealand and across the Pacific. Throughout the entire hundred thousand *li* [40 thousands Nautic miles], only in the Antarctic would the treasure ships have had to sail into the wind or and opposing current.[11]

If it were widely accepted, this paradigm shift would defy the keenest imagination. It certainly deserves a detailed examination beyond the scope of this paper, but if the account took place between 1421 and 1423, then a significant historical change must have occurred around the arrival of Europeans in the Americas. Indeed, the Ming dynasty (1368–1644) made the "mistake" (from the expansionist perspective) of retreating inward and neglecting its global expansion after this feat. The information was used barely seventy years later by the Spaniards, who took advantage of China's scientific and technological knowledge. This event paused the development of China as, overnight, Spain (under the rule of Charles V) became the largest Empire in the world, albeit for a very short time. Despite the relationship with the Americas, "the World economy continued to be dominated by Asians for at least three centuries more, until about 1800. Europe's relative and absolute marginality in the world economy continued despite its new relations with the Americas, which it used also to increase its relations with Asia."[12]

The starting point is the event of the Spanish conquest on American soil, which marks the emergence of Spain as an empire beginning in 1492. It is a moment that sees the force of the Chinese navigation of previous decades fade away. From America's perspective, this politico-military fact of imperial Spain eclipses the interconnections among the interregional systems of Europe, Asia, and Africa. In subsequent centuries, as the Spanish presence faded after the Baroque heyday, the English influence began to emerge through the industrial revolution, when North-Atlantic Europe was able to compete with the Far East, specifically China. This other event fuels the rise of industrial capitalism, as it is easily recognizable today. Of the three parts of the world known before 1492, Europe was still on the westernmost periphery of the West. However, after this year, a New World Order began which "rearranged" commercial relations and the entire planet's cultural universes. Therefore, it is not an Empire like any other. It is worth emphasizing that Europe's centrality emerged only after China's decline during the Qing dynasty, the last monarchy before the establishment of the Republic in the twentieth century. If this happened around 1800, the 500 years of the "first" Eurocentrism are reduced to the last two centuries. That is why a "second critique" of Eurocentrism is necessary.

The reduction in time of the first critique of Eurocentrism entails the adoption of another geopolitical perspective: "The entire world economic order was—literally—Sinocentric. Christopher Columbus and many Europeans after him, up until Adam Smith, knew that. It was only the nineteenth-century Europeans who literally rewrote this history from their new Eurocentric perspective."[13]

The so-called World Wars are intra-imperial struggles that contend for the decidedly global centrality. European regional empires had retreated into African and Southeast Asian enclaves. For their part, the Japanese withdrew toward nearby areas of influence, which resulted in friction with China, while the Americans had already settled in Latin America. Still, their "business model" required greater breadth. The distraction from the center caused relative autonomy in peripheral capitalism. However, Eurocentrism had remained the most entrenched ideology in the academia and culture in general, and attention now turned to the United States. This situation drew a line between new and old empires (as an extension of the Old and New World spoken of centuries ago). Simultaneously, it began the "Cold War," equally Eurocentric, imperial, colonial, and modern.

Drawing from fields like theology, pedagogy, and philosophy, dependency theories in Latin America provided the epistemological bases for liberation thought. These theories considered the relationship between the different geographical spaces, some of which consisted exclusively of merchandise exchange, meeting both material and spiritual needs. It is in this geopolitical paradigm that the philosophies of liberation have spread, offering a story that is consistent with the past (an archeological one); and as a result, they have launched the challenge of a future-oriented (eschatological) postulate. This paradigm has been developed in recent years, and although several aspects will have to be corrected, it is sufficiently elaborated to be the starting point for a global political project. In fact, efforts are already underway to work on the paradigm.

Throughout the history of the Americas, domination has always been denounced. From the Hispanic part, Bartolomé de Las Casas offered a moral evaluation of the conquest and colonization, which, from the validity point of view, was convincing and systematic. It is perhaps the first systematic criticism of modernity in a total sense. Such criticism is strictly philosophical when he confronts Ginés de Sepúlveda (c. 1550) in Valladolid to defend the *pueblos originarios* in the context of the Spanish subjugation. The above became a pattern of discussion in the following centuries until the end of the eighteenth century when the *criollismo* develops more clarity, although not yet fully, of what it means to be born, or in any case, *to be* from a place with substantial differences with Europe. Here is where the dilemma described at the beginning of this document makes sense again: being a Latin American raises cultural questions, and the option for rejection or acceptance places an entire continent at a cultural crossroad. That is why Bolívar can implicitly consider Eurocentrism in his *Carta de Jamaica*, where he denies being "indio" (*pueblo originario*), but also European, to consider himself somewhere in between; or why Hidalgo, in Mexico, can make the classic harangue for the death of the *gachupines* (Spaniards from the peninsula), and not for the *criollos* (Spaniards' children born in America), among many other examples.

The wars of Independence that began with the Haitians triggered the first decolonization. Although the terms "modernity" and "Eurocentrism" are not part of the vocabulary at that time, there is a political transformation with essentially cultural traits, where Europeanizing continuity and anti-colonialist liberation are not incompatible. Regarding the dilemma posed at the beginning, this ambivalence remains throughout the nineteenth century and the first half of the twentieth century. In such a period, a certain consciousness of *mestizaje* appears in society beyond the caste genealogy, which continues implicitly even in the most minimal features of daily activities. That is how the whitening (*blanqueamiento* in Spanish) of society prevails in the highest hierarchy, while workers, or the peasantry, among others of low hierarchy in the social scale, are identified with popular in culture, with poverty in the economy, with illiteracy in education, and with the condition of *pueblo originario* in racial terms. Far from having achieved cultural independence, the affinity for the Catholic monarchy, the support for interventionism, and the obsessive adoption of French taste, among other manifestations, make the new Latin American region an enclave that favors Europeans and North American newcomers to the detriment of the now called *pueblos originarios*. All this situation contrasts even with the attachment to the land (often dispossessed) and the tacit acceptance of family communities in the cities' rural areas and marginal neighborhoods.

This typical stage in Latin America is full of reflections where the emphasis is placed on the most contrasting differences between European and non-European people. However, it should be noted that, from the period of the so-called Independence struggles until the post-war reconfiguration of the world in the twentieth century, there is a consistent existential concern. This concern wonders about those strange *Others* who are neither European nor *pueblo originario* and who are becoming more and more aware of themselves and of the world stage in which they have always existed, albeit covertly. In this accumulation of ancient traditions embedded in a vast continent, Héctor Murena, Octavio Paz, and Pablo Antonio Cuadra, to mention a few,[14] wondered about the meaning of being Argentine, Mexican, and Nicaraguan, respectively. Giving voice and expression to *otherness* becomes as complicated as indispensable and equivocal. Only a few intellectuals who daringly leaned toward deepening their experience favoring the indigenous vein and documenting their reflection gave some sample of authenticity and creativity. And even lesser was the number of cases in which a politician consolidated power as a service to the people. Almost all cultural expressions allude to the same dilemma (acceptance or rejection), but the most creative ones combine some of their aspects. The twentieth century is a display where, for the first time, the Latin American people lend themselves a voice.

There is no "Latin American stage" in the same sense as in the logic of the previous paragraphs. There is constant criticism from the first face-to-face approaches until today, yet with changing circumstances. The indignation triggered by criticism offers continuity, and it is enough to recognize that the common thread is explicit violence against the same human communities, the *pueblos originarios*. Certainly, Zea's work opened an unsuspected path when moving from positivism to questioning the Eurocentrism that his academic work entailed—most of his historical point of view questions the ideological aspect of Latin America's intellectual work. Indeed, framed within the Cold War, it goes through the debates around "authenticity" and "identity" as some of the most visible themes of Latin American thought until the philosophy of liberation arrives to clarify some of its themes.

Along with theology and pedagogy, it also settles in the dependency theory to place the "poor" as a starting point for its reflection. Dependency theories made it possible to look at world history from the perspective of the inequality of countries that, over the centuries, had or had not been, conquered or invaded. Thus, the countries with the highest organic composition of capital (those from Western Europe) had begun an imperial way of governing the planet. Having been exploited from previous centuries, beginning with the violent expansion that began in 1492, Latin America remained an ensemble of countries with the lowest organic composition of capital. Both realities joined through dependency.

Transmodernity as a Postulate

From the above, it is clear that the Eurocentric narrative erases the genuine moral dilemmas that begin with the conquest and extend to the present day to create an ideology that affirms only one cultural block. The perspective issued from this ideology intentionally hides the immorality of explicit annihilation. It covers up the genocide of the *pueblos originarios* of the Americas and other cultures with other rhythms and forms of violence. Simultaneously, it has found very subtle ways to recover history from the victors, showing the adversary's weakness and the Westerners' salvation in a binary and stigmatized history, depending on the time. Second, faced with this fact, this Eurocentric narrative has proclaimed itself as aseptic toward all morality, and, over the centuries, *concealment* has become increasingly sophisticated. The most significant current affectation of the European academy is the appearance of Nazism and its consequent criticism framed in a halo of hopelessness in culture and manifested in multiple ways. This is shown, for example, in the low birth rate since the end of the Second World War, which, together with the gradual growth of the Muslim population, has developed Islamophobia causing the insensitivity of European governments in this first third of the twenty-first century. A supposed morality is rooted in the most intimate of daily acts. In that case, nevertheless, it deposits outside of it the most essential of the ideas that it follows: racial purity or personal perfection. However, it achieves this by placing a border between the One and its *Otherness*.

Eurocentrism is an ideology that frames various manifestations, such as Modernity. Modernity manifests itself as a new ethos born from the almost total extermination of the ancestral population of the Americas. It is a rapid and violent expansion throughout the world that suddenly changes the circumstances to a greater or lesser extent. Indeed, Modernity founded a new era with distinct features at different levels: (1) at a theoretical level, there is a change in world understanding (from *interregional systems* between Africa, Asia, and Europe to the "World-System" comprising the "fourth part of the world"); (2) on a material level, there is a new flow of genes (of all living beings, and specifically of human races with which new subjectivities are also fostered) as well as of products (tools and human artifacts that circulate in previously unsuspected places). (3) At a formal level, there are new ways of organizing States, legitimizing or destroying them, and defending themselves against them. The above implies efficient ways of organizing life because the planet has narrowed since then. This change in the daily life of all the inhabitants (to a lesser or greater extent) is a new cultural phenomenon called Modernity.

The European intellectuals who have been named "postmodern" accept, with internal discrepancies, that modernity begins with Descartes around 1600 to end toward the end of 1900 with Nietzsche as a reference. That erases in one fell swoop the first century of shared history between America and Europe. This way of dividing historical projects' chronological start and end is not at all innocent. Habermas personally considers the second half of the twentieth century to be late modernity, taking as reference the "mature modernity" of around 1800, certainly centered on European geography. From then until the middle of the twentieth century, Europe stood out industrially and militarily until reaching the centrality of the planet, yet this gave way, already in the postwar period, to the political–military presence of the United States. That caused the geopolitical configuration to change radically to this day. In both cases, the provincialization of European culture is itself notorious. In their cultural affirmation, they deny the possibility of other people having contributed to it in some way; and they also deny the possibility of the existence of philosophy in other regions of the planet, or, at least, they consider it insignificant. The need then arises to evaluate such divisions of time from an ethical perspective. In other words, each intellectual project is a part of a larger political project and becomes a game of options from which the most "adequate" or "convenient" is chosen to give consistency to its narrative. The addition or removal of elements from this set of explanations through a thoughtful process of discernment and discrimination becomes political.

Although there is no glimpse of a single consensual project among the mainly Western European intelligentsia, it is possible to see that Latin America continues to disappear, as an "element" of its narrative, its temporal scope being limited to the seventeenth century (Anglo-Saxon America). In other words, none of the two perspectives consider the fifteenth and sixteenth centuries, a moment in which it is decisive to speak of both the military invasion and the subsequent colonization. The "black legend" attributed to Las Casas's seems to have extended to the present day. The important aspect to point out is that this absent factor in the European narrative is the same that would later give it its centrality; namely, an immense space of nature reduced to exploitable "natural resources" and human beings reduced to or rather "enslaved" through "free labor." Moreover, this is a political decision projected toward the intellectual field. However, the Europeans' cultural withdrawal only confirms Eurocentrism.

The argument proposed by Dussel is not only based on the articulation of historical systems and cultural phenomena but also on the temporal and spatial amplitude. If Braudel clarified the importance of *longues durée* to link apparently unrelated and incommensurable events, Dussel extended modernity to the sixteenth century, right at the knot of 1492, where all the problematic threads that concern us converge. So, he brings several themes and categories together to place them in the same interpretive framework, modernity itself. In other words, capitalism (still mercantile and in the process of "primitive accumulation"), a slow construction of the secular State (critical of monarchies and increasingly subservient to the Market), the idea of Empire (from the regional to the entire planet), political philosophy (which justifies violent expansion), and the "World-System" (a category proposed by Wallerstein) among other categories, concepts, and themes, are all used as the starting point of a single argument. Unlike the "postmodernists" who establish the prefix "post" as a state progressively and linearly posterior to their own concept of modernity, this other way of interpreting modernity cannot deny it from a further interpretation: "trans"-Modernity, which is thought of as synchronously linked developments (as they in fact occur in historical development) but which are only happening now as glimpses of what could take place at a later time, perhaps in the very long term. In other words, for the postmodern, once a historical stage is exhausted, it is displaced by the next one in an epistemological rupture, to continue with another supposedly new but culturally enclosed since it can only be thought of as an intra-European phenomenon. On the other hand, the transmodern project implies the simultaneity of several cultural trunks on a worldwide scale, some with a greater presence than others, in clear inequality, but coexisting on the long run. Dussel says:

> Speaking instead of 'trans'-Modernity, [...], will require a new interpretation of the entire phenomenon of Modernity, in order to be able to count on moments that were never incorporated into European Modernity, and that subsuming the best of Modernity European Modernity, and that subsuming the best of European and North American Modernity, will affirm 'from outside' itself essential components of the excluded cultures themselves, to develop a new future politics, that of the 21st century. Accepting this massive exteriority to European Modernity will allow us to understand that there are cultural moments located 'outside' of said Modernity.[15]

Thus conceived, this postulate of transmodernity deals with horizons of possibility still pending empirically. It is theoretically thinkable (and even desirable) to the extent of its geographical and political projection. Only when taking the so-called conquest of 1492 as a starting point is the long argument about transmodernity complete; and, not only because of the prolongation of the chronological line but also because of the deconstruction of the different historical interpretations that, throughout five centuries, have been developed with significant omissions due to prejudices, or with intentional concealments by those standing for a political project that is adverse to the historical liberation of the still subjected peoples of Latin America and the world.

A first description of Modernity alludes to a leaving the state of immaturity (as Kant points out in terms of the *Enlightenment*), which translates into an emancipation led by an exceptional impulse of reason. Then the paradigm of consciousness that dominates Eurocentric philosophy emerges. It is a cultural change deep enough to encompass a change in the organization of the entire world of daily life, with the modern State as the most complete institution of all times. However, this change is postulated as universal even though it is provincial, local, and Eurocentric. Furthermore, it represents the most common opinion of Latin Americans, still to this day, although the same is true for many other regions. It is a kind of "official" history, global and universal in nature, culturally accepted, especially by the subdued peoples. In contrast to this hegemonic description of History, Dussel builds a panoramic scheme of Modernity which divides, as a first approximation, into "early Modernity" (from 1492 to the French Revolution in 1789) and "mature Modernity" (from then until today), certainly with intermediate distinctions. In a decidedly geopolitical vision, the geographical point that defines the first moment of Modernity is the Atlantic Ocean because "there was never empirical World-history until 1492. [...]. The Atlantic supplants the Mediterranean. For us, the 'centrality' of Latin Europe in World-history is the fundamental determination of Modernity."[16] This manifests itself in a divided Christendom between Catholics and Protestants and in a system of accumulation also divided between the annihilation of the *pueblos originarios* by the northernmost Europeans, the Lusitanian slavery, and the eminent Hispanic *encomienda* for most of the Latin American people. In mature modernity, the innocent victim (the *pueblo originario*) is blamed (by the first block of Europeans).

Only in the deep knowledge of the Americas are the communicating vessels seen on a worldwide scale. The concerns of countries under the rule of European states within the last 500 years have been the same as Latin Americans have had. This common adversity is understood because the colonial patterns were similar, although with cultural distinctions specific to each geographical location. Tradition plays a significant role in the cultural invasion and eclipse of cultural aspects of both parties, which common coexistence creates. Apparently, and from the perspective of the colonizer, tradition disappears; or, in any case, current tradition tends to emulate future tradition in such a way that, over the centuries, it would tend to become homogenized to become a distorted copy of the colonizer's culture (a variant of the dilemma posed in the first section of this work). However, it is not so. As time goes by, it is seen that cultural traditions are so deeply rooted in colonized territories that sometimes they are even imposed. Al-Yabri, a Moroccan intellectual with a Marxist orientation, says that,

> The rational and critical treatment of each one of the aspects of our Arab existence—where the traditional patrimony (*turāt*) represents the most current fact and rooted in us—is the only and most genuine tendency towards Modernity. Thus, the 'need to worry about tradition' is dictated by the need to

modernize our relationship with the traditional Arab-Islamic heritage with a double purpose: on the one hand, so that said heritage serves Modernity and, on the other, to root Modernity within our own historical specificity.[17]

As can be seen, it is possible to note the coincidence of the same project. Although it is impossible to register all that could exist for each cultural region in the planet, to a large extent, the criticisms of the other cited authors show that there is always a possibility of resistance that appeals to the hermeneutics of cultures[18]. In other words, the definition of Modernity is in terms of the relationship with excluded, withdrawn, and resistant cultures. Negative aspects can be reproached *ad nauseam*, as occurs in countries in constant tension with the "West," such as Pakistan or Iran, which interpret any interference as a "crusade," alluding to more than a thousand years of history in typical confrontation, while from the Eurocentric perspective, such interference is merely "humanitarian aid." However, the project can be considered a program of mutual knowledge that provides a decolonized future, impossible to conceive only from modernity. The answer to this double aspect is the very meaning of Transmodernity because the premodern interpretation would be the folkloric world of anachronistic proposals that go back to the past. Nor is it *anti*-Modern, because that would be retreating provincially, as the political right wing currently proposes in several countries, especially fascist groups such as those who have tried to destroy the legislative power in the United States and Brazil, as well as the Republican order in general. Finally, it is not a *post*-Modern project, either, which tries to deny all modern rationality, falling into nihilistic irrationalism that translates into cultural hopelessness with manifestations in recent decades that go beyond the academic field.

Today's globalization was the product of Modernity five centuries ago. This is the only way to understand, without omissions or qualitative historical leaps, a *continuum* of related events in the same geography that continue to this day as something "natural" in daily practices. However, this extension is extrapolated backward and forward in time. This is why it is not *post*-Modern but *trans*-Modern; such prefixes require care. It is not because it overcomes or abandons, it rather overcomes and recovers. It has two components: the first is a start from Modernity itself, and the second is a start from the new, from the exterior, from the popular: "*The popular culture of Difference*, of the Exteriority of Modernity, peripheral and postcolonial, will allow us to glimpse the conditions of *Transmodern Culturality* in the full sense of the word."[19]

Transmodernity is a project. However, it is a theoretically possible but empirically impossible *postulate*. At least for the moment, despite the highly fragmented and often ephemeral local examples, there is no such possibility in sight. The approach is very long term. "It is the time of the accelerated cultivation and creation of the development of the own cultural tradition now on the way towards a transmodern utopia."[20] In a chronological line, it is later, but it does not deny the possibilities of dialogue with the non-modern, the "barbaric," the "insignificant alterity." Only from outside this Modernity ("Exteriority") is it possible to trace new directions and to reorient because Transmodernity is "beyond all internal possibility of Modernity alone."[21] The impossible comes from its totalized self-consciousness, which due to its very nature, does not allow the possibility of *Otherness*. Overcoming this Western Modernity means overcoming Eurocentrism, not by annihilating Europe's *location* in world history, but by subsuming it to its proper dimension, in a *pluriverse* scope. From the ontological perspective, it is a "passage" toward the "New Totality," always necessary, although not always possible. But the fact that it is impossible should not make it discardable beforehand.

Furthermore, it is precisely at that point where political praxis must continue as an imperative for liberation to occur, *always* and *permanently*. As a postulate, Transmodernity serves to guide. It guides in a double sense; on the one hand, it gives the marginalized the possibility to emerge in novelty, and in this process, it forces the totality (Eurocentric, Western, and imperial Modernity) into a transformation (a dialectical emancipation). On the other hand, it is an element of resistance because it is a last resource against the devastating nature of Modernity.

Lastly, Transmodernity is an intervention that crosses times: a utopia from millenary ancestry. It also crosses spaces: there is no corner on earth without a cultural contribution because everything, as excluded and insignificant as it may seem, is an innovative possibility in the future. What is useless for Modernity today is essential for Transmodernity tomorrow. Above all, on a concrete level and in full cultural affirmation, the so-called *pueblos originarios* are the best-kept cultural reserve in the Anthropocene era, representing a source (dynamic and disseminated) for hope in their community praxis and in their silent resistance.

Notes

1   The denomination is always ambiguous due to its general character to cover an immensely large diversity in quantity. The denominations of "indio" ("Indian," "native") or "indígena" ("Indigenous," "native") were terms that seemed pejorative so it was decided to change them to "pueblos originarios" ("native peoples"), that is to say: peoples who had originally been here since ancient times. In Canada they are called "First Nations;" in Australia, "Aboriginals." In France, "indigène" designates second-generation North Africans living in France. I will insist on "pueblos originarios" in Spanish to be politically correct.

2   In contrast to the "universe" which supposes the "unity" in diversity, the "pluriverse" supposes the many diversities in diversity. It is a redundant term, but it adequately illustrates what is being emphasized here. When we speak of a "pluriversalist model" we are referring to different "intentional foci of culture" that may or may not be simultaneous; this is in contrast with the "diffusionist model," which assumes Europe as the first global expansion, prior to all others.

3   Enrique Dussel (2007a).

4   Enrique Téllez (2022a).

5   Samir Amin (2009).

6   Bartolomé de Las Casas (d. 1566) is a milestone in American History as he is the first European to support a criticism of Early Modernity. He is a starting point for all historical criticism from the Americas. The "black legend" refers to the *Brevísima Relación de la destrucción de las Indias*, from 1552. It is a small work that was translated into several languages and distributed throughout northern Europe, used as a kind of pamphlet against the Spanish colonization.

7   Martin Bernal (1987).

8   Edward Said (1979).

9   Ranajit Guha (2002).

10 The book's title is "*Science and Civilization in China*," published in 15 volumes since 1954. In it, Needham considers Wallerstein's theory on "*World-System*."

11 Gavin Menzies (2002).

12 André Gunder-Frank (1998, p. 53).

13 André Gunder-Frank (1998, p. 117).

14 The Argentinian Héctor Murena wrote *El pecado original de América* in 1954; the Mexican Octavio Paz, *El laberinto de la soledad* in 1950, based on *El perfil del hombre y la cultura en México* from 1934, written by

Samuel Ramos; and the Nicaraguan Pablo Antonio Cuadra wrote *El nicaragüense* in 1967. All of those works show the meaning of what is meant here, but they in no way exhaust the substantialist question of national identity from the cultural point of view.

15 Enrique Dussel (2007b).

16 Enrique Dussel (2003, pp. 41–54).

17 Mohammed A. Al-Yabri (2001), pp. 42–43.

18 A hermeneutic critique has not been made from the perspective of the philosophy of liberation around the Conquest and Colonization of the Americas, above all recovering Ricoeur's categories of the "symbolique." A first attempt to indicate the path to follow can be seen in: Téllez (2022b).

19 Enrique Dussel (2007c, p. 213).

20 Enrique Dussel (2004, p. 155).

21 Enrique Dussel (2001, p. 406).

References

Dussel, E. (2007a). *Materiales para una política de la liberación*, 209. Nuevo León: Universidad Autónoma de Nuevo León – Plaza Valdés.

Téllez, E. (2022a). La voluntad material de vida del pueblo. In: *Política de la Liberación. Crítica creadora. Volumen III* (ed. E. Dussel), 238. Madrid: Trotta.

Amin, S. (2009). *Eurocentrism. Modernity, Religion, and Democracy. A Critique of Eurocentrism and Culturalism*, 166. New York: Monthly Review Press.

Bernal, M. (1987). *Black Athena. The Afroasiatic Roots of Classical Civilization. Volume I. The Fabrication of Ancient Greece 1785–1985*, 293. New Brunswick: Rutgers University Press.

Said, E. (1979). *Orientalism*, 204–211. New York: Vintage Books *italics mine*.

Guha, R. (2002). *History at the Limit of World-history*, 54–72. New York: Columbia University Press.

Menzies, G. (2002). *1421. The Year China discovered America*, 448–449. New York: HarperCollins.

Gunder-Frank, A. (1998). *Re-Orient. Global Economy in the Asian Age*. Berkeley: California University Press.

Dussel, E. (2007b). *Materiales para una política de la liberación*. Nuevo León: Universidad Autónoma de Nuevo León – Plaza Valdés (Chapter 13).

Dussel, E. (2003). Europa. Modernidad y Eurocentrismo. In: *La colonialidad del saber: eurocentrismo y ciencias sociales. Perspectivas latinoamericanas* (ed. E. Lander), 41–54. Buenos Aires: Consejo Latinoamericano de Ciencias Sociales.

Al-Yabri, M.A. (2001). *Crítica de la razón árabe. Nueva visión sobre el legado filosófico andalusí*. Barcelona: Icaria.

Téllez, E. (2022b). Ricoeur y Dussel. Simbólica y crítica a la ética ontológica. *Inter-American Journal of Philosophy* 13 (1): 1–14.

Dussel, E. (2007c). *Política de la liberación. Historia crítica y mundial. La Arquitectónica. Volumen 1*, 213. Madrid: Trotta.

Dussel, E. (2004). Transmodernidad e interculturalidad (interpretación desde la filosofía de la liberación). In: *Crítica intercultural de la filosofía latinoamericana actual* (ed. R. Fornet-Betancourt), 155. Madrid: Trotta.

Dussel, E. (2001). *Hacia una filosofía política crítica*, 406. Bilbao: Desclée de Brouwer.

Section II

Gender

4

Reflections on the Erotics of Liberation: A Contemporary, Feminist Latin American Perspective

AFYL WOMEN COLLECTIVE

We are a group of colleagues from different territories and disciplines throughout Latin America who are dedicated to building meanings and theorizing together from and with the Philosophy of Liberation school of thought. In 2021, we generated a meeting and consensus in an internal seminar in which we analyzed the work *Women's Liberation and Latin American Erotic* together with its subsequent edition-correction *For a Latin American Erotic*, both versions written by Enrique Dussel (2007) and published in 1980 and Enrique Dussel (1990), respectively. In 2022, we organized a second seminar that allowed us to share our reflections and receive feedback from colleagues of differing areas of Latin America. The text we present below results from our collective reflections in these sessions.

Our objective has been to trace the contributions and categories within the literature which are fundamental in continuing producing, theoretically and politically, from our experience and testimony as Latin American feminist women. Ours is a critical collective analysis that recognizes the ethical and political commitment within the Philosophy of Liberation against the oppression of women and serves as a strategic categorical apparatus. Still, it also seeks to transcend limits and biases in understanding our alterity and in speaking using the plural first-person, betting on the critical power of the properly feminist horizon of liberation. We also seek to walk together, taking some initial steps in the production of a feminist perspective on the Philosophy of Liberation. This would allow us to share with our movement categories that nourish us and, conversely, enable us to make more complex the theoretical development of the school, of which we are part, through the contributions of the different feminisms in which we participate.

The texts have been intentionally written collectively. This ethical and political approach seeks to de-center the *ego cogito* of the hegemonic academy to position ourselves from a feminist epistemology. This practice is a commitment to building more horizontal spaces where we can speak from our affections, feelings, and bodies, and to produce and create collectively and collaboratively among women.

We have divided this chapter into three main axes: (1) patriarchy, ontology, and colonial modernity; (2) the erotic liberation and the metaphysics of otherness; and, finally (3) toward a feminism of liberation. Although this text anticipates prior knowledge of the theoretical apparatus of the Philosophy of Liberation, we also choose to share these ideas with colleagues who are either not familiar or are not specialists; we are an interdisciplinary group which maintains an openness and collectivity in dialogue.[1]

Patriarchy, Ontology, and Colonial Modernity

> *They feel a deep need*
> *of a coherent explanatory system,*
> *one that does not just tell us what it is,*
> *and why should it be like this, but one that allows*
> *an alternative vision in the future.*
>
> Gerda Lerner

Surrounding the category of patriarchy, we find several feminist discussions which are ambiguous. We will address three of them in this section in order to provide clarity regarding the relevance of using this category, as well as how we will develop it. The first discussion revolves around the convenience, the limits, and the interpretive scope it allows us. The second attempts to understand patriarchy and its historical origin. The third criticizes the use of this category when it refers only to the oppression women face without considering other oppressions that are not exhausted with gender.

Once we have addressed, at least within the confines that the measures of this text allow us, the discussions surrounding patriarchy, we will address the criticisms of the ontology of the Totality from the Philosophy of Liberation in its dialogue with Levinas.[2]

We commence from the intuition that if we make clear the foundations from which we think, some of the discussions we are currently debating may become less convoluted. We will maintain that patriarchy is based on an ontology of Totality, and we will trace the interpretive scope that allows us to understand it from this ontological dimension. In addition, we will carefully consider the relationship between feminism and ontology.

Finally, we will analyze the transit of colonial Modernity throughout the centuries, understanding it as a production of meanings and practices that arise from the very development of Western patriarchal institutions. These have managed to become hegemonic based on pacts and key connections with other patriarchal systems that originated in these latitudes.

Patriarchy

Let us begin by questioning and the relevance and scope of the patriarchy category for our feminist struggle and study. In *The Traffic in Women: Notes on the "Political Economy" of Sex* (1975), the North American anthropologist Gayle Rubin (1975) questions the use of the patriarchy category, considering that it alludes to a concrete historical experience incapable of explaining how societies have organized their *sex-gender systems*. She offers the example of patriarchy in ancient Rome and explains the submission of young men to their parents and of women to both.

Since these particularities are not present in all societies, Rubin chooses to speak of the *sex-gender system* as a neutral notion that accounts for the socially organized political economy of sex. Just as capitalism is a mode of production of a particular political economy and is not the political economy itself, patriarchy would also be an expression of the political economy of sex that occurred in ancient Rome. Still, it does not correspond to the political economy of sex, as such.

The distinction that Rubin makes between *patriarchy and the sex-gender system* is crucial as it allows for the understanding that, although all societies have a system in which they organize sexuality and the reproduction of feminized bodies, they do not do so in the same manner.

Further, her distinction historicizes male domination and calls us to pay attention to its different expressions to better understand how it works. However, it must also be said that the affective burden of *patriarchy* far exceeds that of the *sex-gender system*. It becomes more obvious for example, when we go out into the street; we are not implying that the "sex-gender system" is going to fall, but rather the "patriarchy" will. Patriarchy is a common notion that occupies a crucial place in the grammar of our struggle. Such a category is helpful to us, not only because of its ability to explain some aspect of reality but also because it allows us to interpret and influence that reality with greater conviction and achieving a deep conviction regarding the affective load is fundamental.

In this space, we have opted to continue using the *patriarchy* category, broadening its meaning, and not circumscribing it to the Roman experience but to the historical background of male hegemony over sexuality and the reproduction of life. We assume, however, that said hegemony has been constituted in various ways, depending on geographical contexts, mythical ethical nuclei, and other circumstances that have played into the historical configuration of proximity in the world.

This raises the question: what do we name? What do we mean when we talk about *patriarchy*? What is its origin? Archaeological traces and anthropological studies show a constant relationship which is not universal[3] between civilization and patriarchy. From Mesopotamia to China, Tawantinsuyu to the Anahuac Valley, Greece to Rome, Imperial Christianity to liberal Modernity, the constant is the same: all are expressions of patriarchal civilization. Is patriarchy born with civilizations? Are civilizations the product of patriarchal hegemony, or have only some civilizations been patriarchal? The question remains open. However, history seems to indicate that no human group has become a civilization without maintaining control of sexuality and the reproductive capacity of bodies.

This constant of patriarchal civilizations is not based on biological determinations. Patriarchy is not eternal. It is not the product of necessity nor of physical determinations in the evolution of *homo sapiens*, as explained after the increasing influence of Darwin's theory. Rather, patriarchy is ideologically sustained. To understand patriarchy, it must be defetishized; that is, it must be denatured, which calls for historicizing it and showing its contingency.

Although, over and over again, the *objective, scientific* discourse, which *knows nature* through a process of observation and experimentation, is used to justify the domestication of women, and it is decreed: "Biology is destiny," "nature is prior to culture" or, already at the symbolic level, "God has commanded it so." Although ritualized, the truth remains that its origin is eminently political.

Austrian historian Gerda Lerner (1990) shows that patriarchal hegemony results from a long process of almost 2500 years, between 3100 and 600 BCE in the ancient Near East. Given the interpretation made by Engels in *The Origin of the Family, Private Property and the State* that patriarchy is, on the one hand, the result of a "historical defeat" of women and, on the other, that it occurred "suddenly,"[4] Gerda maintains that there was never a defeat as such; it was not an event in which we can trace major alterations in economic power relations. It is not the case that class dominance brought about dominance over women. Gerda Lerner (1990) shows how, for example, women in Mesopotamia lost their bodies and sexuality without losing property and economic rights.

This is significant for several reasons. First, because it allows us to articulate the class struggle and the feminist without subordinating the latter to the former, but rather understanding that it is from and together with the sexual control of bodies that a series of oppressions that not only affect gender but also class and race, necessarily emerge from it. A historical hypothesis is that from the domination of the bodies of women, such domination will occur to other peoples and will continue with patterns of life itself (or what they have called "nature").

Gerda's point is also important because it allows us to situate patriarchy at some point in history, or more specifically, a moment that dates back to before the birth of ancient civilizations. In this sense, it is not that a given society has been patriarchal, it is that there is a symbiotic relationship between patriarchy and civilization that has produced the world we know today. Although human groups based on patriarchal relationships that have not constituted civilizations can be traced, one cannot speak of civilizations—but of cultures—that have been established without patriarchy.

To us, from the Philosophy of Liberation's perspective, this hypothesis leads us to the need to understand the ontology that founds and grounds the entirety of this patriarchal world that we resist.

The Erotic Liberation and the Metaphysics of Alterity

For me, the erotic is like a seed that I carry inside.
When it spills out of the capsule that holds it compressed,
it flows and colors my life with an energy that intensifies,
sensitizes, and strengthens all my experience.

Audre Lorde

One of the first challenges we faced as we began to think about the erotic of liberation was the narrow and reductionist sense of erotic. Historically related to sexual love, which has been naturalized as heterosexual, the possibilities of thinking about erotic were limited. In our first approaches and from the study on erotic that the Philosophy of Liberation we realized that the study of erotic was reduced to the need to think about the oppression of women in the face of machismo.

The allusions made in *Para una erótica latinoamericana* (2007) ranging from the role of women as mothers and wives in the social reproduction of family life, to the sublimity and beauty of the female body, the criticisms made to feminism and angry women or seemingly selfish single women who decide not to have children, among other opinions biased by the author's veiled patriarchal morality, prompted us to reflect upon what meaning we give to erotic? What place does it hold in our lives? What steps have we taken along these paths of Latin American liberation in which we can affirm our lives and from which we no longer think of returning to the former?

We recall a fundamental text written in Lorde (2017), a black lesbian North American poet, which has deeply moved us in our feminist quest. The text is entitled *Sister Outsider*.[5] It is very significant because the thesis Audre Lorde maintains is that as a strategy of domination, the erotic has been confused with the sexual. Women have been taught to think that the joy of eroticism is in the sexual, and the sexual is properly the experience she can have in a bedroom with a man.

But eros cannot be reduced to the sexual, and the sexual is not limited to the experience of the heterosexual regime. Eroticism is the source of the enjoyment of life itself; eros is a vital drive that is embodied which is present when we smile, when we discover or are surprised by a new idea, when we enjoy dancing, writing poetry, or working, it is the drive of life for excellence. Eroticism highlights our ability to enjoy, to connect with ourselves from enjoyment and not from shame, impotence, or contempt, as we have been taught. It is a power that they fear because a woman who knows and prioritizes her joy became unsubmissive and therefore, dangerous.

The vital drive of the eros is a drive for cooperation, for the sensuality of all living bodies, for the interdependence that produces and reproduces life in an autopoietic flow that does not stop. For us, connecting with this vital drive implies confronting that socially imposed mandate in which "being a woman" is "being for the other." For us, "the drive for alterity," in which the Philosophy of Liberation discusses, has not been a liberating drive but a fetishized one.

We understand the reflection on the narcissist drive that constitutes patriarchy and masculine hegemony as well as the need to position the drive for alterity that breaks with this dynamic of domination. But in us, it is different; for us, the drive for alterity is a mandate. It is fetishized as natural; we are mothers or wives. We are always in function of someone else or from the role that mandatory heterosexuality has entrusted us.

It is not a coincidence that for us, it is so hard to think in a "for yourself" mentality in the erotic drive that reaffirms us internally. This is not to become selfish islands, but to connect with ourselves, with our denied potencies, and also with other women, with other joys, with other ways of possible pleasures in life which have been relegated or hidden from us.

Thinking about the erotic of liberation has led us to wonder about the movement of life itself. Maturana and Varela (1998)'s notion of autopoiesis resonates deeply with us. Life is a system with no exteriority, yet it is always open, moving, reproducing, and multiplying. There is anarchy in this vital drive that does not obey any superior entity nor the supravital laws. It is life itself that creates that paradox in which chaos is harmony; it is efficacy, it is perfection (1998).

The balance of life has taken millions of years of combinations, exchanges, flows, encounters, and complicities among atoms, cells, molecules, organs, and bodies. And there, in that millenary genealogic tree, we found ourselves at some point, in these bodies, in these identities, in these others that we now are. Such a realization raises a myriad or questions. How do we understand the wisdom of life itself to comprehend ourselves in it? How do we release the powers of jouissance in that endless movement of the cosmos that nestles in our bodies while we are alive? How do we untie the knots and chains that constrict and compress our muscles, our vital energies, that prevent the expansion of our strength and our pleasure?

We find ourselves in a fundamental historical moment in which the ethical, mythical, and symbolic foundations of the cultures we belong to are in crises and which justify and naturalize the masculine hegemony and the submission of the feminine to their service. We are doing nothing more and nothing less than rethinking the foundations of a new civilization anchored to the needs and enjoyment of life itself.

An erotic liberation necessarily goes through the recognition of our bodies settled in our territories, a struggle that seeks the liberation of life itself threatened by a system of death that does not allow it to maintain any balance, does not allow it to regenerate, or that objectifies, abuses, and exploits as it does with the body of women. Hence, it is not hyperbole to say that erotic liberation, the liberation of women, and the whole world of the feminine, is the liberation of life itself.

Alienation and Subsumption: The Woman as Different from the Same

The patriarchal system has alienated
women of their ability to
make decisions about their lives and their bodies,
denying their role as active subjects in history[6]
Silvia Rivera Cusicanqui

To start elucidating the question of the alienation and subsumption of women and erotic, it is necessary to return to different considerations that have been transversal in this reflection: patriarchy is a long-standing socio-historical and cultural product that is not limited to colonialism. Female subjugation is crossed by the sexual, without a doubt, but is not relegated to solely that. Although we women have thought of ourselves from the perspective of sexual difference, we know that the experience of being and being in the world of life goes through the crossing and overlapping of oppressions.

It was well evidenced by the Afro-descendant women in the United States with the *Combahee Manifesto*, Audre Lorde herself, Chicanas and lesbians like Gloria Anzaldúa or Cherrie Moraga, or the Asian women like Nellie Wong, that after the seventies and anchored to different social movements, they made harsh criticisms of the woman subject built from the white feminist experience to name and make their distinction visible.

For their part, other authors such as María Lugones, Yuderkis Espinoza, Ochy Curiel, *Mujeres Creando en Bolivia*, Francesa Gargallo, and many other fellow feminists from this great territory of Abya Yala, invite us, on one hand, to think about how these intersections of different oppressions have been woven into the construction of what we know today as Latin America, and on the other hand, how this affects us differently.

In this section of our text, we will try to understand alienation and subsumption taking into consideration these guidelines and criteria that have already been followed, but we will start, as a provocation, with the introduction of the much-quoted *The Second Sex* by Simone de Beauvoir, published in 1949. In it, Beauvoir (2021) affirms that alterity is a fundamental category of human thought and the phenomenon of consciousness, while no community ever defines itself as one without immediately placing itself in front of another.

However, the French philosopher is not defining an epistemological trait when bringing up the concept of consciousness, but rather one that must be apprehended from the Hegelian dialectic to explain the evolution of history which means, from the confrontation between two consciences, that when waging their battle, they assume the roles of master and slave with the latter expressing the alienation of conscience, since it denies itself.

The master needs someone to meet his needs, then he realizes that he needs the slave, he could not have him in the exteriority being "unproductive," and for this reason he subsumes him. Following this hermeneutic key on alterity, it can be seen that patriarchy has known how to wage the battle to establish the roles of master and slave to the extent that throughout history, women appear not as a subject, but as an instrument that satisfies the needs of the master, especially the hegemonic one: the white, heterosexual, and western master.

This analysis that Beauvoir makes about the phenomenon of consciousness since Hegel reveals the logic of alterity as a man/woman binomial, and which Butler will later expand and call the *heteronormative regime.* Further, from the Abya Yala we will nurture from the experience of other alterities traversed by racialization and the colonial experience itself.

The concept of subsumption is equivalent to that of alienation. Alienation is the most concrete and complex of the categories within the theoretical framework of the Philosophy of Liberation, because in this category *exteriority* and *totality* interact. In his youth, Marx speaks of alienation, while in his mature years when he writes *Das Kapital*, he replaces the term *alienation* with *subsumption.*

The word *subsume* comes from *sub* (under) and the Latin *sumĕre* (to take for oneself); to subsume is to put something inside that is below. *Alienation* is closely linked to *totality*, insofar as the latter has an intention and a *project* that lies in self-centering, continuing in the same, the identical. For this reason, it extends over the exteriority to make it part of the totality, subsumes it, and makes it alien to itself.

In this sense, without exteriority, there can be no subsumption. You cannot incorporate into the totality something that is already integrated into it, something needs to be outside the totality to be able to subsume it. Therefore, the woman has two options to (out)last she can consciously affirm herself from the *exteriority* of the *totality*, as a denied *alterity*, or, on the contrary, she can unconsciously participate in the totality as a subsumed (alienated) alterity.

In this order of ideas, it is imperative to think about the condition of the woman who is *subsumed* and located in the systemic totality, since in that totality, roles, functions, a type of subjectivity, and a disposition of the body are imposed on her. All of this is for the fulfillment of a hegemonic project that favors men and places them hierarchically in the structures which they themselves have created.

Although we agree on some points with the criticism of the phallocentric society that is made in *Women's Liberation and Latin American Erotic*, we are also challenged by its limitations when it comes to answering: what is it to be a woman? or what does the feminine consist of? We question it as it provides masculine definitions of the feminine in a binary logic that also confuses sex and gender in the field of erotic.

On the other hand, we do not want to fall into essentialism of what means to be and to be in the world as a woman, but to show the contingency, the historicity of the roles and current stereotypes to denature and delegitimize them, betting on the dismantling of the social constructions that sustain the patriarchal order. To offer an example, the role of the mother in which the woman is still seen from a reproductive role to maintain the traditional family scheme and service functions, sustains at the same time the unpaid domestic work and the abuse of home care, thereby reinforcing the stereotype of what is expected of the mother-wife.

The organization of modern patriarchy in Latin America is sustained at the least by the oppressions of race, class, and gender. The complexity in which each of them is imbricated expresses in a different way, the subsumption and alienation of women in this territory. For example, the voices of racialized, lesbian, and precarious women are located in a very different exteriority from those who occupy class and racialization positions that are more functional to the totality of the heteronormative regime; this is why the subsumption of the latter is probably greater than that of the former.

Now, in a general way we can affirm that, dialectically, to be a woman is to be alienated due to the constitution of her subjectivity and the material and because the symbolic reproduction of her life is anchored to the denial that is imposed on her from the dominant patriarchal and macho ideology. However, concretely we should have to stop to analyze all the forms of subsumption that are expressed in our lives based on our participation or not in this racist, colonial, and patriarchal modernity.

In this sense, we can explore how useful it is to think in terms of degrees or levels of exteriority since this would allow us to understand the root of a multiplicity of discussions, debates, and differences that exist between us. In addition to dismantling the idea of a homogeneous being that can express the essence of being a woman, it allows us to trace possible communication and articulation mechanisms and strategies among the feminisms that rise against modern civilization, but which start from different places of enunciation and from trenches that are often at odds with each other.

Toward a Liberation Feminism

> *Women's liberation*
> *it's not just a political issue*
> *it is also an existential question.*[7]
> María Galindo

Throughout this journey, we have been walking and exploring various paths, finding clues and shared intuitions that allow us to advance in the objective of constituting liberation feminism, not only as a theoretical part of our academic tradition but also as an anti-colonial political commitment that dismantles modern patriarchal epistemology and that it is nourished by dialogue with other Latin American Feminisms and with other women who are fighting, even beyond our region. The advances we have made together are barely incipient, and yet no less significant for that purpose.

More than a closure, in these last pages, we would like to establish some notes derived from the previous reflections, in addition to asking ourselves some questions to continue walking. In the first instance, we will strengthen the need for the analectic method in liberation feminism, and finally, we will carry out a reflection on a possible politics of feminist liberation.

The Analectic Method in Liberation Feminism

The last few years have been a turning point in the history of Latin American Feminism. We have witnessed the advances in our fight against the multiple forms of oppression to which we are subjected. Yet, we have also seen how the differences between us and the repetition of patriarchal ways of doing politics have led us, first, to internal disputes that tend to deny the legitimacy of the struggle of other women, especially trans women; and second, to impose or invalidate our places of enunciation, as if we could not articulate them in a complex understanding of the totality that we are facing: difference is not division, difference is complexity, and our struggle is complex. We need to enunciate ourselves, organize ourselves, and fight to know that there is no single trench.

From our diagnosis, it is necessary to agree on some criteria or principles of a possible feminist ethic which allows us to communicate and articulate between us so that our political bets are viable. Yet, many additional questions arise. How do oppressed people reach a consensus? How, if our oppressions are different and place us unevenly in the exercise of power? The "woman" subject as an oppressed subject is an abstraction that does not work for us in this historical period in which particularity, context, and singularity speak to us of diverse, and even antagonistic, experiences.

The oppression faced by a racialized woman brings her face-to-face with the white woman who benefits from racism, for example. How to agree upon a common struggle between these different experiences? Is it possible?

For the Philosophy of Liberation, the encounter with the face, or, the face-to-face, is a fundamental metaphysical moment in which injustice is revealed and responsibility is founded. There is a primary responsibility in those to whom the totality has granted them more favorable positions. Without acknowledging this responsibility and acting accordingly, it is difficult for us to move toward building consensus.

Once these historical positions that go beyond mere identity frameworks and instead place the bodies in the responsibility that corresponds to them have been assumed, we can then think about the ethical criteria necessary for dialogue. Consensus is built through dialogue and the dialogic exercise starts from the recognition of alterity within our exteriority. We are others among ourselves and, nevertheless, we have a common denominator. There is a similarity, something that operates together with the difference that constitutes us: the will to live, a will to live that, moreover, in negative terms, is denied by patriarchy as a historical civilizing system that has its misogynistic, racist, colonial, and classist expression in the modernity we are going through.

In this sense, the analectic method implies a constant adjustment of focus: it is necessary to recognize my story and my place of enunciation. But, at the same time, to observe my partner in struggle, it is in our closeness face-to-face that I can listen and learn of her life story. However, at no time can I forget the framework of the patriarchal regime where his story and mine are framed.

This task remains to be developed later: drawing ethical criteria that allow us to dialogue among ourselves without our differences destroying us or weakening our movement. However, we are advancing in the sense of proposing the recognition of historical responsibility and the starting point, which is the will to live that must be respected. Without these conditions, a dialogue would not be possible; we would have a dialogue only with those with whom the degree of similarity is greater, which always leads us to the risk of building new totalities of meaning that exclude and oppress, even in their exteriority.

Yet, the multiplicity of subjectivities that are constituted as anti-patriarchal is not reduced to the female subject, not even with all its expressions. We are witnessing an overflow of multiple experiences that disagree with the totality and that have fractured the binary sex-gender system. The broad spectrum of the trans and the increasingly strong criticism of the compulsory heterosexual regime have brought practices that operate by deconstructing the modern conceptions of sex, gender, sexuality, and identity. Beyond heterosexual and cisgender men, other experiences and expectations of the body and desire are being instituted and challenged in the generation of a critical and dissident Latin American feminist erotica, which goes beyond modern phallocentrism. If we bet on substituting an ontology of totality for a metaphysics of otherness, all these experiences challenge us and lead us to an even broader dialogue.

Toward a Feminist Liberation Politics

Everything to live loving, live[8]
Baltasar Eliso de Medinilla

To think about Latin American Feminist Liberation Politics implies starting from our ethics, one that is born from the horizons of liberation that we wish to achieve together. It is not possible to build a Feminist Liberation Politics on the foundations of patriarchy; it is necessary to tear them down and abolish the practices that would suffocate our life drive.

There is a desire to live that we share, and that is why we fight; there is a will to live that we defend when we fight for the autonomy of our bodies, for the dignity of our stories, for the liberation of all material and symbolic chains that prevent us from deploying our power. Modern patriarchal politics is anti-erotic. Capitalism commercializes, deteriorates, and devastates life. Racism seeks to lower, subordinate, and annihilate worlds of life (as ways of being) based on the Western white supremacism on which modernity has been built. The cisgender binary heterosexual regime denies and condemns the multiplicity of experiences of the body and of desire that do not fit into their reduced biologist and/or religious frameworks. A Feminist Politics of Liberation should aim to strengthen the will to live denied by these imbrications of modern patriarchal domination.

It is necessary to continue exploring outside the framework of the ontologies of totality and instantiate the radical nature of our exteriority that is not subsumed, but rather rebels. We are not asking the being of the patriarchy to include us in its regime as an equivalent to men, nor are we asking to leave the place of the other to fit into the totalizing being of the male. We do not seek to exchange the leadership roles of the oppressive machine that has led us to the extinction of life, but to dismantle it. Feminist power is creative and transformative; it is born from ourselves, from our life stories, and our bodies. It is a common force that demands and walks toward the collapse of the patriarchy, a vital expression that, however, does not assume it as an interlocutor.

We also need to continue reflecting critically on the place that Latin American women occupy in colonial modernity, as well as the burdens, and the wisdom that we share for five centuries of imperialist history in our territories. This common history allows us to position ourselves antagonistically against capitalist civilization while also challenging other anti-patriarchal struggles that are unfolding in the global south. This is an interpellation that does not necessarily make the classic call to union but to recognize ourselves, weave networks, and articulate knowledge and efforts for our liberation.

It is essential to learn from other political and social movements, from their strengths, and from their mistakes. Our dynamics, as a living feminist movement that is making history, must be different from those of the movements that, even with liberating horizons, remain within the frameworks produced in the patriarchal totality. This is an intricate task because the rules of the game of politics, how such are conceived, and the hierarchical structure in which they are resolved greatly limit the possibility of thinking about feminist politics of liberation. As such, deem politics as erotic as this allows us to start from the territory that is our body, from the desire and will to live itself in its complexity, outside the narrow frameworks of anthropocentrism, and modern hegemonic rationality.

In our experience as feminist women who coexist and dialogue with other women, we have corroborated that the entire structure of the patriarchal regime is designed to deny us jouissance, to repress the vital drive, and wrap our bodies in the kidnapping of life that is racialized capitalist production. It is precisely for this reason, although the desire to experience enjoyment may seem obvious, that connecting with an eroticism of liberation and finding the necessary strength to break down the barriers that separate us from it is a task that involves effort and transformation. And, like any transformation, it is to some extent painful, since it entails the fracture of the ways of being in the world that the patriarchal regime normalizes and promotes.

When we observe that the domination of the patriarchal regime reaches even the smallest corners of the social organization and that it tries to govern our bodies, our daily lives appear as a scenario in which we must constantly monitor and dismantle patriarchal mandates, and our bodies take on a fundamental importance: it becomes the territory from which we must expel the conqueror and, at the same time, the source of the power that we spoke of above. The body, as Leonor Silvestri (n.d.) says, is capable of the most radical transformations when it transgresses its limits and surrenders to constant change to rebellion against any totalizing category or system.

All this leads us to think that it is in the daily and rebellious movement of the bodies where women make the most important discoveries that mark the point of no return on this marvelous path that is the struggle for the individual and collective liberation of women and life.

We know that this transformation process is complicated, the world that was familiar to us begins to collapse and challenges us to live in a constant battle that is waged inside and outside of us: we question the obligatory nature of the heterosexual regime and we begin to suspect the authenticity of the desires that we thought were free. We question the totalizing categories, and we reformulate our life decisions and the expressions of our bodies. We understand the overlap of racist and capitalist domination, and we organize ourselves in defense of our bodies and our territories. We discover that the sanction of jouissance can even come from ourselves, from the women we love and who love us, and, before judging (us), we notice the importance of seeking structural transformation. These discoveries that break through and fracture our grasp of meaning, simultaneously, feed the power of our desires and actions for liberation, and it is for this reason that we celebrate and appreciate them.

Although the reflections and liberation practices that we describe in this text may resonate with many of us, the truth is that they correspond to a small portion of Latin American and women beyond that scope. The majority live a day-to-day routine that we cannot give a direct account of. However, beyond this common thread that weaves part of our lives, there is this power and this desire to enjoy freedom that binds us and that imagines the possibility of a world in which we can express our vital force without fear of being outraged or murdered. Despite the fact that this world does not yet exist, we are convinced that women are becoming stronger and more powerful. We are not waiting for the arrival of this new world, but we are building it. We are not paralyzed by fear and threat, but rather we rebel and resist day by day. Just as anything that wishes to live must defend itself, we are no exception.

Notes

1   Sienten una profunda necesidad de un sistema explicativo coherente, que no nos diga únicamente qué es y por qué ha de ser así, sino que permita una visión alternativa en el futuro. (Translated by the authors).

2   At the end of the 1960s, Dussel met Levinas, from whom he learned categories such as Other, Totality, and Exteriority, which would be understood from the Latin American horizon itself, reaching theoretical drifts in productions of the moment such as *Method for a Philosophy of Liberation* (1972), and that would form a substantial part of his work since then.

3   In her work *The Invention of Women*, Oyěwùmí, Oyèrónkẹ́ shows how in the pre-colonial Yoruba civilization it is not possible to speak of patriarchy, since the categorization of social relations based on gender does not make sense in a culture that does not give it so much centrality to the body or vision. It remains to go

deeper into the debate with the author, since she maintains that the notion of patriarchy assumes (1) the difference between men and women, where (2) the former have an advantage over the latter and (3) women suffer from external domination and own shortcomings (2017, p. 188). However, for us it is important to analyze how human groups become civilizations and the role played by the control of sexuality and the reproductive capacity of the bodies, regardless of whether anyone could rule or if social roles were not so marked, as in modern western societies.

4 Silvia Federici (2010).

5 Audre Lorde (2017).

6 El sistema patriarcal ha alienado a las mujeres de su capacidad para tomar decisiones sobre sus vidas y su cuerpo, negando su papel como sujetos activos en la historia.

7 La liberación de las mujeres no es sólo una cuestión política, es también una cuestión existencial.

8 Todo por vivir amando, vive.

References

Beauvoir, S. (2021). *El Segundo Sexo*. Ciudad de México: Penguin Random House.

Dussel, E. (1990). *Liberación de La Mujer y Erótica Latinoamericana*. Bogotá: Nueva América.

Dussel, E. (2007). *Para Una Ética Latinoamericana*. Caracas: El perro y la rana Publishing Foundation.

Federici, S. (2010). *Calibán y La Bruja. Mujeres, Cuerpos y Acumulación Originaria*. Madrid: Traficantes de sueños.

Lerner, G. (1990). *La Creación Del Patriarcado*. Barcelona: Editorial Crítica.

Lorde, A. (2017). *La Hermana, La Extranjera (Extractos)*. Oaxaca: Fusilemos la Noche.

Maturana, H. and Varela, F. (1998). *De Máquinas y Seres Vivos*. In: *Autopoiesis: La Organización de Lo Vivo*. Santiago de Chile: Editorial Universitaria.

Rubin, G. (1975). *El Tráfico de Mujeres*. In: *Notas Sobre La Economía Política Del Sexo*. Mexico City: Marea Negra.

Silvestri, L. (n.d.). *Primavera Con Monique Wittig, El Devenir Lesbiano Con El Dildo En La Mano de Spinoza Transfeminista*. Queen Lud., S.F.

5

Sylvia Wynter's Gender and Genre for a Queer and Trans-inclusive Politics

ELISABETH PAQUETTE

Introduction

Afro-Caribbean decolonial theorist Sylvia Wynter (b. 1928), originally from Jamaica and currently residing in the United States, has produced a significant number of texts since the late 1950s. She writes extensively on the topics of anti-Black racism and the histories of colonialism offering not only critical engagements with historical and current systems of violence but also develops ways of addressing these forms of harm. While underacknowledged in many disciplines, Wynter's work has been highly esteemed throughout the course of her career and continues to hold significant relevance to decolonial feminist scholarship today.

In my chapter, I provide an account of Wynter's use of gender, and I argue that her gender analysis can be expanded to include trans, gender nonconforming, nonbinary, and intersex folks as well. Such an analysis is possible by attending to her conception of gender *as* genre.

This account of gender in Wynter's work enables forms of resistance to biological and colonial conceptions of gender. While attempting to take care not to subsume one into the others, I aim to demonstrate the expansiveness of Wynter's project and the value that it has for thinking through and alongside queer, and trans forms of resistance.

This paper consists of three sections. I begin with a summary of Wynter's use of genre within her discussion of gender. Second, I turn to her broader work in order to address biological and colonial genres of what it means to be human that she seeks to upend. And third I offer an expansion of Wynter's work to include queer, trans, and gender nonconforming folks.[1]

Gender and Genre

Sylvia Wynter's discussion of gender is premised on a conception of "genre." First and foremost, Wynter leans into the etymological foundation of gender. Gender is a term that is derived from the Old French word *gendre* and *genre*, and subsequently also the Latin term *genus*. In each instance the commonality between these terms is a reference to a kind or a class of noun. As such, in whatever context, we have gender (like genre and genus) as explicitly serving as a mode of classification of a person (and place and thing). As such, differentiation is present here as classification.[2]

Wynter's turn toward genre raises several questions for me as to why she opts for genre over gender. Foremost, I ask: what is at stake in the term gender that is a foreclosure of possibility (whether critique or hope) for which genre offers a different kind of maneuverability and possibility?

According to Tonya Haynes (2012, p. 55), a foremost Wynter scholar, "Gender is always a key feature of how each genre of the human understands itself, but it is not the only feature." Furthermore, "Gender, Wynter insists, is part of genre, or different kinds of the human. Gender is always a key feature of how each genre of the human understands itself, but it is not the only feature. Part and parcel of our globalized understanding of the world is the over representation of a particular genre of the human as the human itself" (Haynes 2012, p. 55).

For my purposes, an important conclusion that we should draw from the above quotes is that first, genre subsumes gender into its analysis, and second, that genre has something to do with what it means to be human. Regarding the first point, the relation between gender and genre are already apparent given the *etymological* source of gender being genre. Of course, there is the way in which both serve a function of classification, whereby gender is often used to distinguish or classify one as woman/man, male/female, or some corresponding binary system. Second, the relation between genre and human is a central one in many essays by Wynter, which will be further developed in section two.

Third, as will be made evident below, Wynter is concerned with the overrepresentation of what it means to be human or of the manner in which genre is imposed as a universal. Or, as stated by Haynes (2012, p. 55): "Part and parcel of our globalized understanding of the world is the over representation of a particular genre of the human as the human itself."

I would like to add a fourth point to the considerations above. While it is true that genre can exist in various formulations, I believe that for Wynter it also holds literary significance.[3] Still serving the function of classification (fiction, nonfiction, autobiography), the implications of this resonance will be made clear in section two as well.

Biological and Human

Many who already know some of Wynter's work will likely know about the way in which she describes and distinguishes different (over)representations of the human. I won't go into great detail here, but a cursory summary of it is needed for the argument that follows.[4] Wynter works out these concepts most explicitly in two essays in particular: "1492: A New World View" (1995) and "Unsettling the Coloniality of Being/Power/Truth/Freedom: Towards the Human, after Man, its Overrepresentation—an Argument" (2003).

She most often begins with that I have elsewhere named "The True Christian Self." This representation of the human is premised on a dichotomy of Spirit/Flesh, whereby what it means to be human is to be a Christian, the opposite of which is to be bound up with the desires of the flesh which is attributed as Paganism. Medieval order of knowledge centers the Christian Church, as the source of eternal salvation. In addition, to refuse the word of God (or to refuse the Christian Church) marks one as an idolator, and ultimately not fully human according to the Christian theological order of things.

Following the Copernican Revolution, a new conception of the human emerges. Wynter names this conception of the human as Man 1, or the homo politicus (or political subject), and it is (over) represented as rationality. In this instance, those who are considered to be human are thought to be rational, and perhaps more importantly, those who are considered to be irrational and/or unrational are *not* considered to be human. Therein too is the rise of modern secularism, and the Enlightenment.

The juxtaposition between The True Christian Self and Man 1 is also locatable between Bartolomé La Casas and Juan Ginés Sepúlveda in the Valladolid debate of 1550, which offered different justifications for slavery and genocide—namely whether subjects had rejected the word of god (Las Casas and the True Christian Self) or whether there exists slaves by nature (Sepúlveda and Man 1). The horrors of the trans-Atlantic slave trade, and the genocide of Indigenous peoples following first contact, are sought to be justified through this debate, whereby Las Casas argues that Indigenous peoples who had not yet rejected the word of the Christian god and therefore ought not be enslaved, and yet presumably peoples from the African continent had rejected the word of god and therefore could be enslaved. For Sepúlveda, ir- or un-rationality is imbued to Indigenous and African peoples by nature, thus justifying their enslavement. In each instance, what it means to be human, for Wynter, is an over-representation, which in short means that it is imposed through a position of power as though it is universal, and as though it can determine who counts as human, and who does not.

Following Man 1, another new conception of the human emerges, this one called Man 2. It is in the era of Man 2 that Wynter claims we currently find ourselves. Man 2 trails the eighteenth century and is situated within a Darwinian, or perhaps more appropriately Malthusian, arrangement of natural selection and scarcity of resources. This homo-economicus determines fitness, or economic survival, to be evolutionarily determined. Therein, the poor and third world are both considered not fit for survival, and thus less than human. The economically successful are so because they are best able to survive within the current context and thus are the instantiation of what it means to be human. Herein, we also have the rise of the biological sciences, taking place following the eighteenth century.

So, in each era, there is a new and distinct conception of what it means to be human, and new criteria used to de-humanize whole groups of people. For Wynter, these organizing principles also have implications for the way in which the world is mapped, the cosmos are ordered, and the way in which sciences and religions are employed.

What is important for my purpose in this chapter, however, is that when Wynter refers to these differing conceptions of what it means to be human, she describes them as *genres* of being human. Furthermore, as noted by Haynes (2012, p. 57), "For Wynter ... all contemporary struggles are essentially struggles against the white Western bourgeois overrepresentation of itself as the human—as The Man—and relegating the rest of us to varying subject positions as lesser Others .... Rather than seeing her analysis as invalidating the entire premise of Caribbean feminist scholarship ..., she insists on a wider project of social justice than that which is made possible by limited deployments of gender. After Wynter's deconstructive work comes her reconstructive project."

I concur with Haynes that Wynter's project is primarily located within a discussion of struggles around what it means to human, and the power relations that seek to delimit this category. And furthermore, that the genres of what it means to be human is where she locates her gender analysis. Such is the case not only because of the relation that she draws between genre and gender, as noted in section one, but also because of the manner in which she discusses manifestations of the human throughout her corpus.

For instance, in her essay titled "Beyond Miranda's Meanings: Un/silencing the 'Demonic Ground' of Caliban's 'Woman'" (Wynter 1990), Wynter states that Shakespeare's *The Tempest* enacts the "mutational shift" from the anatomical model to the cultural-physiognomic model. As such, for Wynter, what is at stake in the narrative of *The Tempest* is the relation that develops between Miranda, the white woman, and Caliban, the ambiguously Black and/or Indigenous man.[5] Therein she notes how Miranda is allocated a position of rationality over against Caliban who is portrayed as irrational. Importantly, this text was written around 1610–1611, during the start of the trans-Atlantic slave trade and colonization of what would become the Americas and Caribbean. This is noteworthy because of the manner in which it makes evident the transition from the True Christian Self to Man 1. The mutational shift I take it to mean a change from the prescription of, the hierarchization of, "sex" (here the anatomical position) to the prescription of, and hierarchization of race (here the cultural physiognomic model).

The Tempest serves here as an example of the shift from the anatomical to the cultural-physiognomic, from the religious to the secular, from sex-gender to race, in part because of the relation between Miranda and Caliban, whereby Miranda the white woman gains power over the Native/Black man. Furthermore, against the backdrop of an explicitly absent Black or Native woman, Miranda is also situated as the proper or rational subject of desire.[6]

While this mutational shift provides us with means to understand at least part of the motivation for where and how gender appears, it is also important to note that these conceptions can change over time. There is nothing that is inherent about them. And yet, in each instantiation it is proposed to be the case that they are inherently true and not dependent upon culture/time/space/politics/religion.

As such, a further point that needs to be made here. In addition to the observation of the shift and the manner in which it invokes gender, she simultaneously addresses the way in which race is implicated. And in each instance, the presumption is that gender, race, the human is pre-determined or at least outside of our control. The Pagan cannot make himself human unless he accepts the word of god (and even that point is contentious—because acceptance is determined by the church), the un- or irrational cannot make himself rational, and the poor is poor because of their predisposition.

It would seem then, for Wynter (1990, p. 358), that with each era there is a mapping of hierarchical relations onto the body, albeit in different ways. Where male/female was mapped onto bodies through the New World order she states the following: "for the first time in history [nature] was no longer *primarily* encoded in the male/female gender division ... but now in the cultural-physignomic variations." Importantly, it is not as though the male/female binary ceases to exist, but that rather it is no longer a primary division. Rather, it becomes important to address the racialization of the body as well through culture and physiognomy.

Furthermore, regarding the invocation of genres of the human and gender, consider this second quote: "If, for Freud, ... biology was destiny ... the variable of *race/racial* difference is, since the sixteenth century, even more primarily destiny."[7] Following the nineteenth century, the rise of evolutionary biology, and the Malthusian-Darwinian-Haeckelian scheme, the purely physiognomic transforms into the "*somatic* mode of difference."[8]

Following the shift from Man 1 and Man 2, with Freud firmly situated within Man 2, we see the rise of biology as the foundation for success, but herein too, biology continues to be mapped onto hierarchizations, such as race. As noted by Wynter (1990, p. 357), "race ... acts so as to place genetically determined constraints on human behaviors [and] ... to *prescribe* a teleology—that is, to imply that 'ends,' ... are still extra-humanly set for the human by *nature*." In Man 2, an articulation that continues to influence the worlds in which many of us move today, in its most basic sense, we see here the rise of biology as determining ones fitness for "survival" or success in the world.

One manifestation of this is genetics, whereby genes provide the clues as to who one is, and who or what one will become. Discussions of the "gay gene" or the "alcoholic gene" are perhaps the more contentious examples of how genetics are utilized to determine ones successes or determine who one will become. And yet "*the* male gene" and "*the* female gene" are often naturalized and therefore determined as true and unchanging. Similarly, for Wynter, race has also been codified in this biological context.

For Wynter, then, the issue is the process through which biologization takes place, a process that implicates race and gender. As noted by Haynes (2012, p. 58), "Wynter is not denying gendered power relations; she is essentially arguing that 'gender' is part and parcel of the Western biologic which naturalized both the human/savage binary and the male/female binary." Importantly, within Wynter's project, it is not the case that systems of oppression are seen as contradicting but rather complicating how we understand and address systems of oppression.

Inherent here is the way in which biological conceptions of what it means to be human becomes naturalized around a binary system. Importantly, Wynter (1990, p. 356) notes the similarities in the ways in which race and gender are constituted, albeit without collapsing them into the same. And yet, she is also careful not to remove the complexity between the two. For instance, she states the following: "Caribbean women writers/critics ... is that of a cross-roads, that is, one in which they experience themselves as placed at a crossroad of three variables" (sex-gender, class, and "race").

Additionally, as noted by Haynes (2012, p. 58), Wynter's project "suggests the simultaneity of 'race' and 'gender' in constituting different genres of the human. Hers is a rejection of a humanist feminist project which would seek to include bourgeois Woman as the counterpart of the Man, which leaving intact a long list of Others." As such, it is on this basis that Wynter (1990, pp. 356–357) critiques conception of *presumed* universal feminism developed by white feminist who fail to understand the ways in that race and gender and class intersect (and thus maybe favor a more anatomical model). For her, it is the variable of "race" that serves to create a contradiction in the field of meaning for the universalizing trajectories of feminism. As such, of the interplay or relation between race and gender, Wynter offers a more nuanced account than white feminists who focus on the anatomical or gender alone.

In summation, in a sense it is the process through which what it means to be human is currently constituted that is at issue for Wynter. Or the genres of what it means to be human is the context against which our gender-based analysis must focus. In other words, rather than attending to race, gender, and class as separate entities that need to be addressed, for Wynter, turning to the conception of what it means to be human (of the genre of human) serves to address each in turn, and the confluence of them at the same time.

Furthermore, and importantly, attending to what it means to be human (and its exclusion) also forestalls the reification or overdetermination of any particular formula as universal. For instance, feminism that fails to address race and class in addition to gender often serves to maintain the conception of what it means to be human that marginalizes women of color.

Beyond Man

Wynter's approach to gender as genre is important because of the way that it navigates attending to the simultaneity of race, gender, and class. In addition, and what I am proposing in this chapter, is that her approach can be extended to address the systems of oppression that impact trans, gender diverse, and queer folks as well. While Wynter herself never names these more expansive forms of gender-based and sexuality-based forms of identity (or oppression), addressing them is not inconsistent with her project, and furthermore, her use of genre continues to be beneficial for addressing a variety of forms of harm.

In what follows I name five different ways that Wynter's project can be extended, and the impact that it has for trans, gender diverse, and queer folks.

First, Wynter's critique of the biologization of bodies as naturalized serves to subdue some of the force of the language of "nature" that is bound up with conceptions of sex and gender. Often gender and sex are divided into two distinct categories, whereby gender is performative and sex is bound up with nature and thus (often) thought of as unchangeable. We can recall here Wynter's use of Freud to name biology as destiny. Within studies of sex and gender writ large, there are an array of positions that assume (or enforce) a "nature" about sex, and furthermore its determinateness.

For instance, Luce Irigaray's "Why Different?" (2000) proffers now well critiqued trans-exclusive position that sex cannot be changed. Similarly, a key component to many Trans Exclusionary Radical Feminists is this assumption that sex itself it determined, embodied, and thus unchangeable.[9] As a result, Wynter's critique is consistent with the writings of various scholars. Furthermore, Wynter's critique is not solely locatable within the realm of sex but also seems to pertain to gender as well. For instance, Haynes (2012, p. 58) notes the following:

> Western feminist concerns with defining gender away from sex, and therefore away from biological determinism, are unnecessarily distracting ... and is the point that, within Western bio-logic, sex is inseparable from gender. Gender may be understood as part of genre, of which race, ethnicity, class, sexuality and other relations of domination and subordination are a part, and are all grounded in a Western bio-logic.

Read in this way, Wynter's project can open up for trans folks, and gender queer folks, for whom the nature of sex/gender is often used to cause harm. Addressing biologized gender is central to Sandy Stone's (2006) "The Empire Strikes Back" and similarly, M. Jacqui Alexander (2006, p. 47) critiques the use of quasi-science and physiognomy and anatomy for the purpose of homophobia. And furthermore, C. Riley Snorton's (2017) *Black on Both Sides* seeks to offer an analysis or engagement with trans experiences that exceed anatomical framings.

Second, Wynter's attention to undoing binary systems, such as male/female, serves to create spaces for gender diverse, and trans folks as well. The point that Wynter repeatedly makes is that culture informs the biological, and any denial of this presumption is misguided. Her intention is not to absolve any faith in science whatsoever (especially at a time when science denial and misinformation is steadily increasing or at an all-time high) but rather to understand that as human beings, we must understand that literature imposes upon science and that culture imposes upon nature. For Wynter, these binary systems are created to serve particular ends, often for exclusion. Wynter is attentive to the harms of binary systems of genres of the human, an attention that can be extended to sex/gender binaries as well.

In "The 'S' Word: Sex, Empire and Black Radical Tradition (After Sylvia)," Greg Thomas (2006, pp. 77–78) discusses Wynter's distinction between ontological and political sovereignty as it pertains to sex. Therein Thomas engages with a number of Wynter's essays[10] and demonstrates the "historical contingency," "cultural specificity," and "sociopolitical undesirability" of the gender binary and heteronormative concepts,[11] engaging with such concepts as sexual responsibility.[12] Furthermore, Thomas brings Wynter into conversation with Toni Cade Bambara, Merele Hodge, Ifi Amadiume, Nkrumah Nzegwu, Oyèrónkẹ́ Oyěwùmí, Cheryl Clarke, Elaine Brown among a number of other authors, offering a narrative of Black women writers, which for him culminates in Wynter's work.

But in addition, and importantly for this chapter, Thomas aims to denaturalize dominant sexual ontologies in an anti-imperialist fashion,[13] to the extent that "sex categories [are treated] as explicit categories of empire,"[14] a treatment he claims that can begin and end with Wynter.[15] As a result, Thomas (2006, p. 93) describes "Wynter's anti-imperialist denaturalization of sex, her demystification of gender and sexuality, [as] amazingly complete." Furthermore, according to Haynes (2012, p. 59), "Wynter does not provide a theory of gendered power within heterosexual relationships; nor does she provide a theory of power relations between generic men and women. What her work does, by not accepting these relationships as given or as the norm, is provide the tools, not for bargaining with patriarchy but for undoing gender altogether."

Given Wynter's general interest in dismantling binaries that serve to maintain hierarchies and that sex categories and gender categories seek to maintain empire, it seems to stand that Wynter is also interested in undoing gender binary systems. Such a move is consistent with the work of various trans and queer theorists. For instance, Stone (2006, p. 231) describes a desire to turn to "a productive force to multiplicatively divide the old binary discourses of gender." Toward this end, Stone (2006, p. 231 emphasis original) states the following: "I suggest constituting transsexuals not as a class or problematic 'third gender,' but rather as a *genre*—a set of embodied texts whose potential for *productive* disruption of structured sexualities and spectra of desire has yet to be explored."

Third, Wynter (1976) frequently seeks to address the ways that one can write oneself into being, or what she names auto-poiesis. While she names the way in which writing oneself into being can be problematic, of course, when it seeks to maintain or create a hierarchy, there is also a liberatory aspect of auto-poieses. For the purpose of this chapter, consider the following examples: there are collective spaces in which one might write out what feminine, masculine, queer, gender-queer, cuir, and two spirit means, away from systems of oppression named above. Importantly also is the way in which such writing necessitates how these conceptions will change over time. To this point, Wynter states the following:

> When I wrote—in a 1997 essay—about feminist thought and Western thought in general as being a-cultural, I meant to underscore that they are a-sociogenic or a-autopoietic. These areas of thought define the human as a purely biological being; their intellectuals cannot therefore recognize their own culture's autopoeisis field as being the genre-specific field that is, assuming instead that its field is simply reality-in-general.
>
> Wynter and McKittrick (2015, p. 30)

Such a position is consistent with various queer and trans authors who seek to re-name and revise what these terms or concepts might mean, and the way in which they are employed. For instance, citing Jack Halberstam, Jacob Hale (2006, p. 286) lists a multitude of self-categorizations that exceed the category homosexual and heterosexual such as "guys with pussies, dykes with dicks, queer butches, aggressive femmes." Similarly, Sara Ahmed (2017, p. 230) seeks to "to create new ways of being in the world" as it pertains to gender, and Susan Stryker (2016, p. 230) calls for a reinventing of essentialist female language or Stone's calls for a counterdiscourse from "outside the boundaries of gender." And Rinaldo Walcott (2016, p. 138) notes the power in reclaiming and in self-naming.

Fourth, I hold that Wynter's approach inherently requires solidarity given that her approach to gender is located within a critique of genres of the human and furthermore, that such framing co-extensively determines or structures racism, sexism, classism (for instance). As a result, this means not only that one does *not* have to choose a particular form of oppression to address (as though that were even possible), but also that addressing systems of oppression requires an inclusive and expansive framework.

Wynter offers a critique of various theorists who fail to offer expansive projects. For instance, Wynter (1990, p. 355) describes Irigaray's project as a "purely Western assumption of a universal category 'woman'." Similarly, whereby for Wynter (1990, pp. 363–364), womanist is both the same as feminist and different; the difference therein

> serves, diacritically to draw attention to the insufficiency of all existing theoretical imperative models, both of "voice" the hitherto silenced ground of the experience of "native" Caribbean women and Black American women as the ground of Caliban's woman, and to de-code the system of meanings of that other discourse, beyond Irigaray's patriarchal one, which has imposed this mode of silence for some five centuries, as well as make thinkable the possibility of a new "model" projected from a new "native" standpoint, we shall need to translate the variable "race," which now functions as the intra-feminist marker of difference, impelling the dually "gender/beyond gender" readings of these essays, out of the epistemic "vrai" of our present order of "positive knowledge," its consolidated fields of meanings and order-replicating hermeneutics.

Whereby sex-gender and class might be shared with European women, race "strongly demarcates" their situations (Wynter 1990, p. 356). As such, it becomes imperative to be attentive to the totality of the position that is operating and maintaining systems of hierarchy, power, and exclusion, rather than seeking to address one issue in particular. And of course, there are a number of queer scholars who advocate for the importance of solidarity across (seemingly) distinct identity positionalities, including Judith Butler (1990, p. 127) or the interdependence of systems of domination as noted by Cohen (2005, p. 42).

And finally, Wynter's approach also leaves open the possibility of addressing other forms of harm in the future, harms that are not yet named. Not only is there a lack in the prioritization of any particular form of harm, but also it does not require that harm be named explicitly. Such a position is possible because Wynter's attention to genres of the human. As noted by Haynes (2012, p. 58), "Challenges to gendered power relations must be made from a vantage point outside of the episteme, not from within it." This means that Western feminism fails if it perpetuates the biocentric model of what it means to be human, and more importantly, that feminism must begin from the margins, from liminality.[16]

Similarly, in "Beyond Miranda's Meaning," Wynter (1990, p. 364) notes the imperative of not offering another alternative definition, "but rather to a frame of reference which parallels the 'demonic models' posited by physicists who seek to conceive of a vantage point outside of the space-time orientation of the homuncular observer." There is no predetermined position from which struggles for justice can be fought, other than to be outside of the system of hierarchization. An attention to futurity is important to a variety to queer and trans theorists as well. For instance, Walcott (2016, p. 134) emphasizes the importance of a politics of a possible future.

Conclusion

Wynter's approach to gender as genre offers a nuanced approach to addressing multiple and intersecting forms of oppression. While she herself addresses race, gender, and class in particular, her approach is also fruitful for addressing the forms of harms that impact queer, trans, and gender diverse folks. As such, her project offers a useful intervention in gender politics writ large.

Notes

1   This analysis could be expanded to include intersex folks as well. However, because I have not here included writings by folks who identify as intersex, I have not made it a central aspect of my analysis.
2   "The etymological link between genre and gender is key, as gender provides an example of how biological differences can be inscribed with social meaning. Both gender and race are forms of differentiation produced by genre." Therein, the issue is not race, rather "Our issue is the issue of the genre of 'Man'"—Darryl Li (2021).
3   And of course, genre is also a literary term. Sylvia Wynter and Natalie J. Marine-Street (2017).
4   For additional summary of Wynter's articulation of the human, see Katherine McKittrick (2006) and Elisabeth Paquette (2020).
5   There is significant debate around whether William Shakespeare sought to name Caliban as Black or Indigenous. As a result, he has been taken up by various authors as both.
6   Wynter, "Beyond Miranda's Meanings," p. 360.
7   Wynter, "Beyond Miranda's Meaning," p. 357.
8   Wynter, "Beyond Miranda's Meaning," p. 359.
9   As a citational practice, I have decided not to include names of any Trans Exclusionary Radical Feminists (TERFS). That said, there exists a rather lengthy list of scholars who have already critiqued this position. Including the following: Sandy Stone (2006).
10   Most notably are the following essays: Sylvia Wynter (1972, 1979, 1995, 2000).

ELISABETH PAQUETTE

11 Thomas, "The 'S' Word," pp. 78–79.
12 Thomas, "The 'S' Word," p. 79.
13 Thomas, "The 'S' Word," p. 78.
14 Thomas, "The 'S' Word," p. 78.
15 Thomas, "The 'S' Word," p. 79.
16 Therein too, she describes the way in which womanist must be "projected from a 'demonic model'" by which she means it ought to address the humanist foundation.—Wynter, "Beyond Miranda's Meaning," p. 364.

References

Ahmed, S. (2017). *Living a Feminist Life*, 230. Durham: Duke University Press.

Alexander, M.J. (2006). *Pedagogies of Crossing: Meditations on Feminism, Sexual Politics, Memory, and the Sacred*. Durham: Duke University Press.

Butler, J. (1990). *Gender Trouble: Feminism and the Subversion of Identity*, 127. New York: Routledge.

Cohen, C.J. (2005). Punks, Bulldaggers, and Welfare Queens: The radical potential of queer politics? In: *Black Queer Studies: A Critical Anthology* (ed. E. Patrick Johnson and G.H.'s. Mae), 21–51. Durham: Duke University Press.

Hale, J. (2006). Are lesbians women? In: *The Transgender Studies Reader* (ed. S. Stryker and S. Whittle's), 281–299. New York: Routledge.

Haynes, T. (2012). The divine and the demonic: Sylvia Wynter and caribbean feminist thought revisited. In: *Love and Power: Caribbean Discourses on Gender* (ed. V.E. Barriteau's). Jamaica: University of West Indies Press.

Irigaray, L. (2000). *Why different?: A culture of two subjects* (ed. L. Irigaray and S. Lotringer) Translated by Camille Collins. New York: Semiotext(e).

Li, D. (2021). Genres of universalism: Reading Into international law, with help from Sylvia Wynter. *67 U.C.L.A. Law Review* 1686: 1688–1719.

McKittrick, K. (2006). *Demonic Grounds: Black Women and the Cartographies of Struggle*. Minneapolis: University of Minnesota Press.

Paquette, E. (2020). *Universal Emancipation: Race Beyond Badiou*. Minneapolis: University of Minnesota Press.

Snorton, C.R. (2017). *Black on Both Sides: A Racial History of Trans Identity*. Minneapolis: University of Minnesota Press.

Stone, S. (2006). The empire strikes back: A posttransexual manifesto. In: *The Transgender Studies Reader* (ed. S. Stryker and S. Whittle's), 221–235. New York: Routledge.

Stryker, S. (2016). Another dream of common language: An interview with sandy stone. *TSQ: Transgender Studies Quarterly* 3 (1–2): 294–305.

Thomas, G. (2006). The 'S' word: Sex, empire and black radical tradition (after Sylvia). In: *After Man, Towards the Human: Critical Essays on Sylvia Wynter* (ed. A. Bogues'), 77–99. Kingston: Ian Randell Publishers.

Walcott, R. (2016). *Queer Returns: Essays on Multiculturalism, Diaspora, and Black Studies*, 138. Toronto: Insomniac Press.

Wynter, S. (1972). One love: Rhetoric or reality? Aspects of Afro-Jamaicanism. *Caribbean Studies* 12 (3): 64–97.

Wynter, S. (1976). Ethno or socio poetics. *Alcheringa* 2 (2): 78–94.

Wynter, S. (1979). Sambos and minstrels. *Social Text* 1: 149–156. doi:10.2307/466410.

Wynter, S. (1990). Afterword: "Beyond Miranda's Meanings: Un/silencing the 'Demonic Ground' of Caliban's 'Woman'". In: *Out of the Kumbla: Caribbean Woman and Literature* (ed. C.B. Davies and E. Savory), 355–372. Fido. Trenton: African World Press, Inc.

Wynter, S. (1995). 1492: A new world view. In: *Race, Discourse, and the Origin of the Americas: A New World View* (ed. V.L. Hyatt and R.M. Nettleford), 1–57. Washington, DC: Smithsonian Institution Press.

Wynter, S. (2000). "The re-enchantment of humanism: An interview with Sylvia Wynter" with David Scott. *Small Axe* 8: 119–207.

Wynter, S. (2003). Unsettling the coloniality of being/power/truth/freedom: Towards the human, after man, its overrepresentation—An argument. *CR: The New Centennial Review* 3 (3): 257–337.

Wynter, S. and Marine-Street, N.J. (2017). Sylvia Wynter: An oral history. *Stanford Historical Society Oral History Program, Interviews* 1999–2022. https://purl.stanford.edu/vt433pj3894.

Wynter, S. and McKittrick, K. (2015). Unparalleled catastrophe of our species? Or, to give humanness a different future: Conversations. In: *Sylvia Wynter: On Being Human as Praxis* (ed. K. McKittrick), 9–89. Durham: Duke University Press.

Section III

Education

6

Struggles to Make Black Lives Matter

ERNESTO ROSEN VELÁSQUEZ

After the licensed public lynching of George Floyd and ensuing mass cross-racial protests in which people faced police and state sponsored military violence in the form of tear gas, rubber bullets, tazers, beatings with batons and imprisonment, westernized universities across the United States issued public declarations of commitments to anti-racism and expressed support to Black Lives Matter. The methods by which some of these documents were produced did not involve listening to, reading, thinking with, critically evaluating and learning from the dead. Those generations of ancestors who worked on the complex problems of racism and colonialism and have offered the world various creative proposals for addressing them were not in those consultations. Neither were much of the living learning community that has worked on racism invited to collaborate on the production of the anti-racism document. No members of Black Lives Matter or teams of Black Indigenous People of Color (BIPOC) scholars with histories of working on these issues produced these public statements. This critical learning community of the living and the dead that collectively constitute centuries, decades, years, hours, minutes, and seconds of sweating, bleeding, dying, reading, analyzing, writing, re-writing, critically evaluating, discussing, speaking, arguing, singing, organizing, protesting, marching, going on hunger strikes, creating art, and resisting racism were not consulted (see Figures 6.1 and 6.2).

Instead of reading ancestors who analyze racism and are no longer with us in body but in spirit through their writings, films, speeches, and other archival remains that enable us to connect with, learn from and with them, something else happens. The justified rage of the people and fires do not become a moment for listening to historically neglected voices. It does not become a moment of humility, embarrassment, or recognition of why it has realized its cowardice so late and opening itself up to learning and collaborating with living experts, social movements, and community-based organizations that historically work on and creatively struggle to reduce various forms of

---

Struggles for Liberation in Abya Yala, First Edition. Edited by Luis Rubén Díaz Cepeda and Ernesto Rosen Velásquez.

Figure 6.1   Black Heaven. Source: Neveah Wade

Figure 6.2   Resistance. Source: Antonio Flores

racialized dehumanization in the United States and the planet. Primarily administrators produced the anti-racism documents.

We should not discount the fact that there are administrators who have awareness of issues of racism and work to decolonize the westernized university. Furthermore, sometimes faculty can inhibit substantive change because their disciplinary decadence registers anything from administrators as problematic because it appears to come from up above. Or sometimes faculty block substantive change when these colonized intellectuals see themselves as gatekeepers to a philosophical tradition that they falsely think is theirs to guard and preserve its purity. This is problematic because it presupposes cultural phenomena such as philosophy are pieces of property that can be possessed by a person or specific community. The absurdity increases when these border patrol faculty guard a field in the face of the fact that the same intellectual tradition, they defend at all costs claim they cannot be a philosopher because of their race or gender. While these horizontal and vertical hostilities may be so, often administrators while perhaps with well intentions lack the knowledge and racial literacies to understand the gravity and complexities of the matters unfolding on the streets. One thing that happens is the original demands by Black Lives Matter such as to defund the police are left out of university public documents and thus neutralize or distort their original creative demands in such a way that their demands are not able to make their way into these education sites to produce transformation and instead produce a form of white justice which is individualist and ornamental (see Figures 6.3 and 6.4). The westernized university operates in a way to either deflect, ignore, or dismiss the original demand or if it is able to penetrate its hallowed walls something very different emerges once the demand goes through the westernized sieve of practices, discourses, and people embedded within these education sites. How, if at all, can demands

Figure 6.3   White Justice. Source: Juan Favela

Figure 6.4   No Justice No Peace. Source: Jordan Hill

of social movements become absorbed into westernized universities so they can become institutional realities? The way the anti-racism documents are produced creates a scenario in which there is a large team of nonspecialists on racism and either one scholar on racism—token representation—or perhaps in some cases none.[1] How does the westernized university create the conditions for the continual proliferation of tokens that focus on difference that does not make a difference? It does so in part through the production of quantitative and epistemological invisibility, reverse empiricism, and rounds of inoculations. Let me explain.

Tokens perform the function of making the people who uphold the system feel as if they are nonracist, tolerant, and open to diversity because they have allowed this one of a kind into the system. This in turn makes people think either that there really is no problem at an institutional level or if there is a problem, it is with a few other racially prejudiced people. Either of these ways of registering the situation entails holding the system intact. If the problem is with a few racially prejudiced people then one way this is addressed is through the common practice reflex response of professional development training. This is an obstacle in the struggle to make Black Lives Matter because this is a highly watered down, individualized, and depoliticized way of attempting to have people quickly acquire racial literacies. Acquiring racial literacies involves an ongoing process of working to understand complex technical terms like white supremacy, racism, the school to prison pipeline, colonization, decolonization, and other non-Eurocentric histories, forms of knowledge production, cosmologies, and doing the community-based work needed to empower a variety of structural victims. While participants in these professional development sessions pat themselves on the back and applaud their performances at the end of these anti-racism training sessions and it is unclear what they are actually applauding, they in fact are not recognizing the gravity and complexity of the problem. It is a wasteful use of funds and people's time. It presupposes scholars working on racism do not produce knowledge. Universities do not have professional development for faculty and staff to acquire literacies in physics or chemistry. One takes courses for that. These institutional practices that fall under professional development assume a hierarchical distinction between knowledge and training. The latter discusses racism in a decontextualized, individualized, moralistic way. It also is a form of reverse empiricism by not drawing on the epistemic diversity available on matters of racism. Instead, it makes an epistemic turn to nonexperts or people lacking a history of working on these complex matters or someone who is taken as an expert because they referred to a minoritized group in their research data and can only use culture of poverty explanations.

Tokens within a westernized university also have a certain significance in that even though they are one they appear as multiple or too much of that kind (i.e., too black) such that one is enough. Lewis Gordon (2021) identifies this is as a form of racial invisibility that focuses on quantity. It is partly why after hiring a token there is a sigh of relief and wiping of hands "there we did our diversity hire now leave us alone for another twenty years." "We already have someone who works in Latin American philosophy we do not need another hire in that area we should hire in . . . [insert you favorite Western European figure, period or tradition]." Imagine a tenure-track or senior philosophy faculty member saying, "Philosopher X is an Aristotle specialist therefore we have Western European philosophy covered." Saying that is logically possible. Is saying that historically impossible in many departments? Tokenized philosophers can experience such hermeneutic marginalization in departments that they often are treated in ways that make them belong to another planet. During the protests after George Floyd, fires, military throwing water bottles from their tanks to the white youth in Kenosha who shot people protesting the police shooting of Jacob Blake in front of his child, the attacks on the Capitol by various white supremacist groups, what did faculty experience in their philosophy departments? When discussions of hires came up, did they witness faculty of, say, 10 (mostly working in various areas of Western European philosophy) with childlike innocence oblivious to its political surroundings say, "We should hire someone in medieval"? This form of epistemological invisibility involves "a form of presumed knowing in which there is, where a particular group is identified, nothing more to know or learn."[2] Faculty such as this either are so steeped in the comforts of the aloof ivory tower of contemplation that they are not aware of what was happening on the streets—only COVID happened—or are aware but are indifferent to anti-black police violence or they do care but cannot see how philosophy (i.e., which is conceptually white) connects to the state of emergency in the cities. These various ways of being a faculty member of a department inhibit us from moving in a direction of making Black Lives Matter.

Often what is happening when tokenized philosophers engage in critical discussions with other philosophers about transforming the curriculum in a pluralistic non-Eurocentric direction, the latter simply do not know much or anything else outside the Western European orbit and tend to operate with a highly provincial notion of philosophy that exclude whole continents of thought.

Consider for instance a philosophy department with four faculties retiring in the context of mass cross-racial protests against the increased visibility on the news and social media of police violence against black people and the impact of COVID-19 on everyone and people of color in particular. Think about a context of unfair housing conditions, environmental hazards, lack of access to public recreation park systems, quality food, clean water, politically responsible education that teaches racial literacies, community-based mental health services, health care, and employment at a dignified minimum wage, all institutional lacks that disproportionally effect black and brown people. Imagine the four retired faculties have the following respective specializations—African, white feminist ethics, human rights, and medieval. One would think in light of all the highly racialized events and universities expressed anti-racism commitments, the department would seek to replace the retirements with hires in Africana and Latinx/Latin American approaches to racism. Minimally one would think there might be a discussion on how we can request a cohort hire of talented intellectual/activists that work in distinct fields, intellectual currents, periods or perspectives, and unified by their work on understanding and addressing the historical global problem of racism. Instead, something else happens.

The African and feminist positions become de-racialized and de-feminized by trying to make the replacement hires into phenomenology or medical ethics lines both of which are understood in a narrow Eurocentric fashion that do not acknowledge diverse lineages and entry points into these fields. The justification appeals to the logic of tokenization. "We already have someone who works in feminist philosophy and black feminism." As if one hire represents a whole, historically complex field with various specializations. "The African hire did some work in phenomenology so we should build on that and hire someone who works in the German tradition, maybe a Heidegger specialist." As if the retired person's four books and numerous articles in African philosophy do not indicate that it is an area of specialization but one article in phenomenology makes his 30-year career into a specialist in that field. It would be inaccurate to understand this as attempts to go back to normal in a COVID-19 context. It is worse than going back to normal. It is as if the only thing that happened was COVID-19. Couple this gap between the department's sensibilities about its future trajectories and the racialized political realities—fires outside the university, tear gas, ensuing 70 million so-called adults voting for a pathological presidential candidate supporting and fueling this toxic racist climate—the historical production of white ignorance with a thick layer of social media circulating misinformation at high speeds. You have an epistemic catastrophe. Imagine a Latinx philosopher trying to explain the significance of the Iberian scholastic tradition to a Euro medieval philosopher that is retiring. Imagine explaining that this philosophical tradition was wrestling with issues of Spanish colonization in Europe and across the Atlantic, war, the proto-racist notion of *limpieza de sangre* (a.k.a. purity of blood statutes), the ontological status of the Indians—whether they had souls or could be converted—the status of Muslims and Jews in the Ottoman empire, international law, etc. Imagine observing that this tradition of thought was deliberately left out of the dominant Eurocentric narrative of the history of philosophy produced by German romantics in the eighteenth century as European colonial expansion was occurring and Europe was redefining itself as it encountered people in the colonies that were viewed as outside history. Imagine talking about why figures such as Francisco Vitoria, Bartolomé de Las Casas, Juan Ginés de Sepúlveda, Vasco de Quiroga, Guaman Poma de Ayala, or others are excluded from the field of Euro-medieval philosophy. Imagine explaining why they have been identified in different ways that assume a Eurocentric chronology and spatiality (i.e., are part of the late medieval period, late scholasticism or silver age scholasticism, etc.). What do you think is the response by the medieval specialist? You can probably guess. Reason tends to exit the room whenever the tokenized enters. The medievalist responds by indicating a candidate with specialization in what Jorge J.E. Gracia identifies as the colonial period of Latin American philosophy could apply to a position with an AOS in medieval if they could teach Jewish and Islamic philosophy together with the potential for "Latin" theology. Notice how three historical intellectual traditions (one identified as quasi philosophical) are conceived as philosophically light and non-extensive?

What is interesting is how the interlocutor is oblivious to the context of the emergence of cohort hires that are meant to remedy the tokenization of minoritized philosophers. In fact, the response and job description that could ensue reproduces the structure of tokenization by working to tailor a job description in a way that seeks a candidate that has specialization in Islamic or Jewish philosophers from the ninth to fourteenth centuries that have no clear connection to grappling with issues of racism very broadly construed. It presupposes a narrow Eurocentric understanding of philosophy that relegates anything else that does not seem to satisfy that standard of rigor as less than, as theology. These kinds of positions can function as gateways for model minorities to enter the westernized university. The absurdity increases when even Latin American philosophy is registered by the interlocutor as simply a European phenomenon that is not even tied to the Iberian Peninsula and the Spanish language but rather Latin theology. There is a liberal trap that tends to emerge when tokenized philosophers struggle to hire more tenure line faculty in Africana or Latinx/Latin American. It is that "we should hire a specialist in disability or tradition A, B or C because we do not have a specialist in that." This continues to multiply the quantity of tokens and passes itself off as caring for diversity. In the case above the philosophy department's Eurocentric curriculum becomes further specialized but is able to pass as ornamental multiculturalism in the sense that you have specialists working on figures with Islamic and Jewish names, who accidentally happen to be Islamic or Jewish but their identities and geography do not inform their mode of philosophizing. They are isomorphic to their Western European philosophy counterparts. Their hires get celebrated as diversity hires, and the department applauds their inclusive work, if the hire is female. You can imagine the paradox increasing when even specialists in feminism—who have token representation—applauding merely demographic diversity which functions as ornamental multiculturalism.

This form of epistemic closure connects to one of the many faces of whiteness identified by Chela Sandoval (2000) through her discussion of Roland Barthes. The notion of inoculation refers to white middle-class postures that take in small doses of difference in order to manage, contain, and deal with difference in such a way that does not disrupt their framework and keeps their sense of self intact. By making ornamental changes that keep the institutional structure untouched a continual source of white ontological density is held in place. Inoculation of tokenized difference is safe and stimulating for its practitioners. These practices of non-relational relationality miss or cover over the complexity and distinctness of tokens visible in plain sight. Can tokens initiate substantive change within the westernized university?

If whenever a person's car breaks down and that person habitually avoids the mechanic and instead consults a chef, a painter, or a team of others who happen to know little or care little about cars, then there would be a problem with the way that circumstance is navigated. The person would either not understand there is a problem with the car, not know about mechanics, or not be aware of how useful they are in solving car problems. If the chef, painter, team of others, and one mechanic produced a document gesturing toward the problems and offered recommendations, the document may capture some aspects of the problem and offer some plausible recommendations but it would be an odd way of going about it. The absurdity increases when there are mechanics nearby, but there is no consultation with them to weigh in on the matter. The university does not ask BLM or specialists in the fields dealing with race and ethnic studies to help them think through transforming the mission of the university, its culture and practices in a careful deliberate way. This practice of choosing to ignore people with epistemic insight on certain matters at hand and having the knack of forming the least competent teams to address certain issues is reverse empiricism. If you want to know what slavery is like you do not first turn to the master enslaver or the politician who is in the country club. Ask the enslaved. While the enslaved does not offer automatic knowledge simply because they are enslaved, their voice should have priority. This is because their social location correlates with certain sets of experiences. How the various aspects of their entangled identity hang together to situate them in a specific set of power relations in the world can shed light on what it feels like to be enslaved. Reverse empiricism is normal in westernized universities when it comes to matters of historical systemic racism and integrating other epistemologies that challenge Eurocentric knowledge production.

Take for example when BIPOC faculty in the humanities and social sciences that work on racism continually express for years the lack of diversity at various demographic, curricular, and cultural levels and the need for transformation. They do so conscious of the double movement context of the westernized university with its 500-year history of silencing other epistemologies and histories of resistance to reverse this epistemic accumulation of authority. They do so aware of the student protests in the late 1960s by the Third World Liberation Front that gave rise to the emergence of ethnic studies as an epistemic insurgence to include other forms of knowledge production that were excluded and that challenged westernized knowledge and offered other conceptual constellations and future visions. Even though BIPOC faculty express the need for more epistemic diversity with this background in mind, the university responds by hiring external diversity consultants to measure the levels of institutional diversity, equity, and inclusion. Quantifying the lack of diversity with data is supposed to help the university gauge what it needs to work on. Instead of initiating conversations with BIPOC faculty who work on racism to think through various ways a university can begin to make the university more diverse and anti-racist and together consider whether it is reasonable to hire an external diversity consultant, it does something else.

Administrators proceed to pay a company to assess a problem that has been written about for a long time in various intellectual traditions and have been struggling against for years. Choosing to ignore what experts in the field have to say about diversity and turning to an external consultant presupposes the scholars specializing in other epistemologies and racism are not producers of knowledge. If the university structure operates in a way that does not view and treat this faculty as knowledge producers, then it is not clear they are seen as experts but quasi-professors. This reverse empiricism is fiscally irresponsible. It functions to contain, manage, and delay substantive anti-racist structural changes. Are mission statements changed? University for the Decolonization of Self and World? University for the People? University for Structural Victims? University for the Poor? University for the Damned? In addition, even when the diversity consultants offer prescriptions for substantive transformation, the university does not follow them.

So, what is the point of wasting money and time on things experts have been indicating all along? What becomes more apparent during the protests in the United States in 2020 is the massive amount of racial illiteracy. Many had to attempt to acquire such literacies on the fly in order to make sense of the systemic racism that was/is unfolding before their eyes. Racism and police violence is more visible in media outlets yet this does not necessarily mean the national discourses ordinary folks are having around these issues are adequate or have sufficient nuance. Imagine if people understood the meanings of technical terms like white supremacy, colonialism, structural racism, white ignorance, resistance, the history of lynching in the United States, the coloniality of time, and other non-Eurocentric renderings of history which emerges not simply from professors but social movements and organizations that have been facing these problems for a long time. People tend to too easily forget or have short-term memory when black youth are killed by police violence (see Figures 6.5 and 6.6). It is clear that one small step in the direction of addressing the active production of ignorance about people of color (that affects white and non-white people differentially) is that all students (i.e., broadly, learners of all ages and positions) need to take required courses on racism and/or ethnic studies that enables them to acquire racial literacies. Creating and supporting race and ethnic studies as central to knowledge production in the natural sciences, humanities, social sciences, and professional schools is another key step in the direction of disrupting the at least 500-year active production of white ignorance in westernized universities and the high-speed production of misinformation and lies that racially criminalize various populations. Does the westernized university do everything else but what is needed? Hiring cohorts of BIPOC faculty in these areas and providing institutional support for ethnic studies departments, centers, and institutes and work with social movements and organizations who address racism are ways to begin to disrupt the aforementioned institutional production of invisibility, tokenizing, inoculating tendencies, and reverse empiricism. Let us consider another way people have resisted this oppressive context.

Figure 6.5   Remember. Source: Kassandra Montes

Figure 6.6 The Invisible Ones. Source: Jada Villalobos

Resistance: Reflections on Breonna Taylor Day

In this context, youth movements declared Breonna Taylor Day and organized events in various cities across the United States as a way of healing, collaborating, protesting racialized police violence, raising awareness, learning from her death, and commemorating her life. An event leading up to Breonna Taylor Day was organized as a way for high school students, youth, social movements, reverends, faculty, staff, and university students to come together and try to articulate the philosophical significance of what that day could mean. It was titled, "Reflections Before Breonna Taylor Day." We held this virtual meeting on March 12, 2021—the day before the anniversary of Breonna Taylor's murder by the Louisville Kentucky police (see Figures 6.7 and 6.8). In order to commemorate her death, we organized a three-part event. In the first part, I framed the event around the discussion of temporality and discussed how Breonna Taylor Day does not fit neatly

Figure 6.7 Pairs of Eyes. Source: Destiny Smith

Figure 6.8   Breonna Taylor. Source: Alexa Brim

within traditional national holidays, academic calendars, black history month, or individualized anniversaries. I tried to sketch another temporality within which this event fit. In the second part, as a way of reflecting on her life and death, we had a film discussion on the documentary "The Killing of Breonna Taylor" which was made available to folks via a link where the film was publicly available. After the film discussion, we had a youth panel of black and Latinx students from an after-school art program of Roberto Clemente High School in Chicago where they presented and discussed their various paintings related to the themes of police violence, the Black Lives Matter movement, and Breonna Taylor's life (see Figures 6.9–6.11). These youth, some of whom were only 15 years old, presented their work to students in my Resistance to the Civilization of Death seminar and my Latina Philosophy and Introduction to Philosophy courses among others I offer at the University of Dayton where I work. In the third part, after the art panel, we had a roundtable discussion with Breonna Taylor's aunt Bianca Austin, Rev. McCorry, the former City of Dayton Community-Police relations coordinator Jared Grandy and the educator and executive producer of the radio show "Talk to Me" Dr. Venita Kelley. We discussed police violence, the city of Dayton, Breonna's life and death, the actual functions of the history of the emergence of police in US history and the role of vocation as a calling to hear and reflect on the cries of marginalized peoples. We then answered questions from the audience. There were 85 audience members from various locations—local, regional, and national.

Breonna Taylor Day does not quite fit into a temporality of national holidays such as Thanksgiving, Christmas, and Independence Day. In many ways, these holidays have become highly consumption-based fitting well into an economy of ornamentations and commodities, some going so far as forming collective bonding through shopping. As these days center on certain kinds of activities and practices, they mystify, cover over, and distort history. Instead of English settlers' stealing lands and

Figure 6.9 BLM. Source: Joanna Rodriguez

Figure 6.10 More in All. Source: Zeke Diaz

Figure 6.11   BLM. Source: Melody Richards

genocide of Native American Indians we get a narrative of a friendly feast misleading one to think settler colonialism was friendly. These national holidays function to cover over the colonial wounds of the nation state. They are able to come into being because of acts of Congress. These national holidays seem to operate in a way that is distinct from the temporality of Black and Latinx heritage months in westernized universities. They tend to involve practices that embody a form of ornamental multiculturalism that conceives of people of color as ethnic exotica that are consumable to a white gaze but do not interrogate it. It in fact inoculates itself with a small dose of racialized difference enough to tokenize the other so they are safe and stimulating (i.e., think of the way "ethnic" foods are taken up) and do not produce any sort of structural or individual change of a westernized frame. The injection of this small dose of diversity functions to provide a white subjectivity a sense that they are not racist but rather, as Shannon Sullivan (2014) notes, the good whites as opposed to the bad explicitly racist whites (i.e., master enslavers, KKK, white vigilantes or "white trash"). To get a month was a struggle. Before it used to be a day. Before that nonexistent. People in the United States fought for all these days. Black and Latinx heritage months came into being by acts of university administrators in response to the demands by BIPOC students, faculty, and staff. It emerges from the educational institution itself. Because the heritage months tend to have these features, Breonna Taylor Day does not quite fit in within academic calendars. It also does not fit within wedding anniversary or birthday kinds of celebrations because these are more personalized, private, and tend to be idiosyncratic to an individual or couple, not so much a public community act.

Breonna Taylor Day aims to affirm her life by humanizing her—discussing her subjectivity, hopes, ambitions, sentiments—her relations to her family and friends and what Breonna meant to them (see Figures 6.12 and 6.13). She was part of a neighborhood and was an EMT that cared for people of all ages and ethno-racial makeups. On this day, we also aimed to shed light on the complexities of the institution of police violence and to try to raise awareness and think of solutions to this catastrophe. Remembering Breonna Taylor and people of color is important in contexts that actively produce collective amnesia/ignorance about the lives, histories, philosophies, and

Figure 6.12 The Light Within. Source: Julieta Anaya Tapia

Figure 6.13 Domino. Source: Julieta Anaya Tapia

languages of people of color. Breonna Taylor Day also aimed to increase the racial awareness and literacies of the people in the community. The event was just the beginning to try to understand a 500-year historic system of racism. Breonna Taylor Day has its own distinct temporality in the sense that it emerges from the people – organizers, the youth, and a new generation of caring people working to build bridges between social movements, young people, community organizations, and the university. For all of these reasons, Breonna Taylor Day does not quite fit within the temporal organization of national holidays, academic black history month, wedding days or birthdays celebrated within a nation state that has legitimacy deficits, and generates and invokes tropes and white vanguard narratives as ways of unifying people around the salvific rhetoric of Euro-modernity. In this context, the Reflections on Breonna Taylor Day event and ensuing protests, art, and political education happening outside westernized universities in cities were ways for people to unify against historic systemic anti-black racism (see Figures 6.14 and 6.15).

How many more black youths, fathers, children, girls, and women have to be killed by police violence and made viral on YouTube in order for the westernized university to take seriously anti-black racism? How many times does the US capitol need to be attacked in order for the westernized university to make substantive meaningful change that takes political responsibility for a 500-year system of racism and plays a role in empowering people so they can effectively address it? How many scores of students do professors have to see who graduate high school enter colleges and universities and are oblivious as to why Christopher Columbus statues are being torn down before change happens? How many more scores of students do we need to see, who were taught an enchanted white-washed narrative of an adventurer explorer that discovered people and places who existed for millennia before his arrival and mistakenly identified them as Indians because he erroneously thought he was in India, before change happens? While different universities have responded in various ways within this context—some being more responsible in trying to meet these ongoing challenges and others being less responsible and more complicit—the future remains ambiguous yet in our hands. As an expression of this uncertainty and taking responsibility for the future and those generations to be whom we may not know, see the painting titled, "Hope?" by

Figure 6.14   Stop Racism. Source: Jocelyn Ramirez Acevedo

Figure 6.15   We Bleed the Same. Source: Hailey Roman

16-year-old Neveah Wade (Figure 6.16). How much data measuring the level of white ignorance—the active production of non-knowing of people of color—is needed before westernized universities make racism and ethnic studies required courses for all at elementary, high school, and university levels? How many times do folks need to see the people being tear-gassed, imprisoned, or killed for

Figure 6.16   Hope? Source: Neveah Wade

protesting police violence or demanding the closure of ICE detention centers before they provide solid institutional support for BIPOC faculty and social movements with histories of work on issues of racial colonialism? How many more times do we need to see successful ethnic studies programs closed because the empowered students are viewed as anti-American in order to create transmodern decolonial studies departments or critical ethnic studies departments that have a history of investigating racism as a global problem from various perspectives and intellectual trajectories and are known to empower the people? Will the westernized university bring its anti-racism declarations into meaningful institutional change when federal executive orders legislate a ban on critical race theory at universities across the United States and mandate a white-washed, color blind, patriot education that evades the realities of racism in the formation of the United States and their remedies? All of these considerations should be kept in mind as tokenized philosophers or scholars struggle in various departments to frame cohort hires within an anti-racism research agenda that makes hires meaningful and can begin to produce some substantive change. If westernized universities do not seriously take into consideration their anti-racism commitments now when it comes to cohort hires then I am not sure there ever would be a right time. In the face of this these challenges, I have learned that one cannot challenge tokenization alone. The catastrophic conditions black lives and others face cannot be analyzed away as if writing alone will produce transformation. Reading books can empower but it can sometimes make us hide from reality and facing others. There also is the power of the pen, but this may not be enough. It must be done collectively with and alongside the youth, organizations, artists, and movements that are part of long histories of resistance. Below is the last painting Erica Obua presented at the art panel (Figure 6.17). She is one of the

Figure 6.17   Breonna Taylor. Source: Erica Obua

high school students from Chicago that participated in the art workshop for the Reflections on Breonna Taylor Day event. All of the art weaved in and out throughout the chapter was done by the 15-, 16-, and 17-year-old youths that are part of the After School Art Program organized by their fun, stimulating, engaging, caring, and talented politically conscious art teacher Mara Ayala.[3]

Notes

1 I grant that there are westernized universities in the United States that have a sufficient critical mass of racism specialists that produce and make public the anti-racism commitment documents. These are more an anomaly.
2 Ibid., 24.
3 I wish to thank my student David Quick for showing me how to integrate art into an article. I also thank the editors at Wiley for integrating the art into the article and the book cover.

References

Gordon, L. (2021). *Freedom, Justice, and Decolonization*, 23. New York, NY: Routledge.
Sandoval, C. (2000). *Methodology of the Oppressed*, 11819. Minneapolis, MN: University of Minnesota Press.
Sullivan, S. (2014). *Good White People: The Problem with Middle Class Anti-White Racism*. SUNY Press.

7

In the Trap of Critique: Making Decolonization Metaphor

STEPHANIE RIVERA BERRUZ

Introduction

Universities are institutions that transfer power, wealth, and privilege. They are institutions that operate through kinship technologies by producing and reproducing ways of relating in the world.[1] In the context of the United States, where I write from today, universities are largely constructed by institutional whiteness. Universities engender ways of relating built on white somatic norms that institute a white body without calling it into view thus forming institutional habits around particular ways of being whitely that transfer privilege and power and at the same time do not draw attention to whiteness itself, rather it recedes into the background.[2] Hence, whiteness is what institutions are oriented around that allows some bodies to move through its spaces more comfortably as others by virtue of repetitive action, precisely the type of action that transfers privilege.[3] The effects of whiteness as an institutional habit also implies that those who arrive and do not belong experience marginalization, which produces hypervisibility or invisibility depending on the space. However, most importantly, the experiences of varying levels of visibility reveals an expectation of who will show up in the first place.[4] At the same time, discourses of diversity are exponentially growing in academic spaces. Offices of institutional diversity along with their administrative roles are growing across the country. The goal, although at times ambiguous, rests on the possibilities of institutionalizing diversity. Said initiatives have transformed the academic landscape for people of color building the possibilities for curricular expansions that justify their arrival to university spaces. At the same time, it institutional whiteness can be reproduced through the logics of diversity and can (and often do) eclipse the histories that tie universities to settler colonial projects.

In the context of institutional diversity initiatives, we have witnessed the increased presence of historically marginalized fields in academic spaces. Philosophy, chief among these, is witnessing shifts in the demand for expertise in areas peripheral to the canon (e.g., Latin American Philosophy, Philosophy of Race, Indigenous Philosophy, Decolonial Philosophy). These demands are often the result of institutional diversity initiatives that claim to work against the institutional habits that have made universities spaces of the habitual and exclusive reproduction of power, wealth, and privilege. Nevertheless, universities in the United States have also taken neoliberal turns that have corporatized their models of education that arrange the possibilities of diversity and thus make possible the reproduction of institutional whiteness through diversity.[5] Yet, we seldom consider what it means to do work from within these institutions in honest ways. I am wondering about the political material realities from which peripheral philosophies draw their livelihoods and consider what we owe those realities as we find ourselves in the throes of academic contradictions. I think we push up against these contradictions by considering the case of Latin American philosophy and the rise of the use of the term decolonial in our disciplinary circuitry. Ultimately, I contend that we owe more to our philosophical commitments than our ability to claim expertise, for even the idea of expertise is predicated on domination and ownership of knowledge.

The University, Emplacement, and Settler Colonization

We as scholars do not exist in abstract space. In the context of the United States, we tend to labor in the trenches of universities as they often provide the only viable routes for scholarly endeavors. Universities are not abstract spaces either. They are built on stolen land, which continues to serve as the capital that accumulates and finances universities. In the words of la paperson (2017, p. 39): "Land is the keystone of the university, yet land is least likely to be discussed in any critical treatment of it." Drawing our attention to the intimate and important relationship between land and universities, la paperson reminds readers that the ongoing histories of universities in the United States are themselves the product of the settler colonial project that turned land into property that could be used to educate American settlers in agriculture, science, and the mechanical arts.[6] "Land as capital and not as campuses is an innovation of the land-grant university."[7] The process of converting land into property that could subsequently be made into capital sits at the heart of the empire-self-making project of the United States and universities have a deep-seated history in the possibilities of emplacement. Universities are land grabbing, land transforming, and land capitalizing machines.

Land is the primary concern of settler colonization in that the settler project is tied emplacement, not merely the seizure and exploitation of people and place.[8] To be clear, the settler colonial project is ongoing, it is actively happening, and universities are one node in the machine – as are we. The recasting of land as property entails severing Indigenous people from land and renders Black and Indigenous people as bodies for disposal. Further, the alienation of land from life produces the possibilities for rights: the right to own (property), the right to law (protection from violence), the right to govern (sovereignty), and the right to have rights (humanity).[9] The mechanisms of settler colonization hinge on the settler-native-slave triad, which serves as a paradigm that captures our skewed participation in colonization and systems of power (not identities). In la paperson's words: "We are all complicit, just some of us a lot more than others."[10] The settler is not an identity, but rather it captures the normative space of juridical rights granted to those who fit within the contours of idealized citizenship. The native is not an Indigenous identity, but rather a site of exception for those who are written as primitive, premodern, and prior to the law.[11] Finally, the slave captures the way blackness is transformed into murderability; a persistent truth which the Black Lives Matter movement centers. The settler-native-triad is a technology framed by land dispossession that presume processes of extraction and fungability.[12]

I write this piece today from the city of Milwaukee, Wisconsin. I am on Potawatomi, Ho-Chunk, and Menominee homelands. I sit on the southwest shores of Michigami (Big Lake), North America's largest system of freshwater lakes, where the Milwaukee, Menominee, and Kinnickinnic rivers meet and the people of Wisconsin's sovereign Anishinaabe, Ho-Chunk, Menominee, Oneida, and Mohican nations remain present. I recognize and acknowledge the labor upon which my livelihood is built. At the same time, I live the reality of living in one of the most segregated cities in the United States where I work for a predominantly white private Jesuit institution. The contradictions abound as the technologies of the Settler-Native-Slave triad operate to occlude the persistent making of settler colonial projects through the university system. I too have a stake in this system one that manically drives me to reflect on what it means to do resistant work from within a system that would much prefer that I stay quiet. Cloistered into a world that sums life in terms of numerical analysis, death tolls, and survivability, I am left wondering about our commitments to the lived experiences that inform our scholarly work. I too am a node in the technology of the Settler-Native-Slave triad and continuously ask myself how to position myself and my work so as to not reproduce the idea of decolonization but enact its possibilities.

I carry said concern because my career has been framed through institutional diversity initiatives that *somewhat*[13] welcomed my work on Latina/x feminisms, decolonial feminisms, and Latin American and Caribbean as well as my body to its spaces. I highlight it as "somewhat" precisely because there is a tension between occupying the privilege that universities can afford and my own philosophical commitment to doing decolonial and resistant work both inside and outside of the university. The tension is profound and in the wake of the murder of George Floyd I started to deeply regret my decisions to be in the academy, I actively considered leaving my job, as I was truly confronted with the lack of regard lives of color have in relationship to the neo-liberal university system; my own included. I participated on a panel for the American Philosophical Association (Central Division) titled Philosophy and Black Live Matters. As I reflected on my remarks with respect to my resistance to my own university as I called the president and the provost hypocritical in a public forum while participating in protests that placed me at the heart of police repression the value of philosophical work started to lose meaning. In the end I was struggling with the contradiction that what I experience and know to be philosophy hinges on the humanity/the futurity/the liberty of lives of color; yet simultaneously I also knew that philosophy has and will continue to exist without any of us mattering. In the end, I had understood the way diversity and whiteness work hand in hand.

In *A Third University is Possible* la paperson draws attention to the way there might be multiple ways of experiencing the university. He describes them in three tiers: the first, the second, and the third. Intentionally drawing on the codifications of the first and third world that structure center/periphery political models, la paperson problematizes the university by advocating for multiple universities in one. They write: "the first world university accumulates through dispossession. The second world university 'liberates' through liberalism. The third world university breaks faith from its own machinery by inspiring the academic automaton with a fourth world soul."[14] In other words, the first-world university is the machine of accumulation, expansion, and debt structured by revenue granting enterprises like PhD programs, D-1 sports teams, highly sought after STEM degrees, MBAs, and medical degrees that count on large grants from state entities like the department of energy, agriculture, defense, and homeland security.[15] The first-world university can turn anyone into a debtor and does so as it fuels its missions of inclusion. You can be educated if you become indebted and indeed debt structures the possibilities for access to the possibilities of the privileges that college degrees can hold *for some*.[16]

A second-world university is marked by investments in critical theory that ties commitments of transformation to critique. The second-world university is often "the house of the hegemonic radical, the postcolonial ghetto neighborhood within the university metropolis."[17] The second-world university creates a trap by presuming that personalized pedagogy of self-actualization is equivalent with decolonial transformation. The problematic assumption is that people will produce freedom through critical consciousness whereby emancipation is enacted through the willingness of the mind.[18] However, the second university seldom attends to the mechanisms by which universities make puppets of us all as we continue to participate in the processes that fuel to the Settler-Slave-Native triad. I find this dimension of la paperson's analysis extremely insightful as it reminds of the multiple university worlds that can be experienced at once. The second-world university is precisely the iteration of the university that positions us as experts in "marginal" fields from the belly of empire and at the same time presumes that if we just talk about marginal identities enough, we will somehow magically come to an emancipatory resolution as if the problem was about identities at all. Identity politics become a smoke screen for larger structural systems of domination built on the seizure of land, capital accumulation, and imperial dispossession. Hence, I want to linger in the space of the second-world university a bit further as I find the presumptions upon which it is built speak to the gap between what it means to do work on the margins of the discipline as well as the rise of the use of the term decolonial as a trending market of expertise.

The Trap: Critique as Decolonial Transformation

The trap of the second-world university is found in the presumption that emancipatory possibilities are encapsulated in the activity of the mind. In other words, if we learn enough about emancipation, liberation, or transformation, they will be enacted in practice. If we study enough, if we learn enough, if we diversify the curriculum and the faculty enough transformation will happen. Scholars in areas like Latin American philosophy, African/a American philosophy, philosophy of race, or decolonial philosophy are situated at the crossroads of critique that leans heavily on the relationship between theory and praxis, critique of Eurocentrism, and the centering of racialized or peripheralized peoples. However, the practice often stops there as if critique is sufficient for change. I find la paperson's diagnosis insightful as it points toward the way in which philosophy (and higher education more broadly) presumes the modern individual divorced from the world and capable of reason where reason is an object of capital exchange in the system of higher education. The danger lies in the de-linking between theory and practice that reproduce colonial and imperial impulses.[19]

In this context, I am not the first to be thinking about the dangers of critique as transformation. For instance, consider Tuck and Yang's piece "Decolonization is not a Metaphor," which in many respects anticipated the very concerns I am trying to draw attention to in this piece. In this article, Tuck and Yang argue that the ongoing adoption of decolonization discourse into educational advocacy and scholarship turns decolonization into a metaphor. The problem, they argue, is that because settler colonization is built on the settler-native-slave triad decolonial desires can be entangled with resettlement and reoccupation that re-instantiates rather than resists settler colonial process.[20] The essay tackles a series of settler moves that reinscribe the structure of settler colonization. Specifically, they note the move of colonial equivocation, which calls out the move of homogenizing experiences of oppression as colonial that rests on the practice of calling oppressed groups as colonized without describing the relationship to settler colonization. In their words: "... describing all struggles against imperialism as 'decolonizing' creates a convenient ambiguity between decolonization and social justice work, especially among people of color, queer people, and other groups minoritized by the settler nation-state."[21] They note that while we may all be colonized may be a truth of the world (albeit partial) it is at the same time deceptively embracive and vague.[22] The ability to be a minority citizen, for instance, means that there is an option to become a brown settler framed by a desire to ascend to whiteness.[23] A second move to innocence, which is necessary to consider here, is what Tuck and Yang refer to as the move to "free your mind and the rest will follow."[24] This critique of the ways decolonization becomes a metaphor echoes la papersons critique of the second university. The project of building critical consciousness, often heralded in origins to the work of Paulo Freire, detaches from settler colonization and engenders a perspective whereby freedom becomes a possibility of human subjects that can be mentally generated. Consciousness building is not the same as decolonization and the same can be said of anti-colonial posturing. Anti-colonial struggles can be, and for Tuck and Yang definitively are, incommensurable with decolonization, because anti-colonial posturing celebrates empowered post-colonial subjects that does not undo colonialism but rather has the capacity to re-make and subvert.[25] Here, I want to link the plethora of anti-colonial critiques found in the length of the Latin American philosophical canon that often ends up falling into the trap of the decolonial – anti-colonial conflation that presumes the modern subjects call to consciousness as sufficient for political (described as decolonial) transformation. The problem it seems is found in the philosophical presumptions of the modern human. In an effort to become modern, that is to become human, Latin American philosophers set forth on projects that identified Westernization and modernization as goals that framed anti-colonial or anti-imperial claims.[26] However, said posturing also entails participating in the formation of modern nation states that are structured in terms of settler colonial specificity.

More contemporarily Mariana Ortega and Gregory Fernando Pappas have taken to task US academic trends on the use of decolonization. Ortega argues that current intellectual interventions by scholars of color regarding decoloniality reinscribes un-knowing. She notes "when resistant epistemic practices enact injustice even in the process of looking for justice, we are faced with the difficulty of what I call practices of unknowing."[27] Practices of unknowing she argues negate knowledge that is disclosed in order to problematize macro-narratives. Asking her readers to consider: "Has decoloniality become the domain of Latin American thinkers and Latin American exiles living in the United States, especially when they are part of elite institutions?" Ortega tracks the way women of color scholarly interventions are largely unseen and unthought in the shadow of the decolonial imaginary, although it has been women of color who have been walking their decolonial talk much longer than the rest of us.[28] Thus, she draws attention to the ways we (academics of color in the United States) have the possibilities of turning into the same thinkers from dominant positions that we critique. Hence, Ortega is highlighting the settler move that Tuck and Yang draw forth when noting that anti-colonial or anti-imperial posturing in no capacity entail decolonial practice, but rather insidious practices that produce not-knowing and unknowing. In a parallel fashion, "The Limitations and Dangers of Decolonial Philosophies: Lessons from Zapatista Luis Villoro" by Pappas (2017) highlights the ways decolonial philosophies (specifically those of the Latin American tilt) presume global explanatory power that undermine their own liberatory promises. Leaning on philosophy of Luis Villoro to elucidate his critique, Pappas argues that the theme of decolonization has become a new synonym for liberation in Latin American thought, but falls short of its own decolonial goal in so far as it begins with a global standpoint about injustice that risks a dangerous oversimplification.[29] It is precisely these the same type of oversimplification that engendered by the conflation between anti-colonial and decolonial that Tuck and Yang actively discuss.

I highlight these two threads of decolonial critique because they sit in different disciplinary camps. Tuck and Yang are seldom considered in conversation with Latin American philosophical concerns, most notably in its decolonial key. However, it strikes me that this outcome is precisely the product of the practices of un-knowing that Ortega describes. Moreover, the global explanatory power that decolonial theories presume, as Pappas describes, speaks to the ways that the modern subject of reason and its global explanatory reach structures how we think about the work of critique. We simply cannot reason our way out of the trap of freeing the mind. And yet, we live in a world of contradictions, where our scholarly livelihoods hold us to living in the trap that if we just dedicate our lives to living in the ghetto of the second-world university critiquing coloniality we will somehow arrive at a better outcome. There is a great danger in the presumption that changing minds is sufficient for action all the while finding subsistence and livelihood from the extraction of the energy that it takes to truly enact decolonial practice.

The truth is many of us (myself included) live in the contradictions of the second-world university and must take seriously the potential harms we enact by doing the "work" we do. I think with Sylvia Rivera Cusicanqui (2010) here when she critiques decolonial theorists in the United States for creating an empire inside of an empire. Her concern is like that of Tuck and Yang in arguing that there cannot be a theory of decolonization without decolonizing practice. The collapse of multiculturalism into decolonization reifies colonial practices. Much like Tuck and Yang, Rivera Cusicanqui highlights the ways that practices that orient themselves around equity do not necessarily serve decolonial ends and in fact might undermine their possibilities. She reminds readers that to do decolonial work in universities in the United States is not simply working within an economy of ideas, but rather it is also an economy of salaries, commodity, and privilege that the university system itself transfers.[30] This is precisely the concern that oriented the opening point of departure for this essay: concerns about what we owe to our philosophical commitments when they are in complicit with practices of harm and extraction. Although Rivera Cusicanqui orients her critique at the academic establishment in the US broadly, I take her push to heart as it highlights the impossible positions some of us might find ourselves in by virtue of moving through the academy. How do we make, *can* we make our work in areas like decolonial philosophy in the Latin American thread commensurate with our positions of privilege as nodes in a system of power that seldom treats us as worthy of arrival. Where do our commitments to our philosophical practices lie?

One of the most important insights gained from the juxtaposition of these different critiques is the importance of understanding what is really at stake in decolonizing practices such that we do not fall into the trap of collapsing critique into transformation. More pointedly, there is the ever present need to consider how our very own livelihoods as scholars rests on the project of settler colonization that follows from being situated in university academic spaces. I offer these reflections as honest contestations of our positionality, of my positionality. We have been and continue to be living in a version of the Rivera Cusicanqui calls the "the world upside down" and Christina Sharpe has captured "in the wake," and Glissant has named "dead end situations" – here there is nothing abnormal or unusual about what has been and continues to be the eternal recurrence of an old scene, an old colonial scene cloaked and performed in new costumes with different words. We live in the world upside down and the persistent moral-political question we ought to be considering is how to traverse this scene, in which we are all complicit, in a way that contends with the inevitable contradictions and traps of critique.

Contending with the Trap

One of the key issues raised by the metaphorization of decolonization is the lack of shared understanding of decolonization. Although I do not aim to provide a definition here, I do want to highlight the fact that one of the most common orientations of decolonial practice found in Indigenous scholarship focuses on the relationship between people and land. To take up decolonial projects is to participate in the re-organization of relations that yield (ongoing) the construction of land and people as property. For instance, Tuck and Yang (2012) describe the project of decoloniza-tion as requiring the re-patriation of Indigenous life and land. It is not, as they state, "a metonym for social justice."[31] The relationship between life and land is profound, and the violent ongoing loss of that relationship via settler colonization is what makes the projects of scholars like Robin Wall Kimmerrer, Dina Gilio-Whitaker, and Kyle Whyte important precisely because they take the land-life relationship as their points of critical departure. As Gilio-Whitaker (2019) writes: "the very thing that distinguishes Indigenous peoples from settler societies is their unbroken connection to ancestral homelands. Their cultures and identities are linked to their original places in ways that define them; they are reflected in language, place names, and cosmology (origin stories)." It is for this reason that Tuck and Yang (2012, p. 21) insist that their readers consider how the pursuit of critical consciousness and social justice can also be, and often are, settler moves to innocence that conceal the need to give up land, power, and privilege. Settler colonization actively produces broken links between land and people and therefore severs the relationship between past and present.[32] However, decolonial and anti-colonial struggles are not synonymous.

The trap of critique that orients so many practices of higher education cannot be read divorced from the context of higher education that requires the on-going project of land-life dispossession. Hence, la paperson activates the possibilities of a third-world university, which defines itself up against the first and second. It is assembled through the scrap material, the salvage capital, that teaches first-world curricula, third-world critique, and strategically re-assembles in attempts to truly de-colonize by putting into practice transformative work that does not seek to stabilize the first-world university, but its demise.[33] The third university is made possible by the scyborg and impure being in assemblage that interrupts the machinist processes of the university that continue to feed the settler colonial project knowing that its ultimate terrain will be the undoing of the machine of the university itself.[34] I would argue it further requires an ethics of incommensurability as discussed by Tuck and Yang (2012, p. 28): "... the opportunities for solidarity lie in what is incommensurable rather than what is common across these efforts." In other words, there will be projects that simply cannot speak to one another and must relinquish settler futurity as decolonization is not accountable to settlers or their reconciliation.[35] However, this argument is not new in philosophy, Ofelia Schutte explored the limits of communication and commensurability in "Cultural Alterity: Cross-Cultural Communication and Feminist Theory in North-South Contexts." In this canonical Latina/x feminist essay, Schutte (1998) argues that the condition of cultural alterity in power differences produces residues of meaning that cannot be transparent and therefore create the conditions of cross-cultural incommensurability. Incommensurability, she argues, is "... inherent to the processes of reasoning itself."[36] As a result, residues of meaning leave untranslatable aspects of communication that requires that we not bypass or subsume our reasoning under familiar categories to make sense of the world. In her words: "I am speaking here of a psychological state in which the stranger is not abjected, derided, persecuted, shut out of view, or legalized out of existence, but – departing from the premise that the other is also human – neither is she subjected to the demand that she be the double, or reflected mirror image, of ourselves."[37] Here, I take Schutte to be flagging the conditions that produce the incommensurability that Tuck and Yang are trying to capture when they note that anti-colonial projects and decolonization should not be commensurable. If we understand incommensurability as inherent to reasoning and knowledge/meaning production, then we must contend with the fact that the presumption of transparency (even in the anti-colonial key) is itself part of the on-going production of the Settler-Native-Slave triad. Ultimately, the goal for Tuck and Yang (2012, p. 31) is to break the relentless structuring of the triad and that process does not require neat closure to the concerns of all involved; it does not require semiotic transparency.

The trap of critique, as I have been describing it, presumes the possibilities of commensurability and distorts the power differentials that bring us all, myself as writer included, to the table. The critique as action model that orients the second university and structures settler moves to innocence is also what keeps us employed, building careers, and in many respects building empires inside of empires, as Silvia Rivera Cusicanqui (2010, p. 58) has poignantly critiqued. Hence, our projects of knowledge production bear the residue of these realities, even if we ourselves stand as marginal subjects within empire itself. We are both producers of the triad as much as we are abjected from certain forms of settler productions. As scholars of color, I think we need to contend with the painful realities that position us as both producers of settler colonization through critique and ardent defendants of social justice practices. Minimally, I think it requires a reckoning with our everyday lived practices. I wonder, and I ask, how do we live out our philosophical commitments? How do we enact the practices that we preach? It was this question that brought me to this piece of writing. In the wake of the murder of George Floyd I rallied in the streets, I was gassed, I was chased, I stared down the barrels of the police. I wrote about institutional negligence, I screamed at the president and provost of my university for loving money more than people. I faced the echoes of unnatural natural disasters: pandemics, hurricanes, earthquakes. I felt alone. I became acutely aware of how decolonial critique moved so many into the comfort of settler innocence, into the comfort of presenting a paper that no one will ever read, about the comfort of the ivory tower even amidst its discontents. Where were the practices? Where were the actions that scholars so passionately write about? Silent.

I am not the first to think these frustrations into words. In *Light in the Dark/Luz en lo Oscuro* Gloria Anzaldúa describes her work through the frame of spiritual activism. In this text, Anzaldúa grapples with the heaviness of grief and the pains of transgenerational wounds produced by the colonial condition. In response, she articulates the imperative of repair. In her words: "I define healing as taking back the scattered energy and soul loss wrought by woundings."[38] Healing requires work, work through culture and being worked through culture such that personal and cultural identity change accordingly making a new cultural story possible.[39] The work of healing requires recognizing that healing is an ongoing process of dismemberment and reintegration where the answers to the problem is found in the wound itself. In this frame, activism emerges as a practice of healing work. It means, in her words, "... putting our hands in the dough and not merely thinking or talking about making tortillas."[40] Spiritual activism, I think, gives us a window into a possible response to the traps of critique. It calls forth the importance of practice in the work of healing not just as a possibility, but as a necessary requirement that nurtures the possibilities of change. There is no idea without practice for Anzaldúa, the gates of change will not open otherwise. However, there is great fear in radical change because we recognize that if we heal we will change, we will have to let go of our surroundings and intimates that make our lives look the way that do. I think it is precisely this fear that drives the comfort of critique to continue to grind its gears and divorce us from practices that can participate in the process of repair. In my reading, Anzaldúa anticipates the ways repair and healing must coincide with sets of practices that reveal our political commitments. It simply cannot be critique the whole way down, in fact the insistence that ideas are enough reflects a comfort with practices of settler innocence. We who labor in universities entrench disenfranchisement even if we also occupy the position of "other" in the context of the United States. We too participate in dispossession by conflating liberation/emancipation with decolonization particularly when we contend with the diverse contexts of Latin America and the Caribbean. We must reckon with the ways settler states are constructed through liberation-independence movements and in so doing we have to, as Anzaldúa anticipates, put our hands in the dough and not merely talk about making tortillas.[41]

Conclusion

Noting the importance of living out one's philosophical commitments is not novel. Hence, I close out this essay with one of my guiding examples: Luisa Capetillo. Luisa Capetillo (1882–1922) was an anarchist feminist activist from Puerto Rico. Contemporarily heralded as one Puerto Rico's first feminist writers, Capetillo defied all categorization. She was a woman, a writer, a working-class activist, an anarchist – spiritist, and most importantly a fervent believer in the practice of her philosophical commitments. For Capetillo, material conditions guide the production of ideas. She famously opens prefaces her book *Mi opinión* with the following words: "I do not believe anything to be impossible; nor am I amazed by any invention or discovery, which is why I do not find any idea utopian. What is essential is that the idea be put into practice."[42] And putting ideas into practice is exactly what Capetillo did over the course of her life. Capetillo lived out her philosophical commitments and leaves us with a complicated archive that is intellectually rich and materially messy, a reflection of a life lived in many constant and brave attempts to not fall into the traps of critique. For her the reality of ideas was in their practice as she truly believed in the possibilities of changing a social order built on false foundations, crime, fallacy, and hypocrisy.[43] I wonder then what it would mean if more of us walked this path, what would it look like for us to disavow ourselves of our comforts and contend with the gaping ocean between theory and practice that shapes the possibilities of our scholarship, what sort of work would we be called to do? I, the writer, read myself into this question. It is intentionally unsettling. I prefer to plant trees instead of going to meetings. I prefer sharing with my communities the stories they were never told instead of teaching predominantly white students how to "be better people." I prefer writing about the pains of life, unruly writing, that reminds readers of the infinite processes that connect our theory and practices.

Notes

1 Sarah Ahmed (2012, p. 38).
2 Ibid., p. 38.
3 Ibid., p. 41.
4 Ibid., p. 42.
5 Taylor and Lahad (2018).
6 Ibid., p. 40.
7 Ibid., p. 40.
8 Ibid., p. 21.
9 Ibid., p. 22.
10 Ibid., p. 25.
11 Ibid., p. 25.
12 Ibid., p. 33.
13 I would come to touch on this topic in one of my first publication: Berruz (2014).
14 la paperson (2017, p. 46).
15 Ibid., p. 46.
16 Ibid., p. 47.
17 Ibid., p. 50.
18 Ibid., pp. 49–50.
19 Mariana Ortega (2017).
20 Eve Tuck and Yang (2012).
21 Ibid., p. 17.
22 Ibid., p. 17.
23 Ibid., p. 18.
24 Ibid., p. 19.
25 Ibid., p. 19.
26 Santiago Castro Gómez (2021).
27 Ortega (2017, p. 511).
28 Ibid., p. 508.
29 Ibid., p. 3.
30 Ibid., p. 66.
31 Ibid, p. 21.
32 Robin Wall Kimmerer (2013).
33 la paperson (2017, p. 86).
34 Ibid., p. 111.
35 Ibid, p. 35.
36 Ibid, p. 61.

37 Ibid, p. 58.
38 Gloria Anzaldúa (2015, p. 89).
39 Ibid., p. 89.
40 Ibid, p. 90.
41 Ibid., p.90.
42 Luisa Capetillo (2005, p. 4).
43 Ibid., p. 59.

References

Ahmed, S. (2012). *On Being Included: Racism and Diversity in Institutional Life*, 38. Durham: Duke University Press.

Anzaldúa, G. (2015). *Light in the Dark/Luz en lo oscuro: Rewriting Identity, Spirituality, and Reality*, 89. Durham: Duke University Press.

Berruz, S.R. (2014). Inhabiting philosophical space: Reflections from the reasonably suspicious. *Hypatia* 29 (1): 182–188.

Capetillo, L. (2005). *A Nation of Women: An Early Feminist Speaks Out* (ed. F.M.R. Matos), 4. Houston: Arte Publico Press.

Castro Gómez, S. (2021). *Critique of Latin American Reason*, 208. NY: Columbia University Press.

Gilio-Whitaker, D. (2019). *As Long as the Grass Grows: The Indigenous Fight for Environmental Justice From Colonization to Standing Rock*, 27. Boston: Beacon Press.

Kimmerer, R.W. (2013). *Braiding Sweet Grass: Indigenous Wisdom, Scientific Knowledge, and the Teachings of Plants*, 264. Canada: Milkweed editions.

Ortega, M. (2017). Decolonial woes and practices of un-knowing. *Journal of Speculative Philosophy* 31 (3): 504–516.

la paperson (2017). *A Third University is Possible*, 39. Minnesota: University of Minnesota Press.

Pappas, G. (2017). The limitations and danger of decolonial philosophies. *Radical Philosophy Review* 20 (2): 265–295.

Rivera Cusicanqui, S. (2010). *Ch'ixinakax utxiwa: Una reflexión sobreprácticas y discursos descolonizadores*, 58. Buenos Aires: Tinta Limón.

Schutte, O. (1998). Cultural alterity: Cross cultural communication and feminist theory in north-south contexts. *Hypatia* 13 (2): 53–72.

Taylor, Y. and Lahad, K. (ed.) (2018). *Feeling Academic in the Neoliberal University*. London: Palgrave and Macmillan.

Tuck, E. and Yang, K.W. (2012). Decolonization is not a metaphor. Decolonization: Indigeneity. *Education & Society* 1 (1): 1–40.

8

Education in Latin America: Decolonization as an Ethical–Political Urgency

NADIA HEREDIA

Reflecting on education in Latin America implies placing it in a historical context of permanent economic, political, and cultural tensions that cross it. From the founding dichotomy of the educational discourses of modernity, civilization, or barbarism, to the deepening of neoliberal policies, Latin America has been the testing ground of the North in terms of educational policies, too. The center-periphery tension planted in the 1970s and 1980s remains intact in its hardest core. It is precisely in this period when the dark alliance between the military governments and the different economic and civil sectors resulted in the implementation of a set of measures aimed for guaranteeing the crystallization of the Latin American turn to neoliberalism. In educational matters, we can mention, as a statistical fact, that as a result of these measures, for example, Latin America is today the region in which the privatization of education has grown more pronounced and constant in recent decades, sharing position with the countries of sub-Saharan Africa. What interests support the fact that education is considered as the privilege of a few? Or rather, what modifies at the geopolitical level for regions such as Latin America, or Africa among others, that education is conceived as a possibility of access to knowledge and feelings of Others? What links can be established between the discourses that underlie current educational exclusions and the discourses sustained by colonial modernity? In the lines that follow, I intend to deepen these questions from the Dusselian Philosophy of Liberation, as a way to contribute to the educational epistemological resistance that tries to raise its voice in favor of life, in this civilizational crisis.

Latin American Liberation: Reflections on the Meanings of Educational Oppression

Education is understood in various ways. Talking about education does not always refer to formal education, much less in Latin America. That the State eliminated the different educational systems of the ancestral communities is a fact. That the State tried to guarantee universal access to certain meanings of what we understand by national culture, is also true.

In this sense, thinking about education from Latin America through decolonizing perspectives implies keeping in mind that it is a field of constant dispute of cultural, historical, and geopolitically situated meanings. Although each era has its particularities, the tension regarding the directionality of education was always present between the church, the market, and the State, between an imperial culture and the local, be it national states, popular culture, or negated culture.

In the present work, I will deepen some lines of Latin American research that go from philosophy, educational policy, and literature. Placing the educational and the discourses on education in a historical framework that starts from the complexity and places us in the exterior, allows us to make the existing oppression visible. The one that makes us identify

> The philosopher Enrique Dussel will tell us, taking up Carlos Fuentes (1971): The poet announces to us that "you will have to fight against everyone and your fight will be sad because you will fight against a part of your own blood. Your father will never recognize you, little dark son," la Malinche cries out to her mestizo son, "he will never see in you [Europa] his son, but his slave; you will have to make yourself recognized as an orphan ..."
>
> Dussel (1980, pp. 71–72)

Modern education, born from the imperial culture of modernity, accelerated the processes of denial of one's own. The national being was imposed from its whiteness. Educational systems made this homogenization possible. Although Latin America has experienced similar processes in terms of its identity formation, and even in cultural proximity, Chile, Bolivia, Brazil, or Argentina have reacted differently to the imposition of neoliberal policies in education. Their greater or lesser adherence to the application of the educational reforms of the 90s, make the situation vary from one country to another. This work is located in Argentina, hence the particularities expressed here. So let's start this way.

Enrique Dussel in the 70s, through his work Latin American Pedagogy (1980), began to notice the vital importance of deepening the questions regarding the interference of any educational project for the liberation of our peoples. The path proposed by Dussel is the following: to talk about liberation, we must first be aware of the structures of domination that have historically traversed us, as an Amerindian continent, as people, at its different levels. Most of the time naturally and inadvertently. Hence its effectiveness and scope.

As part of the ethical–political framework that Dussel develops in his architectonic, the pedagogical is one of its substantial aspects, since it constitutes the passage from the erotic to the political (Dussel 1980, p. 15).

> The passage from the domestic-erotic pedagogical of the child to the political pedagogical also means leaving the game for planned learning, study, education in institutions, without yet being economic

work. The erotic pedagogical says relationship to the father-mother; political pedagogical, on the other hand, opens the scope of the State, social classes, enlightened and popular culture, science, technology, the mass media, etc. It is the passage from the psychic to the social; it is opening to the political space.

Dussel (1980, p. 61)

While classical pedagogy omits to problematize the history that makes up the present of the Latin American cultural world, in this case, presenting itself as something neutrally given, the pedagogical part of the fact that it is a continent marked by the conquest of the European, where "the conquering man became an oppressive father, a dominating teacher" (Dussel 1980, p. 18).

Pedagogy, then, will discover the domain of relations that go from the family erotic level (mother–father/son), to the institutional political level (teacher/student). But it is actually the *imago* of the father and mother, which can also be:

(...) as a teacher, doctor, professional, philosopher, culture, State, etc. [who] prolongs his phallocracy as aggression and domination of the son: filicide. The death of the son, the child, the youth, the recent generations by gerontocracies or bureaucracies is physical (in the front line of armies or human sacrifices), symbolic or ideological, but it is always a type of alienation, domination, annihilation of Alterity.

Dussel (1980, p. 15)

The Dusselian pedagogy is thus presented as a critique of domination relations from an Amerindian perspective, recovering the knowledge of the historical processes that occurred to eliminate otherness.

Although Dussel develops these denials in highly complex schemes, we can say that in a given temporality is imposed a certain. epistemological *corpus*, consolidated as ahistorical, when in fact it is the result of continuous disputes about meaning about what it is. What Dussel proposes is that this ontological foundation is the result of the imposition of one project(s) over another(s). In other words, the pedagogical contains within itself, as part of its ontological foundation, the current Totality project, as the germ of the liberating project. In this sense, it is essential to talk about the ethics of the current pedagogical project. Uncover its denials, its deniers:

Especially in Latin America, where the current systems have as their project the imperial culture of the "center" (almost exclusively European-North American and in 3% of our population with clear Russian influences), and where, furthermore, the enlightened oligarchic elites confuse their own pedagogical project with that of the "center," denying, like Sarmiento, the project of popular culture.

Dussel (1980, p. 71)

Understanding the pedagogical as what we receive from others, this proposal allows us to historicize and contextualize what we usually understand by *one* culture, *one* knowledge, and *one* history. In other words, it allows us to affirm that within symbolic and theoretical constructions presented as universals, there are Others that were denied by the project of the current system or Totality, in Dusselian categories. Pedagogy is then a generational relationship and, for this very reason, it is the bridge that will allow us the establishment of links between the Totalities, understood as systems that we share with the generations that precede us (Heredia, 2019, p. 133) and with future ones:

In this case the son-people are educated in "the same" that the system already is. For this reason the pedagogical project of domination is always the fruit of violence, of conquest, of repression of the Other as other.

Dussel (1980, p. 73)

In this sense, for Dussel it is fundamental that pedagogues and scientists in pedagogy question what is essential: the ultimate project of the system itself. Questioning and interrogating ourselves about the ethics of the current educational project means then:

Consider whether the goal of education is to deny the son-people or affirm it in its own exteriority. It is about judging the projects of the pedagogical systems, the foundation of the objectives, the ultimate goals of education.

Dussel (1980, p. 71)

Problematizing these last ends or the meanings of education is the task of philosophy of education as a discipline, often tinged with a Eurocentric imprint that precisely prevents us from problematizing educational nuclei from geopolitically situated perspectives that are not only Latin American. The pedagogical allows us to situate the criticality of the pedagogical discourse on the side of the oppressed, just like the philosophy that gives rise to it, philosophy of liberation (Dussel 1985).

With what has been said so far, we can see that although these working hypotheses that were formulated in the 1970s, resignifying them in our days allows us to ask ourselves: What is the validity of thinking about the educational project as part of a current Totality and therefore imposed on other ways of understanding educational meanings? What other senses of understanding education and the educational system are in dispute as part of the present ethical project? Are we putting into debate in our educational, institutional spaces, the foundation of the current ethical project, from the place of the oppressed?

It is in this sense that we affirm that reflecting on education in Latin America, from decolonizing perspectives, continues to be an ethical–political urgency, while the senses of cultural whiteness continue to be the foundation of the current educational project. Dussel highlights the ideological aspect of the project, proposing another way to understand ideology as the "existential interpretive totality" (Dussel 1980, p. 76). The interpretation presented as universal, white, European, and patriarchal is therefore ideological, the result of violence imposed on Other knowledge. Ramón Grosfoguel (2013) wonders in this sense:

How is it possible that men from (...) five countries achieved such a privilege epistemic to the point that today their knowledge is considered superior to that of the rest of the world? How did they manage to monopolize the authority of knowledge in the world?

Grosfoguel (2013, p. 34)

The father has killed the son as popular culture, as ancestral knowledge, as women's knowledge. Now his project is universal.

[The] epistemic privilege of western man in the knowledge structures of westernized universities is the result of four genocides/epistemicides in the long 16th century (against the population of Jewish and Muslim origin in the conquest of Al-Andalus, against the indigenous people in the conquest of the

American continent, against the kidnapped and enslaved Africans in the American continent and against women burned alive under accusations of witchcraft in Europe) that are constitutive of the knowledge structures of the world-system.

Grosfoguel (2013, pp. 33–34)

As we can see, the construction of the senses *of* education and *in* education is historical. The dispute over meanings is permanent. The senses of being and therefore, educational in Latin America, continue to be colored by the historical colonial oppositions that cross us. Those that pedagogical currents such as Paulo Freire's or the liberation movements of the '70s categorized as oppressors and oppressed.

I would like to close this section with the Dusselian reflection that states that "It is in the time of pedagogy where the operators of domination, the dominated and the liberators are formed" (Dussel 1980, p. 71). Understanding the depth of this statement gives us the responsibility as educators to be responsible for the passage from the familiar (erotic) to the institutional and social (political). No one who considers himself a critical educator is left out of this responsibility. Either we are part of the current Totality project that reproduces the Same or we are part of the liberation project (Dussel 1980, p. 71). The rest is neutral. And as Dante Alighieri (1921) said in The Divine Comedy "The hottest circle in hell is reserved for those who in times of moral crisis opt for neutrality."

Education as a State Matter

The dichotomy that constitutes the westernist ideological basis of formal education, the Sarmiento premise civilization or barbarism (Sarmiento 1977) seems to have been updated in the neoliberal educational discourses in the opposition private public. The private sector is presented as the destination of the wealthy classes, and therefore white, in society. On the other side, the public appears as a relegated place, where in the past the Indian, the gaucho and those excluded from everything that was considered acceptable citizenship would have gone. If at the beginning of the formal State, the education eliminated everything related to the "Indian," or the telluric, was necessary for the confirmation of a citizenship bleached in its self-perception. At present the dispute of meaning raised with neoliberals in educational matters seems to be positioning themselves in these terms again.

Contemporary neoliberal discourses make these statements find their representatives in current figures of Latin American neoconservative politics. As is happening in a global order, the return of the extremism of the right-wing discourses is also a constant in Latin American territory. From the self-proclaimed president from Bolivia, Jeanine Áñez, who "did not hesitate to declare: "I have a mixture of Aryan and Nordic features, and I have nothing to do with the Bolivian coyas" (Lopez Ocon 2019). Until the statements of the former president of Argentina, Mauricio Macri, when in the celebrations of the Bicentennial of Argentine independence in Tucumán, an emblematic place for the date, for being where the independence of Argentina was proclaimed on July 9, 1816, when trying to feel what the liberators felt at that moment, he maintained: "clearly they should have anguish to make the decision, dear King, to separate from Spain" (Our Voices 2016).

It is difficult to measure the scope of these statements in regard to the construction of an epochal common sense, when it is part of the political leadership, or of the sectors that have in their hands precisely the possibility of building common sense, which is positioned reaffirming the coloniality that so many centuries and blood cost to banish, in some way. If we refer specifically to the educational field, from these political speeches, we can mention another example when in a press conference, the aforementioned former president of Argentina opened up his conception of public education by stating that there is "a terrible inequality, of that who can go to private school versus the one who has to fall to public school" (Telam 2017).

Continuing with our analysis, from these discourses the public sector is related to blackness in the colonial senses of the term. On the other hand, the white of society continues to be identified with the superior, with those who carry the values of a supposed society of free competition of fit individuals, who are educated in the private sector. For the supporters of the Free Market "the Public Education network is intended for those who cannot access private education" (Paviglianiti 1995, p. 130). In other words, from these discourses, those who are part of the public educational systems are simply poor because they cannot pay for a private educational service.

Education ceases to be a right that must be guaranteed by the State and becomes a service, bought by whoever can. The public, in its gratuitous nature, begins to be associated with social discredit, linked to the presupposition of its scarce quality. What neoliberals understand by quality is precisely what depoliticizes the very act of educating. Private teaching usually has little participation in union spaces, since many schools/companies do not allow it, or if they do, this participation is usually taken into account when renewing employment contracts. Added to this is the fact that the private sector receives state economic support, with which the excess amount of the quotas is reflected in inputs and amenities that in the public sector tend to be deteriorated or simply not there, due to underfunding.

On this point of educational financing, under the premise that the State must guarantee the plurality of educational offers to citizens, the neoliberal educational political discourses postulated that the existence of the private sector is a right and as such it must be guaranteed. Thus, the Federal Education Law in Argentina, No. 24,195 proclaimed in 1993, establishes State financing for the private sector. This means that currently all compulsory Argentine education is public, what can change is public or private management.

Through educational reforms since the 1990s, Latin American educators have learned to recognize the scope of incorporating economic categories into educational language. Education ceases to be a right and becomes a service. Education must be of quality and guarantee good results measured in the systematic evaluations carried out at the national level. The best results of the private sector lead to quick conclusions: the private is better, the public is worse. However, studies show that the best results in this sector in national assessments are due to:

> Enrollment in private schools tends to come from professional sectors or with higher cultural capital, their levels of knowledge are higher, but not as a result of private school teaching. There is no scientific basis to affirm that private schools are better, in terms of learning, than public ones.
>
> Tenti Fanfani and Grimson (2017)

In this sense, the growth of private schools in Latin America is linked to economic growth:

> In Latin America, private education has grown even in contexts of exit from neoliberal models, when all countries have experienced economic growth that improved family possibilities to spend on non-essential goods (that are not for mere survival).
>
> Tenti Fanfani and Grimson (2017)

Neoliberals, far from problematizing the impossibility of access to cultural resources that broaden general knowledge that is reflected in educational performance, at any level, place the responsibility on the individual to obtain them. Poverty and inequalities are never a structural problem, they are always the responsibility of the subject, his temper, his personal effort, or at most, his own and his family. What they need to question is the role of the State.

If the neoliberal discourse in its origins criticizes the State of well-being, in its interventionist excess after the economic crises of the post war, currently, it does so to the State in general, in any of its forms of intervention. Especially in those that limit the Free Market considering that this "prevents the force of progress (...) from working correctly" (Paviglianiti 1995, p. 127). Progress is directly linked to the business sector and its delay falls on the mismanagement of the State and its excessive spending (in these terms) of economic resources on the popular classes. Neoliberals consider that the greatest threat comes from the do-gooder bureaucracies and that:

> The ideal is to move from state benefits to subsidies directed to individuals or in the second instance to private institutions so that in this way everyone can buy their services in the market.
>
> Paviglianiti (1995, p. 127)

What the neoliberals do not make explicit is that if the monetary subsidies are directed to families, individuals, and private institutions:

> This position leads in the long term to the abolition of the Public Education system and its replacement by a system of vouchers that can be used in the market to buy education in combination with the resources available to families or individuals.
>
> Paviglianiti (1995, p. 129)

Of course, the disparity of resources that families or individuals have to gain access to education, understood as a service, is not under discussion.

In neoliberal discourses, education at any of its levels is losing its meaning as a builder of valid knowledge or as useful for the demands of the world, the market. It is true that we can and must question what type of knowledge is transmitted in educational institutions, questioning the bases of the current pedagogical project, as we saw with the Dusselian pedagogy. But ignoring the importance of public education for the popular sectors, putting private education as a viable option, is an ill-intentioned fallacy.

The incorrect use of social pillars in education as fundamental as equity, equality, and rights are postulated in directions contrary to all criteria of justice, understood as the principle that leads to acting in favor of those who need it most. That is to say, for the neoliberals, the benefit of a fair state action will be aimed at protecting those who can, have, or have the most. In this way, María Eugenia Vidal, governor of the province of Buenos Aires during the period 2015–2019, for the PRO (Republican Proposal) will ask: "Is it equity that for years we have populated the Province of Buenos Aires with public universities, when all of us who are here know that no one who is born in poverty in Argentina today reaches the university?" (CPB News 2020).

From this point of view, what would equity be? What would be an equitable State action? Would it be fair to populate the richest cities and sectors of the Province of Buenos Aires with public universities? What right to education would be defended from such an action? Clearly the popular sectors are taken as having no right to access public education. At this point, I would like to return to Apple (1997) when he posits that "as educators we are inevitably engaged in a struggle over meanings" (Apple 1997, p. 52).

We live immersed in discourses that discredit the public and ponder the private, which seek to establish that equity educational policies are in favor of those who can, as a way of guaranteeing state investment in human capital. This sense of whiteness "is deeply built into our understandings of common sense, of everyday life" (Apple 1997, p. 52). The internalization of coloniality manifests itself in the public sphere, creating shared opinions and senses of community identification. How should we position ourselves before the neoliberal discourses that update the meanings of an internalized whiteness, not only educational meanings?

> The fact that someone is a political militant does not guarantee that they are free from the dynamics power differentials, dynamics that penetrate our daily lives in very subtle ways. This may require a conscious act to disarm our common sense and make this participation clear.
>
> Apple (1997, p. 51)

As educators we have to be aware of these uses and discuss them. The equity, equality, defense of rights, works like ethical–political *praxis* when applied in favor of the excluded(s). It is necessary to be clear on this point.

Third and Last Part

My paternal grandmother's name was María, that's why I also call myself María. My maternal grandmother's name was Margarita, and she is the one I knew the most. I remember, from when I can have a record, that she was a very quiet woman and always looked toward the window. Like remembering something, like waiting for something. Maybe she wasn't quiet, but she didn't talk much anymore, when I got to know her. However, as I grow older, her story gains relevance in my own story, in the family story that, on my mother's side, is a story of women.

My grandmother's voice comes through my mother's words, in anecdotes that she tells whenever she can, and of course. She tells that from the deepest poverty, my grandmother confronted my grandfather Julián, to leave the field because her son and daughters had to study. Thus they began their journey, from the countryside to the nearest town, where there was a school, in the singular. The field they left behind was not romanticized by urban thinkers. It was the one that hurts in the dark of night, due to lack of services. The field that requires staying and living there as the only possibility of life. From there they left, my grandmother and her daughters. Some to study, all to work in the houses of the ladies of the town. His daughters all finished school. Her son died young. They learned to read and write as a first legacy and gift from my grandmother, who died illiterate. My mother repeats with an emotion that I even think she doesn't measure when she repeats my grandmother's words "Study!! You have to study." She told them.

Those words resonate with me through my mother as a legacy. A mandate? Maybe. An echo that has always been with me, especially when I also remember my enthusiasm when reading the newspaper to my grandmother, even before starting school. My grandmother saw her granddaughters finish primary and secondary school and she saw them starting at the university. She did not come to see me graduate from almost nothing. She has gone, but it was part of everything. Those words resounded in me like an echo, an invitation on the other side of a door that would take me to a better place, of course. They functioned as a hope that something better would come. Something that she surely longed for and to which she could never have access to: education. Bringing her to these stories is also putting into words the emotion of being part of the first generations of the family that could have access to higher education. We arrived, again, the majority women. It could be in our horizon of possibilities. We know that in Latin America, in Argentina, being a woman is a lot. Not to mention, having a disability.

Being the first generation with access to all educational levels in Latin America continues to be a privilege, an achievement of few. Something that many cannot even think about within the horizon of possibilities. I discovered myself, as Dussel would say, with a Mapuce identity thanks to the University and the discourses of liberation and decoloniality that I assumed were not out there. Nor outside of me. They told my own family stories. Those that my mother told about how her paternal grandmother remembered that they were brought running from Buenos Aires: Trapalque. That name over and over again. From there they went south to the mountains. Fleeing from soldiers on horseback, in what was misnamed Conquest of the desert, which was never such. They saved their lives while sheltering in caves, in Aluminé, eating pine nuts, the fruit of Pewen, a food that carries ancestral value for the Mapuce community.

Inquiring into regional, Latin American literature, I read about herding stories in Argentine Patagonia. These stories were my story in other voices. Those stories help us situate ourselves in the world, as part of the denied stories: "It is in the final stages of the so-called Conquest of the Desert (1878–1885) and Occupation or Pacification of Araucanía (1860–1883), who begins to be herded is not the animal but the persons" (Mellado 2021, p. 50). There was in front of me a new truth discovered: part of my family was herded.

These practices in our territories continue to be hidden by any pedagogical curriculum today. We learn nothing from these stories in schools and even in many universities. The discourses based on the Eurocentric civilizational myth are reproduced. How do we generate a liberation project, in the terms of Dusselian pedagogy, if the bases of the current system remain intact, without being questioned? The history that is our territorially and geopolitically situated history continues to be denied. It should be clarified that the "systems of herding and confinement of native peoples by military campaigns in Patagonia [are] actions understood as genocide (Lenton 29–49)" (Mellado 2021, p. 53).

Liliana Ancalao, a Mapuce poet and writer, recounts when on a trip, on her way to a conference where she was invited to say something about another Argentine national date, May 25, when the May Revolution and the formation of the first national government are commemorated. Ancalao remembers the voices of the old people who lived the herd in Patagonia,

I brought something to read (...) And Felix Manquel said ... a compilation by Enrique Perea. I can imagine the worn voice of Don Manquel,
And so ... that ... also kind of sad that ... that
matter ... what I ... can talk about ... because ... they cry there

after. I remember when I talked my father cried,
when he remembered; the way they walked, on foot ...
they drove ... like animals like that to Buenos Aires ...
(...) I keep reading
(...) My old man was talking to another old man, right? Known of him;

Of course they are the same age, they are. The way they lowered it ... one
if he got tired out there, on foot everything, they got tired they took out the saber they cut it in the
garrones. The people who got tired and ... went from to foot. There it was just, alive, torn, cut. And that
of course ...
very sad, very long too I cry, while I look at the immensity of the sky through the window, looking into
the distance comforts me. I ask myself again, will someone ever ask for forgiveness?

Ancalao (2014, pp. 166–167)

The genocide of 1492 and those that followed in the Latin American territories in the nineteenth century are a fundamental part of our history. A part hidden by the educational systems, a part silenced by the pain of the elderly. Dussel's words resonate with me when he affirms that the civilizational myth was irrational, it was a sacrificial myth.

I am questioned by Mellado's voice when she says that the literary investigation regarding the ways in which current texts resignify what happened in the nineteenth century, and the herding in particular, "taking not only the hegemonic stories but the voices of minor, family or communal memories" (...) is moved "by a desire for restitution, (...) of a humanitarian trail in relation to oral memories" (Mellado 2021, p. 58).

I share these final reflections because I want to finish this writing, highlighting the value that public education has for families of the popular classes, for many women, in Latin America. But I also want to emphasize that what public education assumes as a political responsibility to teach must be from decolonizing perspectives, in the specific sense of the term. The specificity that the situated discourses will give it, the recoveries of Other stories, like those of Don Manquel, like those of my great-grandmother. We carry coloniality and the possibility of decoloniality in our lives, bodies, and memories, as is the case with the founding ethical project of the current system, according to Dussel. Education can be part of the project to come, one of liberation.

I recover the voices of other women, who question my own voice with their voices. I remember that my grandmother died being illiterate. She didn't read letters and words. As a child I was intrigued to think what a world without reading words would be like. However, now I can think differently, my grandmother knew how to read the world, her reality. She knew how to read that a world without education offered fewer opportunities. She offered that opportunity to her daughters and sons. Now that I think about it, it was my grandmother, in the voice of my mother, who from her humility taught me that education is an offering of love to the world and to those who come to continue the task.

References

Ancalao, L. (2014). That is what is in Mellado. In: *The Uncomfortable Dwelling Studies on Mapuche Poetry: Elicura Chihuailaf and Liliana Ancalao* (ed. Silvia). PubliFadecs.

Apple, M. (1997). Education, identity and cheap French fries. In: *Culture, Policy and Curriculum: Essays on the Public School Crisis*. Paul Gentili (comp.) Michael Apple/Thomas Tadeus da Silva Losada.

125

CPB News. (2020). *Vidal: "Nobody who is born in poverty in Argentina today goes to university"* [Video]. March 12, Youtube. https://www.youtube.com/watch?v=Nt38XeQr_iA&ab_channel=CPBNoticias

Dussel, E. (1980). *Pedagogical Latin American*. New America.

Dussel, E. (1985). *Philosophy of Liberation*. Orbis Books.

Fuentes, C. (1971). All cats are brown. In: *The Original Kingdoms*.

Grosfoguel, R. (2013). Epistemic racism/sexism, westernized universities and the four genocides/epistemicides of the long sixteenth century. *Tabula Rasa [Online]* 19: 31–58. ISSN 1794-2489.

Heredia, N. (2019). La pedagógica de la liberación de Enrique Dussel: Inakayal y lo que la pedagogía nos negó. *Revista Del IICE* 45: 131–142. https://doi.org/10.34096/iice.n45.7129. Accessed June 3, 2023.

Lopez Ocon M. (2019). *Ambitions of a Superb Indian*. Argentinian Time, November 17. https://www.tiempoar.com.ar/cultura/ambiciones-de-un-indio-soberbio/

Mellado, S. (2021). Words up to date: links between "that's what he is" and "so that this memory drains" by Liliana Ancalao; National University of Cordoba. Faculty of Philosophy and Humanities; heterotopias; 4; 8; 12-2021; 1–21

Our Voices (2016). Macri apologizes to the "King of Spain" on behalf of the patriots at the Bicentennial celebration. [Video]. July 9. Youtube. https://www.youtube.com/watch?v=PafUPMlufOO&ab_channel=NuestrasVoces

Paviglianiti, N. (1995). The Federal Law of Education as an element of regulation of the socio-educational reality in Argentina: Its orientations towards privatization, provincialization and withdrawal of the National Government from financing the public education system. *Pedagogical Series* (2): 123–146. In Academic Memory. Available in: http://www.memoria.fahce.unlp.edu.ar/art_revistas/pr.2535/pr.2535.pdf.

Sarmiento, D.F. (1977). *Facundo or Civilization and Barbarism*. Ayacucho Library.

Telam (2017). *Macri:* "Seven out of ten boys do not have basic knowledge of Mathematics". [Video]. March 21, Youtube. https://www.youtube.com/watch?v=yjuJA1zF8OM&ab_channel=Télam

Tenti Fanfani E. and Grimson A. (2017). Public and Private Education. Fall in public. UNSAM Amphibious Magazine, March 22. https://www.revistaanfibia.com/caer-publica/

9

Philosophy of Liberation Praxis in Mexico City

GABRIEL HERRERA SALAZAR

Introduction

In 2001, after the Zapatista Army of National Liberation command passed through Mexico City, I decided to study Philosophy of Liberation in practice. What followed were five years of training research in action.

My collaboration with NGOs led to the construction of community-based groups. The direct contact that I had and have with the people of these communities made me descend from the abstract to the concrete of philosophy, it also caused me to rethink the methods learned in universities in order to try to understand the complexity of our reality as a peripheral, Latin American country.

My theoretical approximations at the time attempted to criticize the academic philosophers who made abstractions from logical statements without having as a reference the real of reality—the supposedly "scientific" theories were not neutral and lacked facticity. From the perspective of Philosophy of Liberation, the implementation of a methodological participatory proposal for the social sciences aims to leave as something discontinued *the object of study*, giving greater emphasis to intersubjective communities as groups of non-objectifiable human beings, like Marcela Lagarde (1997) analogously thinks with regard to women when she says: "profound epistemological changes make women appear as subjects and not as an object of research, especially from the perspective of female anthropologists."

The practical experience was carried out through an NGO whose strategy at that time was to initiate resistance processes in communities of Mexico City with the end of confronting the so-called

Struggles for Liberation in Abya Yala, First Edition. Edited by Luis Rubén Díaz Cepeda and Ernesto Rosen Velásquez.

Puebla-Panama Plan, today the Mérida Initiative. The actions of the NGO were aligned along two main axes: gender equality and sustainability. A series of economic alternatives were created that were insufficient in solving the underlying problem of social inequality; however, what we learned with the people in these communities enabled us to understand that consciousness raising, and the ethical–political position that goes with it, are fundamental actions in the long-term transformation of the global situation of the peripheral countries of the world.

Subjective Learning from Existential Experience

In the insurgency work carried out in the mountains of Xochimilco not everything went as expected. Throughout the entire process there was constant confusion, errors, and discouragement, and perhaps we did not achieve what we had ideally wanted: a profound transformation that would generate community development alternatives for the construction of another possible world.

Motivated by the guerrilla front, I joined the organizations of organized civil society as a militant in 2001 to begin a learning process with those actors who had participated in the social movements that were persecuted by the State in the 1970s and 1980s, but now with new learning, since civil society had shown another path for transformation; the ethical obligation for the poor had not fallen with real socialism, but rather brought together and united the different liberation fronts that fought in isolation for justice, autonomy, and dignity.

I began to collaborate as a community organizer. My intrasubjective intention, trapped in postmodern meaninglessness, was a kind of socially conscious suicide attempt. Today, with everything I have experienced, I have learned that the death drive is a way of reaffirming life.

The resistance, militancy, and ideals of liberation inherited from my family provided me with some hope that the postulates of the historical revolutions and clandestine struggles were not completely defeated. I clung to the communiqués of the Zapatista command and its struggle for a dignified life.

In this way, looking for signs of life among the rubble, I decided to start a focoist struggle—a crazy and anachronistic idea, old-fashioned for my contemporaries; for the time in which we had to live, it was an idealism that according to many was "outdated." However, with the wind against me and advancing against the grain, the praxis of liberation was the only reason that gave some meaning to the meaninglessness of the chaos of my existence. It was a choice driven by anguish, between cutting my veins or that ideal of a messianic future that conservatism dismisses as "immature."

Upon arriving in Xochimilco I met a group composed mostly of women. In the exchange of conceptions of the world and liberation projects it was clear that while the armed struggle was one among many others, it was not the most important, however it was not ruled out. It was a strategic means for an anarchic moment of destruction, not an end in itself, nor the ultimate end. Very quickly I began to notice that there was a lot of work to be done and very few hands to do it.

It is at work where we learn together, we make mistakes like every human in constant learning. Human errors, of imperfect beings, we make mistakes with love and with the love that gives the will to live, we get up to continue walking.

With the constructive criticism of my friends, classmates, in the intersubjectivity of the group and the self-critical reflection of my subjective experience lived in the carnality of my existence,

I can say, always with some inevitable degree of error, that it is a fact that it was not possible to meet strategic objectives in the field of local economic development that could promote root transformations proposed as medium and long-term objectives.

However, such a situation should not lead us to disqualify or minimize the need for structural change, that is, the need for an anti-systemic social movement of the local peripheries that destroys the structure and economic logic of the current capitalist world-system, to create a fairer system for the excluded. Neither should the analysis of the strategy and tactics of the various liberation fronts, nor their genuine, authentic, honest ideals, purposes, and claims of transformation be demerited. In the same way, the effort, creativity, the limitless sacrifice, and dedication of the people and families who jointly committed themselves to seek and believe in a change, in a new beginning, should not be ignored.

The planned objectives were not always achieved, nor was what was expected received, but we learned in practice. From all the experience, I point out only four factors that we constantly faced throughout the entire process of the experience of insurgency. They are key to understanding the minimum but sufficient regarding the failure to achieve strategic objectives: (1) the lack of economic resources, (2) intolerance to criticism, (3) lack of compliance with ethical principles, and (4) a solid political definition of liberation. We lacked the time to change our habits that the ethics of neoliberalism obliged us to purchase, we lacked time to mature in the interiority of the mother, we were born before the necessary time, imperfect, we were born so as not to die in the womb, to know a dignified life.

The Material Foundation for an Ethics in Social Research

Our methodological proposal is based on the philosophical-categorical framework of *Ethics of Liberation* by Enrique Dussel, which, from a distinct point of departure, provides the grounds for a practice in social research and is situated in a concretion and complexity beyond the epistemology of modern philosophy that boasts of being empirical, neutral, and objective, that is, apolitical, since it aims to objectify the subject, dehumanizing them by way of a modern instrumental rationality and, in doing so, eliminate the material content of ethics (Herrera, 2016, 2018)[1] and the practical consequences of political action intrinsic to all human action.

For Enrique Dussel (2013), in his *Ethics of Liberation*, or his mature ethics, *human life* is the material content of the *Ethics of Liberation*, and, unlike formal ethics, it does not leave out the *living corporeal subject*. In this book he tells us:

> This is an ethics of life; that is to say, human life is the content of ethics. For this reason, I want to forewarn the reader, here and at the outset, about the meaning of a material ethics or ethics of content. The project of an ethics of liberation unfolds in in its own way from the exercise of an ethical critique [...], where the negated dignity of the life of the victim, oppressed or excluded, is affirmed.

The purpose of ethics for Dussel is not the "good" or "bad" act as it is for other ethics, the former must occupy itself with the universal conditions of the norm, the act, the micro, or macro structure as an institution. There are no good or bad decisions, since no action we perform is perfect, there are always unintended consequences, so none of our actions are good or bad, but rather have a claim to goodness. An act with a claim to goodness must take care of its unintended consequences, that is, it must correct its actions. The fact that our actions generate unintentional negative effects does not mean that they cease to be unjust, they cease to be when the negative effects of our unintentional actions along with those anticipated are corrected, that is, when there is a sincere and effective claim to justice with the victim who suffers the unintentional negative acts.

That is why all human actions have political implications and social research methods should contain in their foundations a "political claim to justice" that is supported by an ethical position. The implementation of the *Philosophy of Liberation*, like the *Ethics of Liberation*, has as a categorical imperative: the duty to produce, reproduce and develop human life in community, ultimately that of humanity, this gives it a character with a claim to universality.

So for us, human life, as the material content of the *Ethics of Liberation*, is the necessary and inevitable material principle upon which to base the social sciences, since social research has the ethical and political duty to produce, reproduce, and develop the life of all humanity, since the scientist (and not only the social scientist), is a living, material, empirical, ethical corporality before an epistemic one.

Release Methodology

The praxis that we present is only a proposal to be considered and criticized with empirical arguments by future, young social scientists. It is one proposal among many to be put into practice. It does not claim to be a finished work, but only to point out or situate a problematic to be deepened by those who share the same concern, with the end of surpassing or corrected it materially, formally, and factually and with this contribute to the development of our critical social sciences. I understand critical social sciences as those that are not mediocrely satisfied with being functional to the system that created them but go further by constructing another possible world with their criticism, a world where many worlds fit or an "analogical pluriverse" as Enrique Dussel likes to say.

The objective of this research praxis, unlike others, does not have the ultimate goal of exploiting and extracting information in order to accumulate knowledge, and then invest it and generate a monopoly of power to dominate and manipulate in a more subtle way the objects of the world that surround us, where alterity is always a possible object of study. What this methodology intends is to humanize, raise awareness, liberate, and decolonize in the development of dialogue and intercultural exchange of knowledge, to learn with the wisdom of the other person, and together achieve a common goal with a claim to justice for the oppressed, the victims, that is, those excluded from any field (such as the ecological, economic and cultural fields) of a system.

So the ultimate goal is not to conduct research in order to have prestige, a job or a privileged hobby in the complicit comfort that justifies the inequitable distribution of material goods for the lives of all humans in the *Pachamama*; but to transform the material conditions to achieve a life with dignity, with which we can change the course taken by the world system that destroys human life and the planet's other species, which if not accomplished, leads us toward a collective suicide.

After putting this methodology into practice in social research, we can conclude that the identity between theory and praxis, their unity or embrace of love, is contained in the reflexive paradox that exists in human interiority, in its dialectical contradiction lived as aporia within the interior of subjectivity, as Kierkegaard had already suffered. Thus, an "analectic" logic opens the possibility of having another alternative option, and not a single, universal, and unequivocal truth, but an *analogic pluriverse*. The minimum unit that is paradoxically composed of a minimum of two complementary elements, yields a multiplication of found and intersecting interpretations, making it complex, since there is more than one path, more than three reasons to dialogue. The principle of male–female *complementarity* of native Amerindian cultures is and has been since before the European invasion the denial of the monoculture of thought, it is now for us a position in favor of pluriculture in the social sciences.

The first step that we recommend to begin a methodology of liberation for social research is to have the will as a base of support or foundation. To have the will to live is to have the will to want, then, for this methodology, the starting point is to have the *will to power*, to transform and transform oneself in an uncertain and complex process. The *will to power* is understood as that *will to live* that uses power to get out of marginality or exclusion and generate the conditions to achieve a life with dignity in community.

This starting point implies leaving the certainties of our cultural world in suspension and returning to have the attitude of beginning to learn. Wanting to learn, in the methodology of liberation, means unlearning the unique and universal principles of the modern scientism of Western culture. It is a willingness to detach from the single theory and its absolute truth, which has shaped modern subjectivity. It is to open our perceptual panorama that carries in its genetics another way of internalizing the material world that surrounds us. It is teaching by learning, sharing other cultural truths to which we do not belong, since the epistemological fence imposed by modern scientism of the late nineteenth and early twentieth centuries has excluded us from the way of accessing the world of other cultures, and thus from the dialogue with another type of "social sciences."

It is wanting to establish an intercultural dialogue with a claim to true honesty. It is having the will to learn together with anthropological alterity, that is, with the loved one, the partner, the sister, where no one teaches anyone and we all learn from everyone, as Paulo Freire taught us to understand. But even beyond anthropocentrism and human alterity along with which learning is taught, dialogue is pending with our relatives with whom we share the world, the species prior to the human, the older brothers, that is, the stones, the plants and animals—for this dialogue it is necessary to situate ourselves at the starting point of decolonial epistemology.

Having the will to power to break the epistemological fence is to go to the roots and look for analogous principles in the culture of the other that are compatible with the principles of our mother culture, that is, it is to look for a positive point of support in both cultures in order to have a solid foundation, it is to find a material principle that is shared in an analogous way, it is to leave negativity behind with the mutual intersubjective help of criticism and self-criticism of principles and to come out to exteriority leaving behind marginality and exclusion. It is having faith in the word with a claim to truth of the other, taking each other by the hand and confidently undertaking the adventure of knowing and building a different and new world.

The second necessary and inevitable step is to make a geopolitical analysis of the real context of a locality, social group or interpersonal relationship, within the reality of the world system, then, this methodology aims to make a contextual analysis of the global situation from the local perspective. The study of the reality of the context implies analyzing globalization and acting in response with local strategies from communitarian or intersubjective ethical principles. It is to recognize the feasible resources and means for the real transformation of our world. Without this analysis, one can fall into idealistic activism without a concrete material foundation; one can also fall into other extremisms from alienated and uncritical actions that have dehumanized deculturalization as the engine of their action, where the human loses its dignity and is transformed into merchandise with use and exchange value.

This context analysis must be inserted in long-term historical processes, that is, it is the irruption, turn, or contribution that can give innovative continuity to the processes of cultural resistance, always with the authorization and participation of the communities or directly affected actors. It is like listening to a command by giving us the opportunity to change our perception by closing our eyes; or de-hegemonize the sense of sight and recognize the local world through the other senses that had always been timidly contributing their knowledge, but now in a symmetrical, not oppressed way.

To free the senses from visual hegemony is to break the epistemological fence of modern scientific and objective observation. For example, having the intention of listening to the vocation of the one who calls or shouts in pain demanding justice, if the metaphor is accepted, it is like listening to the flower of the word that has life in the heart. It is to place as a starting point, not the sight, but the senses that have been excluded by the hierarchical imposition of the impartial observer, it is to stop being objects of knowledge and recover human dignity by sensing the taste on the lips of a loving kiss, smell the natural perfume of a lover's warm body in the semi-darkness of erotic intimacy, exploring the soft caress and gradually discovering the response of a silence that approves and calls for a response.

The third step of this methodology is the aperture and entry to the field work, it is "breaking stone" or "opening a gap." An ethical and political decision is implicit in this action. It is approaching the people and having the courage to accompany them in a human and fraternal relationship, share their crisis, and assume it as our own. It is to detach ourselves from our known place, a safe abstract center, it is to unhinge the psyche by entering a terrain that is new for us and known by human alterity, it is to de-center ourselves and, insecure, to put ourselves in their hands, always with an honest "claim to goodness," offending unknowingly and unintentionally, in our innocence without guilt, because the "claim to justice" is implicit.

In the mutual solidarity that is born from our similar oppression, compassion of brothers and sisters from different struggles, but who at some point intertwine and each suffers their pain, we suffer, we pity each other. By compassion we understand "to suffer with," that is, to laugh with the same joy at the feast of the brothers of life who free themselves from their suffering. It is assuming, together with the other, a commitment to the consequences of our acts of transforming and transformation, it is making ourselves responsible for history and its new time that is to come.

Patience finds its moment, because we are going to wait for the cornfield to grow to collect the fruit and the new seed, it implies arming ourselves with hope and thinking about the future project, it is taking care, with effort and affection, of the seed that will be sown in communal work, elbow-to-elbow with the participation of those who opened the door of their home to us and welcomed us into the simple and humble warmth of the family.

It is learning to walk again, stepping into the unknown with our eyes closed and controlling the anguish caused by the imaginary nothingness and the chaos that will eventually settle down. Without fear, we can trust the people who will now be the teacher who leads us by the hand. It is to be seduced by their wisdom, by a knowledge that is very much their own, to know their dreams and secrets that have been hidden for so long for fear of censorship and repression. The community, only they know their body and know what the most sensitive parts of their feelings and emotions are, those utopian chimeras that have always generated passion and an ardent desire to wake up with a new sun.

The fourth step is perhaps the most important for the methodology of liberation, that is, the training of local organizers. Our methodology undoubtedly has a preference for young people, since, in the future, the project under construction will have to be deconstructed with the vital impulse of criticism, new proposals, and perspectives that would avoid dogmatism, it cannot be otherwise, if it were, it would fall into the conservatism of corruption and moralism, it would fall into immobility, into the only truth that does not accept corrections. To be united with the energy, enthusiasm, joy, and creativity of the youth made us begin to know the culture of the locality, since friendship and solidarity turned out to be very natural elements in our actions and relationships with people, generating a fraternal atmosphere.

With the natural friendship of the human and the fresh smile of youth, we present ourselves to the other as a presence. The real and material epiphany of our presence in the community brings us closer to its reality, with which another existential analysis of the context begins, but now much more embodied in our physical body and subjectivity. This analysis is not merely "theoretical," but with training action, it is existentially theorized in subjectivity. The relationship with the community becomes more intimate and consequently one begins to work on common objectives. Along with the training action of local organizers, a first participatory diagnosis or a "participatory proto-diagnosis" is put into practice, which is given from the conduction of surveys, which will help us to have a general opinion of the people of the area, who live and suffer from the favorable or unfavorable conditions of their locality on a daily basis. For the systematization of the information collected in this part of the methodology, the tools of university sciences will be very helpful.

The team of local community organizers who are prepared in "training action" is the seed that must be cared for with patience, working so that it grows in the field and the fertile land can bear fruit like a mother. In "training-action," the whole team learns to combine the experience of the best-trained cadres through the existential experience of the years, the wisdom of the grandparents, and the new contributions of the youth society in motion. It is like the aesthetic enjoyment of the beauty of the morning and its new shine, it is to have the certainty that the love of life cannot be wrong because the night has given up its place to imagine and believe in the utopia of those who promised the future of a new day in the dark night. It is like waking up embraced in history and making conscious, in a mystical silence, of the joy that the company of alterity and its fresh and sincere smile causes us.

The fifth step is the construction of the foundation that will support the entire organizational architecture of the community. With the knowledge of the local organizers and the hard data systematized from the first participatory diagnosis, locations are excluded and others with greater possibility and conditions are delimited to begin a joint work process. After an intersubjective dialogue between the team, leaders are appointed to form groups in the communities. In this step, a new ethical and political definition is given that makes the seriousness of the actions to be developed together with the people of the town mature.

Organizers alone or in a team integrate into the work with a community group, together in community assemblies they seek to detect weaknesses, threats, strengths, and opportunities, to create common objectives to improve the community, community group, and common life. From the many voices arise personal objectives, the least viable are excluded under the principle of feasibility, until reaching a general one with real reach for the community itself. The real of the community, the community itself knows, pride has no place, nor the great fashionable scientific theories. The people set the limits and scope for us, we simply have to place ourselves in the place of the student and know how to listen to the voice of the people. It is the community that decides the objective to be investigated, the mandate of the community is the beginning of the investigation for the academy.

The local problematic analyzed makes apparent immediate actions to be solved by means within the reach of the community itself, the common objective is defined always keeping in mind the principle of facticity, that is, keeping in mind actions that can be carried out, specifically, and in the short term. Without the participation of the community and the seriousness of the local organizers, it is impossible to advance in this methodological step.

Theoretically, it is a dialectical transformation from the ideal to the real, it is to discover the imperfection of the human condition, it is the disappointment of platonic or ideal love and to enrich oneself with a more real and true love. It is a love that promises to be lasting and to learn to mature with the mistakes and failures always possible in us and in the people we love. It is the tension between dreaming a perfect love like Marx's communism and recognizing each other face-to-face in a more mature, concrete, and consolidated love relationship by finding our own limitations. It is making a commitment with responsibility and honesty.

The sixth step is the exercise and strengthening of the organizational structure to consolidate community groups or support bases. This methodological step is taken when making a second participatory diagnosis, or self-diagnosis, in the communities where there is a significant presence. Then a third context analysis is carried out; but now with a greater degree of interiority in our work, according to the word of the people. This diagnosis for us was the door that was opened to pass to a praxis of liberation, since it threw us directly into the production of creativity with which one could begin to imagine and generate the minimum conditions for the transformation of negativity.

The actions taken in the praxis of liberation at this moment of the investigation become practical cultural dialogues, that is, the human culture of production is shared, dignity is recovered through work, side-by-side, under the sun, working we become closer.

In solidary work, friendship and trust are consolidated, it is the response to the faith placed in the word of alterity. The intention of learning by teaching leads us to try to listen to the diverse voices of the people. Articulating the valuable contributions of all people in common work for the benefit of the community is a challenge, it is the pluriversality in concrete, inevitably with some unintentional exclusion. With the natural fluidity of friendship and trust, it is possible to strengthen the internal communal organization of the groups and thereby carry out exercises to make political-democratic decisions that help the benefit of the community, for the common good.

Intercultural exchange is reciprocal, co-responsible, and mutual, since the teacher in the field, of construction, of the house, of the education of the smallest, exchanges wisdom and knowledge with another type of teacher who teaches to read, to write, to add, and to build history through engineering and art.

In this cultural exchange, the social scientist does not have more hierarchy in knowledge, he does not know more than another type of teacher, but neither less, they are simply different knowledge that require different artistic skills. In the differentiated but symmetrical work, the secrets of the trade are shown, they are revealed by showing to alterity as they are, without masks or disguises, both learn by teaching their art. It is the clothing of the bodies that falls in front of alterity to show the hidden beauty of the scars and the face worn by the sun and time. It is the naked encounter of the truth that walks without shyness or dissimulation through the intimacy of the house, without prejudice it erotically hides what is necessary, but lets the feelings emerge enough so that the message is clear and transparent like the crystalline water that flows in the rivers and springs of the mountain.

The seventh step of this work for us is the withdrawal and beginning of a new process. Just to put a limit, it is the last step that this methodology of liberation is composed of. It does not necessarily have to be this way, since more elements can be added; however, for academic, pedagogical, and formal purposes it is a sufficient minimum framework. What is described here is a minimum framework proposed to begin a constructive dialogue and to be able to criticize this methodological proposal.

With the training of local organizers from the communities themselves, a new and more lasting self-organizing commitment is guaranteed, and we go from defining medium-term objectives to building long-range objectives. In this step, a deeper ethical and political commitment of the local organizers is defined, they will have to assume the mandate of the community, which will decide between staying forever in the community or leaving to return soon, or paradoxically both. It is the appointment of specific jobs, of historical positions. The mandate of the community is to listen to the voice of the people, in the construction of this participatory methodology it is categorical because the mandate has to be obeyed, one has to lead by obeying.

When organizational strengthening and community participation begin to be a daily part of the community, self-organization begins to solve small but essential objectives for the people's spirits, that is when the pedagogical dependence begins to break and with it comes the feeling of nostalgia knowing that detachment has to be attempted again. It is time to pack your backpack, put it on your shoulders and once again set out on your way to find another side of the mountain uphill. It is like the prophet who announces the good news of some community similar to any, who has solved by his own means, small objectives that represent great achievements for the benefit of the community.

The farewell of the leaving, never total or final, is to feel the embrace of the parents and the knowing smile of the grandparents who understand that the withdrawal is a momentary withdrawal. The one who has to leave takes a part and leaves something of his heart that can never be recovered, that will be the witness that maintains the memory of the history. The one who leaves and the one who stays is the daughter who has decided to begin to experience autonomy, she has already learned what had to be learned to walk on her own feet in search of the part that is missing to be someone complete and true.

The feeling is mutual because the commitment is long and life is too short not to seek to build a dignified life. Grandparents are too old to not know that the path of the sun and the moon is cyclical, like the sowing of the cornfield and the harvest of corn. The withdrawal is a goodbye kiss that makes you have a memory of happiness, that loving kiss implies the hope sustained in the faith that we will be together again in the future. It is looking at the light that filters through the open window and illuminates the semi-darkness of a simple and humble room, discovering sitting down, a silent and uncomfortable peace that makes us think. However, deep in the bewilderment there is a happiness in knowing that the memory will not disappear. It is an uncertain new beginning, a new beginning, one begins again, but now with another understanding of the world.

By Way of Conclusion: From the "Death of the Subject" to Political Actors

Faced with the "death of the subject" of postmodern philosophy and the "crisis of Marxism," the problem of the "historical subject" in social movements has to be rethought, that is, it is the opportunity for a decolonized redefinition of the subject that occurs through their actions in the political field.

As Pierre Bourdieu (1998) has shown and taught: "In fact, 'subjects' are active and knowing agents endowed with a practical sense ...," that is, the subject is an agent that acts in various practical fields, within of a material sphere such as the ecological, economic, and cultural. The subject is not exhausted in a field but is articulated in an interlocking manner in infinite combinations with respect to each and all the fields through which daily life is traversed. All the practical fields of a subject are constitutive or intersected by a system.

Public institutions created in the political field inevitably intervene in the social life of the subject. The participating actors within the political field press from their unfulfilled material demands, thus the revindicating action occurs from the participation of the social actor as an agent of transformation.

It is in the search for material justice that awareness of the responsibilities for a dignified life is achieved. The learning process of the revindicative struggles is the one that throws us directly into the praxis of liberation that with its political action tries to go toward the root of injustice. Praxis is the element that makes one become aware of the material conditions needed to achieve a life with dignity, moving from the social subject to the social actor and, if possible, to the political actor, this within social movements.

Thus, and only thus, the one who acts under responsibility in solidarity with the other—excluded from a current system—and meets the ethical or material requirements for social change, can be consistent with the claim to promote a more just order. The act of liberation is the effective response to the demands of the oppressed.

Thus, the militant subject-actor is implicated with the social organization that form or adhere to in this relationship both (the militant and the organization) must be at the service of the mandate of the community to which they belong, in a constant leading by obeying to learn and teach to live with dignity, in the inalienable responsibility to produce, reproduce, and develop human life in the world, through the networks built and under construction of the different political actors or liberation fronts that revindicate and transform with their regional movements relations of domination and exclusion.

Note

1   In my work entitled *Vida Humana, Muerte y Sobrevivencia. La Ética Material En La Obra de Enrique Dussel* (México: CESMECA-UNICAH, 2015). I dedicated myself exclusively to comparing the ultimate foundation of three philosophers who have been concerned with building an ethical philosophy. In that work, I sought to understand the differences between the formal and the material in the ethics of Aristotle, Kant, and Dussel. At the end of the last century, with the advances of the different philosophical currents, Latin American thinkers sowed the possibility of an ethics that was beyond Europe or the United States of

North America. In the architectonics of the Ethics of Liberation by Enrique Dussel "human life is the content of ethics," therefore, ethics itself is human life, "life" considered not as a soul, but as the most radical materiality, that is, Heidegger's metaphysical entity, seen not as an entity, but as a victim of world geopolitics.

References

Bourdieu, P. (1998). *Practical Reason: On the Theory of Action*. Stanford University Press.

Dussel, E. (2013). *Ethics of Liberation: In the Age of Globalization and Exclusion*. Duke University Press.

Herrera, G. (2016). *Ensayos Heréticos. Crítica a La Subjetividad Moderna, Posmodernidad y Nihilismo*. México: La tinta del silencio.

Herrera, G. (2018). *Metodología de La Liberación Para Las Ciencias Sociales. Una Experiencia Práctica*. Chile: Cuadernos de Sofía.

Lagarde, M. (1997). *Los Cautiverios de Las Mujeres: Madres, Esposas, Monjas, Putas, Presas y Locas*, 70. Ciudad de México: UNAM (My translation).

Section IV

Social Movements

10

Experiences of Weaving: The Chilean Social Revolt as an Esthetic Proposal[1]

PALOMA GRIFFERO

The Fabric[2]

During the year 2019, I worked as a teacher in a school in Recoleta, a commune with great formal and informal commercial activity, and many inhabitants with scars resources. This commune is located in a popular and multicultural sector of the city of Santiago. In the school, we shared our space with people from different countries, mostly Latin American, and in each classroom we met people from the Dominican Republic, Costa Rica, Venezuela, Argentina, Bolivia, Chile, Peru, Colombia, Brazil, Haiti, among others. During that year, I was the teacher in charge of the visual arts class of the second cycle of elementary school, fifth to eighth grade, boys and girls between 10 and 14 years old. I worked with a little more than 500 students, whom I saw twice a week.

There was one question, posed at the beginning of an activity conducted in all classes, that changed the way we related to each other and to our diverse family/cultural backgrounds. The question was *why do we wear "parka"?* The activity was to make a small wallet, woven on a cardboard loom ready-made during class. The children, a bit surprised by the apparent absurdity of the question and without thinking too much about it, answered that it was to avoid the cold. Then, I questioned them again, this time about why a parka or jacket and not something else, which caused all the classes to look at me with some uneasiness, without understanding the question too much.

Therefore, I propose to the groups that we talk about the thermal oscillation of some European cities, such as Berlin, where in winter it is $-2°C$ in the morning and $3°C$ in the afternoon, which justifies the use of such a garment both in the morning and in the afternoon. However, in many of our Latin American countries, in the morning, both in autumn and winter, it is between 5 and $7°C$

and justifies its use, but at three o'clock in the afternoon, when we have reached 22°C, we carry the parka, scarf, and vest on our arms because it is too hot to wear them.

Leaving that image of the clothes in the arms, I show a video with images of different types of fabrics and looms, where it is clearly seen that there is a common garment that has different names depending on the Latin American country, but the same purpose: to protect from the cold in the morning, it does not cover the sun in the afternoon and is much more practical than the parka for our climatological reality. Garment that are named, according to their country of origin as poncho, sarape, blanket, shawl, aguayo, ruana, rebozo, or echarpe, and then I ask them if they know any of it.

At that moment, the children of all the classes open up and tell us about their experiences such as where and when they have seen these garments in their countries of origin. At the beginning of the unit, the students participate with a certain shyness, but during the weaving that we do during the classes, the children converse, they open up to the narration of their family experiences, they tell us how they progress in weaving with their mothers, uncles, grandmothers, and grandfathers; some teach us different ways of using our loom and different stitches. As Paulo Freire states in his *Eighth Letter*, "educators need to know what happens in the world of the children they work with, the universe of their dreams [. . .] What they know and how they know it outside the school" (Freire 2010, p. 120). The instance of collective weaving opens us to the knowledge of what each child is inside and outside the school.

They weave in groups of 2, 3, and even more than 10 children. We left the classroom and occupied the entire school with groups of weavers. One girl brought the aguayo where she had been transported as a child and taught us how to use it with a doll that we borrowed from another smaller class. Another girl brought and showed with great emotion, the bag that her grandmother knitted for her before she died and that was very similar to what we were doing. Many people, family members, teachers, girls, and children from other classes participated directly or indirectly in the creation of our weavings.

Weaving opens us up, excites us, summons us. We recognize ourselves as part of a grassroots community and share what we know to give meaning to the community we are as a school, and the one we build as a class.

At the end of the unit, at the end of our knitting, I ask again the initial question: *why do we wear a parka*, but today the answers are radically different. Children express themselves in a fluid, emotional, and profound way. They make reflections such as "because we do not know what we are," "because we want to imitate the Europeans, but I am Mapuche and I am proud of that," and "we can no longer feel ashamed of our families." It even happened that a group of migrant children, from the older class, asked to go to the younger class to talk to them about the importance of feeling proud of where they come from and of their families.

While the activity was taking place there was a change in the entire educational community, many of the students and even some teachers and workers began to attend school with blankets, sarapes, ponchos, shawls, and aguayos. With hand-woven bags, with pictures of their communities, with lunches more related to the land and less to fast food.

Almost simultaneously, at the end of this activity that lasted a little more than a month, in the news appeared groups of students who decided to jump the turnstiles at the entrance to the subway, demonstrating against the increase in public transportation fares. This action was the detonator of a great popular revolt that had been brewing throughout the year and that inspired the awakening of all our territories, an expression of protest to which the whole country joined, demanding dignity, claiming the possibility of collectively weaving our future. The Social Revolt was being woven in all territories.

Social Revolt

The Social Revolt was named by the press as a "Social Outburst" because of its supposedly unforeseen and surprising appearance on October 18. However, from the data of some situations prior to that date, it can be recognized that it was not something spontaneous or an outburst, but a revolt that took place prior to the date indicated by the press.

During 2019, numerous demonstrations called by various organizations took place. The first mass action of that year was the feminist march called on March 8 by the Coordinadora Feminista 8M, who estimated that around 400,000 women occupied the streets only in Santiago and close to one million throughout the national territory.[3] The demands raised ranged from stopping violence and abuses against women, through equal rights and opportunities, to the vindication of sexual and reproductive rights, such as free abortion. This march was the largest and most peaceful march to date in Chile since the return to democracy after the Pinochet dictatorship and could be considered the beginning of the Revolt. The occupation of the streets during the march was characterized by the number of performances, chants, and colors that covered the main avenues throughout the country. Feminist demands were thus made visible.

Another significant action that began the first semester of 2019 was the national stoppage of activities called by the Teacher's College, which took place in schools and high schools across the country from June 3 and lasted for 51 days, time in which around eighty thousand teachers participated and just over one million students stopped receiving classes normally. Regarding the reasons for this mobilization, the president of the Teachers' Association, Mario Aguilar, points out:

> We are asking for improvements in working conditions and, above all, attention to public education, which today is falling apart. There are schools that have plagues of mice, schools that do not have supplies to clean the bathrooms, schools where, on June 1st, teaching materials have not yet arrived (. . .) For all these reasons we are calling for an indefinite national strike. We hope that the Government comes out of its arrogance, its intransigence and resolves these issues that we are raising.[4]

During the period of the stoppage, numerous marches were held and spaces for debate and reflection were generated within the schools, but what characterized this mobilization was the enormous amount of videos that circulated through social networks with performances and protest songs interpreted by the teachers of each school. There were hundreds of songs and dances invented by teachers to generate popular awareness of the demands that led to the strike.

The ways of communicating the uneasiness of each of the school communities had a triple development: in the schools themselves, which were configured as a place of meeting and debate. The streets, through marches, murals, and performances. And in social networks, thus fulfilling the role of facilitator of the "social network" and fabric of demands and complaints, which are intertwined mainly on Facebook, Instagram, and Twitter. In this way, demands for education were made visible.

In parallel to the teachers' strike, on June 20, more than 150 people belonging to the movement for the right to housing, Ukamau, entered the offices of the Housing and Urbanization Service (SERVIU) of the Metropolitan Region, remaining inside the building for about four hours.

The demonstration was carried out due to the delay in the delivery of housing for more than 400 families, a fact that was committed for that month of June but that would have been postponed to March 2020.[5] Regarding this action, from the movement they declare: "We burst into an indolent institutionality, which did not respond to the right to Housing and City for the workers, for the popular sectors, for women and young people of our people."[6] Thus, claims for the right to housing are made visible.

Subsequently, in September, a large nationwide mobilization in defense of the environment took place. The cities with the largest gatherings were Santiago, Concepción, Antofagasta, and Valparaíso, where tens of thousands of people gathered to demand the improvement of environmental public politics in our country and around the world. Two of the reasons for the call are the scarcity of water in some cities due to the overexploitation of this resource for monocultures such as avocado for export and the massive intoxication of the population of Quintero and Puchuncaví, two cities in the region of Valparaíso, territories environmentally devastated by the high industrial concentration and product of that called "sacrifice zones," seriously affecting the daily life of the inhabitants of these sectors.[7] Thus, like this, different environmental claims are raised.

In August 2019, faced with the discontent of different sectors and the need for organization, a space for coordination for action was born, which was called Social Unity. Under the slogan "We are tired, We are united" this space is configured as the place of national articulation, originally configured by the main unions of the country, and subsequently brings together more than 250 social organizations Trade union, human rights, environmental, indigenous peoples, settlers, migrants, artistic-cultural, health sector, people with disabilities, feminists, university and secondary education, teachers, and academics organizations.[8]

During that year there were hundreds of calls of different nature and magnitude, since June there were strikes and mobilizations every week. Here we have only mentioned a few that give a glimpse of the feeling of a country with heterogeneous demands, with inhabitants who build different ways of linking and strengthening the social fabric, who seek in different ways to make themselves heard, using various strategies and the means at their disposal. Throughout 2019 a loom of polychromatic demands was woven and from within the communities emerged the force that allowed in October of that year, the outbreak of the Social Revolt.

On October 18, 2019, Chile faced the most critical moment for the government and for democracy. Of the 136 Santiago subway stations, 118 were damaged and, within this group, 32 were set on fire,[9] in the face of which the then president Sebastián Piñera mentioned "We are at war against a powerful, implacable enemy, who does not respect anything or anyone, who is willing to use violence and crime without any limit,"[10] declaring a curfew throughout the national territory, which extended until September 30, 2021, more than a year and a half, *supposedly* as a result of the COVID-19 health crisis.

All Metro stations have numerous surveillance cameras and constant surveillance by Carabineros (police force). However, more than three years after what happened, there is still no clarity about the real perpetrators of the arson attacks, it is only known that they emerged from restricted places and there are some recordings where unidentified police man are inside the metro station La Granja[11] and others where they are leaving just before the fires, but strangely there is still no record in the investigation, nor those responsible for burning or damaging simultaneously more than a hundred stations.

Let Them Eat Cake

Legend has it that in the midst of the famine that France was experiencing prior to the Revolution and faced with the impossibility of the population to buy even a loaf of bread, Marie Antoinette would have proclaimed the famous phrase *"Qu'ils mangent de la brioche"* (let them eat cake), which would have provoked the wrath of all the people. And, although there are numerous texts that deny the attribution to Marie Antoinette of that phrase, the nature of that statement and how credible it was for decades in various contexts makes evident the forms of power exercised during that period, with huge economic inequalities and the indolence of the monarchs in front of the precarious situation of the people under their command, which resulted in a Revolution that ended with the absolutist monarchy of Louis XVI and the guillotine as a symbol of justice.

That phrase, wrongly attributed to Marie Antoinette in various accounts, is credible because it reflects the feelings of the people about their rulers and makes evident the despotic attitude of the monarchy prior to the French Revolution. This situation can be compared with the attitude maintained by Sebastián Piñera and the people linked to his Government, who made numerous statements during 2019 and the period of Social Revolt, which only increased the discontent of the population. According to a survey conducted by Centro de Estudios Públicos (CEP), Piñera had only 6% approval of his presidential administration and 81% of those surveyed assured that the Executive acted "badly" or "very badly" in the face of the Revolt.[12]

Some of the statements that resonated the most from Piñera's environment were those made by the Minister of Finance, Felipe Larraín, at a press point, regarding the country's economic stagnation, he said that "for romantics, the price of flowers has fallen,"[13] which concluded with a laugh that made social networks burn expressing the widespread discontent at what was considered a mockery, similar to the invitation to eat cakes in the absence of bread.

Another phrase remembered was the one issued by the former president of the Santiago Metro, Clemente Pérez, who stated in an interview for national channel, "Dudes, this did not catch on. They are no more bullies, they have not won the support of the population (...) Chileans are much more civilized,"[14] regarding the demonstrations and evasions of students from paying for public transportation, actions generated in response to the increase of approximately 5% in fares ($30) and that marked the mediatic beginning of what the press called Estallido Social (Social Outburst).

José Antonio Kast (2020), an ally of Piñera and his government, who was later candidate for the presidency in the election together with Gabriel Boric, in March 2020 declared on his Twitter account:

> The marches have only brought violence and desolation for millions of Chileans. Criminals get on the social protest just to destroy the country and after five months, this has to stop. If we want to get to the Plebiscite, #NoMásMarchas #SalvemosChile.[15]

In this context, Sebastián Piñera became what Alberto Mayol (2021) pointed out as "the King Midas that Marxism had always dreamed of: everything he touched he turned into class consciousness," because every appearance or statement Piñera made, consequently provoked diverse and massive manifestations of criticism and disapproval. This annoyance was justified, since his statements did not differ too much in content from the phrase attributed to María Antonieta, ignoring and rejecting the national reality. Some of his most polemic phrases pronounced in different moments of that period of Revolt were:

> In the midst of this convulsed Latin America, our country is a true oasis', 'There was intervention of foreign governments', 'We are at war with a powerful enemy', 'I will reach the end of my government. I was democratically elected by an enormous majority of Chileans', 'No constitutional accusation against me will prosper', 'Human Rights have not been violated in Chile.[16]

In this same context, an audio message that the First Lady, Cecilia Morel, had sent to a friend was leaked:

> We are absolutely overwhelmed, it's like a foreign invasion, alien, I don't know how to say it (. . .) Please, let's keep calm, let's call people of good will, take advantage of rationing meals and we will have to decrease our privileges and share them with others.[17]

From these and other statements of a similar nature, it can be seen that people linked to the Government, instead of feeling challenged by the *face of the Other*[18] that manifests itself in the main avenues throughout the country, decide to act under civilizing principles similar to those put forward by the European invaders, for whom "the so-called conquest, in reality, is an emancipatory act, because it allows the barbarian to emerge (Kant's *Ausgang*) from his 'immaturity,' from his barbarism."[19]

In Chile, like the conquistadors, the numerous human rights abuses[20] would have been ignored as such, because it was the necessary mechanism to confront the *powerful enemy* and return to the *oasis* mentioned by Piñera, to the *civilized Chile* of Pérez; the violence exercised was the way to end the *delinquency* proposed by Kast.

However, despite the attempts of the hegemonic powers to stop the Revolt, the mechanisms used by the demonstrators meant a reconquest of the symbolic spaces of all the main cities of the country. This could be due to the fact that they would have followed the same phases of conquest developed by the European conquerors, retaking control of the bodies, the imaginary and the geographical spaces.

Conquest Phases

Modern Western thought, according to Boaventura de Sousa Santos (2010), divides social reality from what is *on this side of the line*, which responds to hegemonic and solipsistic thinking, from what is on *the other side of the line*, where there would be no real knowledge and would only be constituted by opinions, beliefs, superstitions. It can be argued then that the actions carried out by the demonstrators during the Social Revolt would be *on the other side of the line* proposed by de Sousa and, therefore, there was never respect or listening to what was manifested during the Revolt. An example of this was what happened with the Centro Cultural Gabriela Mistral and the Cine Arte Alameda,[21] both located in the Alameda, the nerve center of the Revolt in Santiago, and the quick intervention of the Government to dismantle statues and paint walls where numerous murals made spontaneously and collectively were painted during the marches or rallies,[22] and which reflected the diversity of demands that were being raised during that period.

The people who express themselves in the streets and their aesthetic manifestations are positioned *on the other side of the line,* just as the Indians were during the period of conquest. According to

Dussel (2011), in this colonizing principle the Indian is concealed, subsumed to the dominant culture, and would appear only as an anecdotal and folkloric fact, but in no way as a culture-other, in equal conditions for its experience and transmission. In this context, Enrique Dussel (1994) recognizes and defines three phases of conquest:

> After 'discovering' space (as geography), and 'conquering' bodies, as Foucault would say (as geopolitics), it was now necessary to control the imaginary from a new religious understanding of the world of life. In this way the circle could be closed and the Indian could be completely incorporated into the new established system: the nascent mercantile-capitalist Modernity—being however its 'other-face,' the exploited, dominated, concealed face.
>
> (Dussel 1994, p. 81)

The Indian, according to Dussel, is denied as an "other" and must assimilate the European forms, an invading culture, which permeates his symbolic world and takes him to a space of "non-being"; impeding, fetishizing, and making invisible his representations, forms of socialization, and conditions of his own existence. The same thing happened during the period of social revolt.

In recent decades, we have witnessed how the phases of conquest are still being applied. Geography, body, and spirit are configured as spaces in dispute. Geography is intervened, removing the ritual space of the encounter, the inhabitants are extracted from the roots, and the streets are paved for them to walk on.

We begin to move through what Marc Auge calls *non-places*, spaces that are spaces of transit or consumption, such as shopping malls, where there is a large confluence of anonymous people. They are spaces empty of symbols and meaning for the construction of community affectivities, they are "useful" places, they would not allow proximity, and proximity would be utilitarian and/or fictitious. They are random crowds of faceless beings, where bodies disappear in swarms without form or historical narrative that appeals to the collective memory.

As we are inserted daily in *non-places* and our bodies are placed at the service of the production and reproduction of capital, we can conclude that our ancestral spirituality would be asleep under the cloak of overmodernity, where the individual is exacerbated, the culture of individualism and consumption, as defined by Auge.

The third phase of conquest, that is to say, the domination over the imaginary, caused in Chile the uprooting and invisibilization of the archetypes and original myths, which would endure, however, in the unconscious of the peoples, but lacking a host to inhabit or a rite that could summon them. Nevertheless, during the protests developed from October 2019 to March 2020, different rites, expressions, and aesthetic manifestations took place throughout the national territory, thus awakening the deep and Indian soul of our country. Thus, as forms of anchoring with the territories, the bodies were manifested together and the different cultures were made visible in what could be called the Awakening, the Reconquest.

The Reconquest

During the Social Revolt developed in Chile, the three phases of conquest proposed by Dussel for the conquest of America can be appreciated, but this time it was the people who manifested themselves for the reconquest of territories, bodies, and the imaginary. The calls to take to the streets to express discontent were numerous, multitudinous and of different styles. Little by little the forms and times of demonstration were ordered.

Given that the Social Revolt was a moment of expression of diverse denunciations and social demands, it was initially developed without an order to unify, organize, or convene the different initiatives, such as marches and "cacerolazos" (pots and pans).[23] However, little by little and as the days went by, the meeting places, schedules, and forms of demonstration were organized.

The reconquest of geography developed at different levels, from the micro level through the organization of each neighborhood, to the macro level through the massive marches and mobilizations organized at the national level. But, in each instance, it was possible to see that, although the general demand was for greater democracy and social justice, demands linked to the cultures of each particular territory were simultaneously expressed.

Crucial to this organization was the creation of Unidad Social, a space for articulation mentioned above, which brought together more than 250 social organizations of all kinds. From this space were convened the Territorial Councils or Territorial Assemblies, instances that allowed the link between neighbors of most of the sectors that adhered to the Social Revolt. Likewise, in an interview, historian Daniel Fauré points out that the Assemblies and Territorial Councils allowed the articulation of dispersed groups that only met in instances of protest.[24] There were also cultural, feminist, environmentalist, and other cabildos of different motivations, which were not necessarily linked to Social Unity. Another instance of Cabildos that had an important presence during the period was the CAT, Coordinadora de Asambleas Territoriales (Coordinating Committee of Territorial Assemblies).

In the territories where the Cabildos took place, *whatsapp* groups of neighbors were set up, which later during the pandemic, were spaces that allowed organizational instances such as the Ollas Comunes[25] that sought to provide food for an important part of the population, since about 30% of workers in Chile, work informally.[26] In the absence of aid from the Government and the impossibility of going out to work in the streets, from Unidad Social we raised the slogan "Only the People Help the People" calling for the creation of grassroots popular organization, proposing instances of barter and collaboration, maintaining the motivation of the Social Revolt, and giving continuity to the political work of that period.

From a general organization at the macro level, people organize themselves at the micro and local levels. In the neighborhoods, neighbors gather in neuralgic spaces to demonstrate (caceroleos), to get to know and educate each other (Cabildos Territoriales) and, later, to feed themselves together (Ollas Comunes). In these spaces *the other* appears as an equal, with valid demands and the demands are accepted from the individualities, for the strengthening of the collectives.

In the sites convened for the large rallies, the spaces that Marc Auge points out as *non-places* are intervened. Train stations, bus stops, avenues, squares, sculptures, and monuments are intervened by the demonstrators. Altars with images and objects commemorating the dead and wounded; victims of police violence.

In the main avenues of each city, central squares, and at the exits of the busiest train stations, altars were built with images and objects symbolizing the demands of the different sectors and symbolizing the dead, wounded, and victims of police violence of the period. In downtown Santiago, interventions were made along the Alameda, where the display on the facade of the Gabriela Mistral Cultural Center (GAM), located 500 m from the Plaza de la Dignidad, stood out. The demonstrators turned this space into an "open blackboard" where they intervened collectively and spontaneously.

Different objects, paintings, fabrics, handkerchiefs, mosaics, flags, and posters were installed. The intervention varied constantly both in terms of messages and composition. Despite the government's insistence to dismantle this street art exhibition, it was constantly renewed and to this day it is still used as a blackboard open to the samples of passersby.[27]

As well as the facade and the street adjacent to the GAM, numerous transit spaces, clearly identifiable as *non-places*, were then configured as *places* with history, with social and political significances that are still maintained. Through the interventions of almost all the walls where the demonstrations circulate, the identity of those who are in the protest spaces is captured, the geographical conquest of the *places* of popular demonstration is achieved.

In the marches, our bodies congregate and become one that walks confidently and becomes unstoppable. Our bodies, different and complementary parts of a whole, of a great indivisible, polychromatic, and polyphonic body. As we present ourselves from our identities and demands, we see the colors that make up this pluriversal social fabric bloom and what were initially political marches become carnivals in which tinkus, music bands, poets, dancers, people dressed as different characters, giant dolls, banners and flags of all kinds, congregate, putting their bodies at the disposal of the collective through the expression of different artistic manifestations. Simultaneously, during this period, numerous slogans were created, and songs were sung in large numbers, such as "el Derecho de Vivir en Paz" by the communist musician Víctor Jara, murdered during the dictatorship, or "El Pueblo Unido," a protest song created by the composer Sergio Ortega and the group Quilapayún.

Dances and performances are created in which thousands of people participate, as in the case of the one developed by the feminist collective Las Tesis, who never imagined the impact that their performance "un violador en tu camino" ("A rapist in your way") would cause both nationally and globally. Regarding this, the member of the collective, Paula Cometa, says: "We did not think of it as a protest song, but as part of our performative work (. . .) But the truth is that the performance got out of our hands and the beautiful thing is that it was appropriated by others."[28]

The bodies inhabited what were once *non-places*, now conquered *places*. In these spaces, each body manifests its individuality, but not from individualism, but rather it raises its demands and gives its cultural practices for the weaving of a collective body. The bodies are made available in these marches/carnivals for the construction of the collective body. We reconquer our bodies.

By January 2020, at least 329 urban monuments throughout Chile would have been plastically intervened, reconfiguring their original function, 24 of them would have been removed or replaced, as happened in the city of La Serena, where protesters replaced the monument in honor of the Spanish conqueror Francisco de Aguirre by an indigenous sculpture, Milanka, installed as a tribute to the women of the Diaguita indigenous culture. As well as in La Serena, also in Concepción, in southern Chile, where hundreds of people tore down the sculpture of the Spanish conquistador Pedro de Valdivia.[29]

The statues and monuments that were intervened represented the conquest and the hegemonic powers. Faced with these symbols of power, the communities decide to intervene and give them a meaning that identifies them. The original political meaning of the monuments is changed, through interventions of different nature, these are re-signified and configured as spaces of ritual and memory. They become spaces comparable to sanctuaries, as they are configured as places of the extraordinary, of recognition of the original myths, as sources of collective and community strength.

During the protests that took place from October to March, rites, expressions, and esthetic manifestations appeared everywhere, awakening the deep and Indian soul of our country. They awakened forms of anchorage with the territories and their cultures. Ironically, the meaning of the monuments was reconfigured. In the end, the Government decides to remove many of the intervened sculptures, recognizing that it no longer exercises that symbolic referent, those monuments are no longer a referent of the citizenship. Mythical spaces are collectively created to reaffirm the identity and belonging of those who make up the community that rises in each territory. The imaginary is thus reconquered, completing the three stages of conquest proposed by Professor Dussel.

The Social Revolt, the Outburst of Aesthetics

In times of Revolt in Santiago, the Avenida Libertador General Bernardo O'Higgins, mostly known as La Alameda, was configured as the main space for marches and mobilizations. At one of its ends is located the former Plaza Baquedano, also called Plaza Italia, renamed by the protesters in 2019 as Plaza Dignidad or Plaza de la Dignidad[30] and was configured as the neuralgic place of the Social Revolt.

The "Plaza Baquedano" owes its name to a monument installed in the middle of the square, in honor of General Baquedano, military chief of the Chilean army, who played an important role during the War of the Pacific. This statue, due to the numerous and constant interventions of the demonstrators, had to be moved to the Military Historical Museum in June 2022. Thus, the hegemonic power must leave that significant territory configured as a conquest of the Social Revolt.

The now popularly known as Plaza Dignidad, most of the time it was constituted as a place of transit and could even be thought of as a clear example of a *non-place*. However, it could not be defined as such, since this is the space that summons the spontaneous meeting of the people before the great national joys such as the triumphs in soccer, the death of Pinochet, feminist marches,[31] and that, since October 2019, was a space in dispute, where constant and very violent clashes developed between the *First Line*, which is the most radical group of demonstrators, and the police, those who responded with bullets, pellets, tear gas, pepper spray, caustic soda in the water of the water car or vulgarly called *guanaco*; to stones and slogans, leaving dozens of dead, thousands of injured, and more than 400 people with eye damage.

The National Institute of Human Rights (INDH 2020b), an agency that is part of the Government, states that as of February 2020 "A total of 3,765 people have been injured, of which 427 cases show eye injuries, 34 of them with a diagnosis of eye loss or eye bursting."[32]

Plaza Dignidad is the border, the limit, the dividing point of the city of Santiago into two social classes. To the east is the "upper neighborhood," where the communes with the highest *per capita* income at the national level and, of course, the highest right-wing vote are located. And to the west are located the "slums" and less economically favored. This Plaza is the territory where the *abysmal invisible line* materializes, as stated by Boaventura de Sousa Santos,[33] who calls modern Western thought as an *abysmal thought*. Regarding this type of thinking, he points out:

> It consists of a system of visible and invisible distinctions, the invisible ones constituting the foundation of the visible ones. The invisible distinctions are established through radical lines that divide social reality into two universes, the universe of 'this side of the line' and the universe of 'the other side of the line'. The division is such that 'the other side of the line' disappears as reality, becomes non-existent, and is in fact produced as non-existent.[34]

Thus, social reality is divided into the universe of "this side of the line," the hegemonic, and the universe on the *other side of the line* or non-hegemonic, which disappears as a possible epistemic reality. "On the other side of the line, there is no real knowledge; there are beliefs, opinions, magic, idolatry" (de Sousa Santos 2013, p. 33).

From this colonizing principle, the protesters would be subsumed to the dominant culture[35] and would appear only as an anecdotal and folkloric fact, but in no way as a culture-other, in equal conditions for their experience, therefore the claims raised would not be considered as enforceable rights and are publicly minimized and even ridiculed, as it was exposed in previous pages, in the subchapter "Let them eat cake." The invisibilization toward those who are *on the other side of the line*, executed by those in the spaces of hegemonic power, is evident in statements such as that raised by Luis Castillo, Undersecretary of Assistance Networks, in July 2019, regarding the long waits of people in public health services. Faced with this, Castillo states that "patients always want to go early to a doctor's office, some of them, because they not only go to see the doctor but it is a social element, of social gathering,"[36] which is evidently a mockery of the needs of the people who are attended under this health system.

This contemptuous manner of those who are in the hegemonic spaces of power differs profoundly with the feelings of the general population. The results of a study carried out by the University of Chile assures that 85.8% of the population supports the Social Revolt and its demands,[37] which would indicate the null reception on the part of the Government to the citizen's feelings, to those who are installed *on the other side of the line*. The 85.8% of the national population would not be valid interlocutors, without voice, without rights. Those who demonstrate would not be *another* for the hegemonic power and would only exist as useful bodies for the production of capital and reproduction of labor.

The Social Revolt resignifies the territories, through its occupation and interventions, they are transformed into a lived text. In this context, the Plaza Dignidad is then configured as the maximum symbolic space of conquest, the struggle for the defense and occupation of the Plaza becomes crucial, since it is established as the symbolic *place* of Dignity. The *First Line confronts* the police in its contours, while inside the square, during the days of protests, a brass band plays a brass band that accompanies the demonstrators, while along the Alameda, numerous demonstrations are interwoven, which as we pointed out above, are true carnivals full of bodies expressing themselves, artistic displays of all kinds and diverse flags, being the most present the *Wenüfoye*, Mapuche flag that has become the main emblem of the germ of a new society that was clearly born and struggles to democratize the scenario,[38] vindicating the struggle of this people subjected for centuries. Also, as a symbol to highlight, the Chilean flag could be seen modified and dyed black, a design that began as an avatar in the Instagram profile of the Chilean composer Paz Court and spread quickly. This is how,

> In this context, an image emerged that went viral to such an extent that it became the unmistakable symbol of the outbreak: the Chilean flag stripped of its characteristic white, blue and red to show itself as an emblem in mourning, completely in black, where only the solitary star stands out, also darkened, but with its outline in white.[39]

These flags and others of all colors and diverse organizations could be seen every day around the Plaza Dignidad, territory that is established as the most mystical geographical space of the Revolt: the place of the meeting, the place of the rite. There, all the signs of transit are destroyed, the once established relationship of the body with the territory, functional to the transportation of the workers, is destroyed and we transform it into a residence, a settlement, people take root, settle down, it becomes a place of parking, of belonging. The resignification of the territory from the inhabiting of the bodies; the conquest of the square.

Faced with the numerous interventions made, the government decided to remove the statue of General Baquedano and leave the platform empty, which affirms the conquest of the space, the final transformation in the symbolic *place* of the triumph over the hegemonic and military power that was present throughout that period and maintained the dispute of the Plaza.

In this context, and as part of many of the activities that took place there, three indigenous totem poles built by Colectivo Originario were installed in front of Plaza Dignidad. In an interview, Mauricio Soto Paillalef, one of the members of the collective, explains that the three totem poles represent the three zones of the country. The northern zone is represented by the *Petroglyph Shaman Tilama*, belonging to the Diaguita culture and composed of three parts: the head symbolizes the deity Sun Inti, the heart is the spiritual portal and its belly is a flower, which refers to fertility. The center zone is represented by a *Chemamüll*, from the Mapuche culture. Specifically it is a *Domomamüll*, which refers to woman, life and nature and the energy that allows us to be reborn as people. And finally, the southern zone is represented by the sculpture of a *Selk'nam* spirit, which represents the Onas, to remember and represent the extermination to which they were subjected by the conquerors.

In the interview, Soto indicates that many people do not know the meaning of the statues, they come to ask and when they hear the explanation they feel represented by them. In that sense, Soto points out, "and that has been super good because in the end the sculptures are no longer ours, they belong to everyone."[40]

The installation of the totem poles places, at the center of the revolt, the struggle for the recognition of the indigenous peoples, the strength and perseverance of the struggle for autonomy is recognized in them and those who see them. As Mauricio Soto mentions, even without knowing in depth the meaning that these would originally have, identify with the struggles that these totem poles represent and the Plaza is further consolidated as the mythical place of the Revolt.

From the Aesthetic Object to the Aesthetics of the Object

In relation to these totems, Professor Jorge Martínez (2019) would say that they cannot be recognized as an "aesthetic object" under the consideration of what a "work of art" traditionally means, which must be transcendent to its context and historical time; it assumes a use value and exchange value, it calls for alienation as its observation becomes the relationship of people with "the thing," individually and preventing the relationship between people.

On the other hand, we will now talk about what Professor Martinez points out as indispensable for the construction of a Latin American Aesthetics: the consideration of the Esthetics of the Object. By the way, he mentions that now the object will appear as a space of semiosis, as a carrier of information and meanings for people in a community. The estheticity of the object would be granted by its cultural and communicative functionality, as specific expressive, and that goes beyond the mere utility of the object as an instrument.

Mauricio Soto, in stating that the three totem poles "now belong to all of us," agrees with Martínez, inasmuch as it is the community, from the social fabric, which gives them a significance that does not necessarily coincide with the meaning originally given by the indigenous peoples, or the reasons that the members of the Original Collective had for their construction. The totems would possess in themselves an esthetic constructed by a diverse community that defends the Plaza as a space of settlement during the context of the Revolt, a space that becomes the *place* where poly-chromatic claims are woven.

During the demonstrations, police forces try to retake control of the Plaza Dignidad. The confrontation between demonstrators and police becomes a symbolic struggle. Just as the statue of General Baquedano was imposed in the middle of the Plaza, so was the parka imposed on us for our winter days. The familiar fabric was replaced by the garment that is bought in a shopping mall and has a brand, but in no way a story. The foreignness of the parka could be likened to the *non-places* through which people without name or memory are forced to circulate, and the aguayo and the poncho is the *place*, the space with memory, where belonging and identification are evidenced. The struggle for the defense of the Plaza is the struggle for memory, for the dignity of the cultures that are interwoven in this territory.

The social movement reveals the true nature of the aesthetic object, as a fabric or a totem, which is not an autonomous value, but resides in the relations of belonging of the subjects in the communities, and each totem, fabric, song, dance, flag, actions, and objects present in this context is a mediation of the relationship between people and allows the experience of being community. A sense of community that Mariátegui gives to the force that lies in the myth. The author indicates that this is the genesis of the movement of the people. The Amauta points out that:

> The strength of revolutionaries is not in their science; it is in their faith, in their passion, in their will. It is a religious, mystical, spiritual force. It is the strength of the Myth. Revolutionary emotion, as I wrote in an article on Gandhi, is a religious emotion. Religious motives have moved from heaven to earth. They are not divine, they are human, they are social.[41]

The myths crystallize in those totems of the square, which in turn become icons that demarcate the ritual space as the space of the extraordinary. A ritual space and a space of encounter in the struggle that weaves diverse claims and makes evident the interdependence between different groups, but that walk together.

Dignity Square becomes, almost instinctively, the space of ritual pilgrimage and multitudinous encounter where people from everywhere claim the geographical conquest, the bodies dance as if they were one, and we recognize ourselves in the same rite of defense to our dignity and right to life. Place of symbolic persistence, ritual place that connotes the extraordinary, that gives you the strength of the community, you will receive strength by belonging, insofar as it is the ritual community that recognizes each singular person as belonging to it, and identification, insofar as each person recognizes in the symbolic values of the community his or her own space. Therefore, there is a double bonding mechanism, from the community to the individuals through belonging and from each person to the community through his or her own identification with the community's values.

Weaving the Reconquest

The Social Revolt made it possible to recognize the strength achieved by weaving together the different demands of the various communities that inhabit the different territories, when it is possible to place dignity and good quality of living at the center of the intentions, approached from the particularities of each organization, community, or territory. The strength, then, would be given by the notion of plurality and interdependence from the articulation of particularities.

The polychromatic and pluriversal organization reveals itself in the face of all signs and structures linked to uniformity to the order imposed from above. All the elements that are in the way of the marches and mobilizations are destroyed, those that represent the imposition of hegemonic power, such as statues, traffic lights, and signage. Likewise, elements and spaces that symbolize capitalism and its reproduction, such as large commercial monopolies or banks, are also intervened.

The Social Revolt allowed us to make ourselves heard from the streets, putting our bodies to work for the destruction of everything that prevents us from living the imaginaries and cultures of those who are located on the *other side of the line* and, also, allowed us to reconfigure spaces that before could be clearly identified as *non-places*, into spaces of meeting and listening. The signs of hegemonic external power are dismantled and in their place signs are constructed that allow the identification of the diverse communities that make up the social fabric.

Throughout the country, the struggle of the indigenous people is recognized and their cultures are vindicated, the value of the esthetic manifestations that emerge from the territories as an expression of the pluriversal, polyphonic, and polychromatic fabric that makes up this country is established as a principle. Today, Chile is a divided country, the marginalized assume awareness of marginality as a value, they become art occupying the streets, where culture is expressed in as many ways as the communities that inhabit them, from the diversity of the groupings present in the manifestations. Polychromy was the language that gave strength to the Social Revolt.

The three phases of conquest proposed by Dussel: geography, body, and imaginary are clearly reflected in the phases of reconquest developed by demonstrators throughout Chile during the Social Revolt, Plaza de la Dignidad being the neuralgic and most mythical space of the whole period. And as well as Plaza Dignidad, the squares and meeting spaces of the communities of different territories are constituted as ritual places of pilgrimage and meeting for the recognition *of the other*. They are configured as *places* of confirmation of belonging and identification with the community, the *place* conquered and defended even with life, mutilated bodies, and the eyes of the demonstrators.

The carnival is established as the conquest of polychromatic bodies, those who give themselves to the construction of a collective, indivisible, and pluriversal body. Spirituality emerges from the notion of the search for the roots, the mystique of the community and the original cultures of our territories, spaces of decolonization that come from a deep and collective feeling, which leads us to think about the construction of participatory democracy as new ways of relating to each other and building national politics.

However, something went wrong along the way and the result of the plebiscite on the new Constitution was rejected by an overwhelming 62% of the voting population and, consequently, the Constitution established in 1980, during the dictatorship of Augusto Pinochet, is still in force today.

Prior to the beginning of the Revolt, we articulated Social Unity, which functions as an assembly that brings together hundreds of organizations and defines as a fundamental principle the transformation of representative democracy toward a participatory democracy, for the definition of actions, so that everyone has a place both to give their opinion and to act. However, after a short time, situations began to emerge that made it clear that they were only declarations without support, because the declarations were contradicted by the actions.

The Social Unity Union Block was the strongest space, it brought together more people and more organizations, and they were not able to transform their traditional political practices. They were not listening to the other twelve Blocks or to what was happening in the street.

An example of this is the "Dignity Camp," which they organized behind the backs of other organizations. It was set up in front of the Palacio de Tribunales in December 2019[42] and could be thought of as an imitation of the *Occupy Wall Street* protest, the encampment set up in Zuccotti Park in October 2011.[43] In the Dignity Camp, the leaders of the most emblematic movements of the first marches, NO + AFP, Teacher's College, Ukamau, and a couple of other organizations that they define that should accompany them, converge. The members of the camp state that one of the purposes of the camp is to generate in this space a constant debate during the time they remain in this place.

However, there is a stage where people defined by the heads of the aforementioned movements speak, artists invited by personnel in charge of that, who are paid for their management perform. There was never a defense of the space, because they were never a threat to the hegemonic power, because they rigorously followed the verticalist ways of doing politics, contrary to the principles declared by Unidad Social.

There was no *place* to defend, there was no space for community building, they did not know how to read or respect the mystique of the Revolt and its polychromy, nor the spirit of the people mobilized and confronting in the Plaza Dignidad the violence of an entire system embodied in the Carabineros institution, which tirelessly and unethically attacked demonstrators.

The Camp was the unmistakable sign that the political practices of the leaders who were trying to lead the movement did not differ from the traditional political practices of representative democracy, thinking and deciding for the people they claimed to represent. As a result, a deep division was created in the protest against the system.

One could even suggest the existence of an abysmal line between the social leaders who behave or adhere to traditional political parties, being inserted and relatively comfortable in a political system of representative democracy. And on the other hand, the demonstrators came from the territories, from environmental, cultural, feminist groups . . . who shouted in the Alameda and in the Plaza Dignidad, for a Popular Constituent Assembly, a Constitution written from the territories and with active, deliberative, and situated citizen participation.

From the demonstration spaces that demanded a Constituent Assembly and that were convened in the Dignity Square, the People's List emerged as a functional political party for the election of candidates to draft the New Constitution based on the principles exposed during the Social Revolt. They managed to win 27 of the 155 seats, but quickly lost strength as a political party, because most of them did not meet the profile of a traditional politician and, in a large percentage, were people without previous militant life in political parties. That was precisely one of their qualities.

When confronted with the writing of a new Constitution, those candidates followed the same logic put forward during the Social Revolt. They presented a proposal for a Constitution for a participatory people, concerned about the environment, indigenous peoples, feminists. They were concerned about the Political Prisoners of the Revolt and also to vindicate inclusive participation. It was even a revolutionary Constitution from several aspects.

The proposed Constitution could be openly called decolonial, because of the content worked on, because it's made with contributions from the citizenry, it addresses the diversity present in the country, among other factors. But, neither the people of the Government, nor the leaders of the political parties of the center and left, wished to approve it as it was drafted by the 155 Constituent Convention members elected by popular vote for such purposes.

These advances, not even the traditional left was able to understand it, let alone the right, who were in charge of convincing, even from some television programs, that the new Constitution was communist and giving such absurd arguments as that there would be no right to property rights over their houses. In general, almost anything can be expected from the right, but leaders of the traditional left betrayed the proposal built in the Constitutional Convention, because they were not willing to support a Constitution where they did not have the influence that, they thought, corresponded to them for being "the left."

As a result, the left fractures.

It is not by chance that it was Guillermo Teillier, leader of the Communist Party, who had the mission of reading the agreement made with the political parties of the center and left, the agreement made behind closed doors, to approve the constitutional proposal, but then to carry out the relevant reforms.[44] It could easily be interpreted as a subtle (or perhaps not so subtle) way of expressing their dissatisfaction with the lack of participation of traditional politicians in the process of drafting the new Constitution.

Finally, the Constitution proposed by the Constitutional Convention was rejected by 62% of the country and, today, a proposal for a new Constitution is being drafted by the Commission of Experts elected by the Senate and the Chamber of Deputies, but without direct citizen participation. When the proposal is finished, it must be delivered to the Constitutional Council of the Congress, who may modify it to elaborate the final text.[45]

At the same time, Congress is passing laws that are deeply repressive toward demonstrators and others that grant greater freedom of repression to the police forces,[46] who still remain largely unpunished for the systematic violations of human rights that took place during the Social Revolt.

The struggle for the reconquest is not only political, it is the struggle for the dignity of the peoples that inhabit this territory, it is the recovery of our bodies, it is the freedom to think from the imaginaries that inhabit and coexist subsumed before the hegemonic narrative.

In this context, it is urgent to remember and to feel ourselves again. To remember together that we have the strength to rise again, that in our hands are the threads ready to weave again a network that brings us together, that unites us in a definitive way. To weave together from the inside out and from what we are, to weave again together, our emancipation nets.

Notes

1 This article contains several references, directly or indirectly, from the text I wrote, "Revuelta Social En Chile, La Reconquista Desde El Estallido de La Estética." *Anánsi. Revista de Filosofía* (2022). As part of the Centro de Investigación de Estéticas Latinoamericanas (CIELA), Universidad de Chile.

2 This section has been built based on a text I wrote as part of Centro de Investigación de Estéticas Latinoamericanas (CIELA), Universidad de Chile (Paloma Griffero 2021). Organized by the Iberoamerican Research Center in Education.

3   CNN Chile (n.d.).
4   Diario UChile (2019).
5   Rodrigo Fuentes (2019).
6   Ukamau Chile Administrator (2019).
7   Michelle Carrere (2019).
8   Paloma Griffero (2020).
9   Rodolfo Carrasco (2020).
10 Meganoticias (2019).
11 Mentiras verdaderas La Red (2022).
12 Tómas González (2019).
13 The Clinic (2019).
14 Estallido Social (2019).
15 José Antonio Kast (2020). *Twitter*, March 2, https://twitter.com/joseantoniokast/status/ 1234577702125998081.
16 El Periscopio (2020).
17 BBC News World (2019).
18 Emmanuel Levinas (2005).
19 Enrique Dussel (2012).
20 INDH (2020a).
21 El Mostrador (2020).
22 El Mostrador.
23 The cacerolazo is a form of protest, in which discontent is expressed through the noise caused by banging pots or pans, usually with a wooden spoon. The cacerolazos can take place from homes or in specific spaces. During the Revolt, the cacerolazos took place in meeting points defined by the neighbors, most of them participants of the Territorial Councils and later, in pandemic, leaning out of the windows.
24 José Ojeda (2021).
25 The Ollas Comunes are instances of self-management and popular organization to solve food problems, which usually operate through the donation of food or money. A group of volunteers cooks the food in specific spaces and then distributes it to those who need it.
26 National Institute of Statistics (2020).
27 Variuos Artists (2022).
28 Ana Pais (2019).
29 R. Montes (2020).
30 Cristóbal Hernández Serrano (n.d.).
31 Alejandro Gana Nuñez (2021).
32 INDH (2020b).
33 Boaventura de Sousa Santos (2009).
34 Santos, 31.
35 Dussel, *Filosofía de La Liberación*.
36 El Mostrador (2019).
37 Sandra Serrano and Daniel Vázquez (2013).
38 Fernando Pairican (2019).
39 César Tudela (2020).
40 Karen Astorga, Mauricio Soto Paillalef, and Mapuche Sculptor (2020).
41 José Carlos Mariátegui (1950).
42 Sebastian Barraza and Emol (2019).
43 Javier Antonio Enríquez Roman (n.d.).

44   CNN Chile (2022).
45   Senate (2023).
46   Latin American Observatory on Environmental Conflicts OLCA (2023).

References

Astorga, K., Paillalef, M.S., and Sculptor, M. (2020). That they burned the totem only made the material burn, but not what it symbolizes. *El Desconcierto* February 8. https://www.eldesconcierto.cl/tipos-moviles/2020/02/08/mauricio-soto-paillalef-escultor-mapuche-que-hayan-quemado-el-totem-solo-hizo-que-ardiera-la-materia-pero-no-lo-que-simboliza.html.

Barraza, S. and Emol (2019). Mesa de Unidad Social Initiates New Protest and Sets up Camp in Front of the Palacio de Tribunales. *Emol* December 9. https://www.emol.com/noticias/Nacional/2019/12/09/969812/Nuevas-formas-de-manifestarse-campamento.html.

BBC News World (2019). Chile protests: Controversy after first lady cecilia morel compares demonstrations to "an Alien Invasion". *BBC News* October 23, https://www.bbc.com/mundo/noticias-america-latina-50152903.

Rodolfo Carrasco (2020). *Piñera Calls to Take Care of Public Transportation Is Total Reopening of Santiago Metro Stations.* September 23. https://www.df.cl/economia-y-politica/gobierno/pinera-llama-a-cuidar-el-transporte-publico-en-reapertura-del-total-de.

MichelleCarrere(2019).*Mongabay.*November 13.https://es.mongabay.com/2019/11/puchuncavi-quintero-crisis-social-en-chile/

CNN Chile (n.d.). Coordinadora Feminista 8M puts the number of people who marched in Santiago at 400thousand.*CNN*https://www.cnnchile.com/8m/coordinadora-feminista-8m-cifra-en-400-mil-las-personas-que-marcharon-en-santiago_20190309/.

CNN Chile (2022). These are the 5 points of the officialist agreement to reform the eventual new constitution. *CNN Chile* August 11, https://www.cnnchile.com/pais/acuerdo-reformas-oficialismo-nueva-constitucion_20220811/.

De Sousa Santos, B. (2013). *Descolonizar el saber, reinventar el poder*. Santiago: LOM.

Diario UChile (2019). *Colegio de Profesores Convoca a Paro Nacional Indefinido*. June 2. https://radio.uchile.cl/2019/06/02/colegio-de-profesores-convoca-a-paro-nacional-indefinido/.

Dussel, Enrique, (2012). 1492, El encubrimiento del otro. Hacia el origen del mito de la modernidad. Obras Selectas XIX, Buenos Aires.

Dussel, E. (2011). *Filosofía de La Liberación*. Fondo de Cultura Económica: Ciudad de México.

Dussel, E. (1994). *1492, El encubrimiento del Otro: hacia el otrigen del mito de la modernidad*. La Paz, Bolivia: UMSA Facultad de Humanidades y Ciencias de la Educación. Plural editores.

Freire, P. (2010). *Cartas a quien pretende enseñar*. Buenos Aires: Siglo veintiuno editores.

Fuentes, R. (2019). Ukamau movement protests for delay in housing delivery. *Uchile Newspaper* (June 20): https://radio.uchile.cl/2019/06/20/movimiento-ukamau-protesta-por-retraso-en-entrega-de-viviendas/.

González, T. (2019). Historic: CEP survey places Piñera as the president with the lowest approval in 30 years. *Uchile Newspaper* January 16. https://radio.uchile.cl/2020/01/16/historico-encuesta-cep-situa-a-pinera-como-el-presidente-de-mas-baja-aprobacion-en-30-anos/.

Griffero, P. (2020). Social unity: Where we are and where we are going. *El Desconcierto* (February 4): https://www.eldesconcierto.cl/opinion/2020/02/04/unidad-social-en-que-estamos-y-para-donde-vamos.html.

Griffero, P. (2021). Tejiendo Nuestras Redes de Emancipación. In: *100 Cartas Para Paulo Freire de Quienes Pretendemos Enseñar* (ed. F.G. Vergara). Santiago: Ariadna Ediciones.

INDH (2020a). *NHRI Delivers New Report of Figures Four Months After the Beginning of the Social Crisis*. Insituto Nacional de Derechos Humanos (INDH) https://www.indh.cl/indh-entrega-nuevo-reporte-de-cifras-a-cuatro-meses-de-iniciada-la-crisis-social/.

INDH, (2020b). *NHRI Turns in Balance a Year After the Social Crisis*. October 16. https://www.indh.cl/indh-entrega-balance-a-un-ano-de-la-crisis-social/.

Mentiras Verdaderas La Red (2022). *Telesurveillance Footage of the Day the La Granja Subway Burned*. April 27. https://www.youtube.com/watch?v=6QWoV9mAf9k.

Latin American Observatory on Environmental Conflicts OLCA (2023). Ley Gatillo Fácil y Conflictividad Socioambiental: Los Derechos Humanos En Jaque. *Uchile Newspaper* April 7. https://radio.uchile.cl/2023/04/07/ley-gatillo-facil-y-conflictividad-socioambiental-los-derechos-humanos-en-jaque/.

Levinas, E. (2005). *Humanismo Del Otro Hombre*. México: Siglo XXI.

Mariátegui, J.C. (1950). *El Alma Matinal*, 22. Lima: Amauta.

Martínez, J. (2019). *Materiality and Transmateriality in Mariategui's Aesthetics*, vol. XLV, no. 89 (1st semester):, 65–82.

Mayol, A. (2021). The oclocracy of disagreements. In: *Analysis of the Year 2020. Society, Politics, Economy, Culture, Issues*, 77. Santiago: Universidad de Chile https://www.uchile.cl/dam/jcr:aa2fe8fb-fa71-4160-a3b3-0dba8b1a3664/analisisdelanio2020.

Meganoticias (2019). *President Piñera: 'We Are at War against a Powerful Enemy'*. October 19. https://www.youtube.com/watch?v=r8BrqEDLEIs.

Montes, R. (2020). Chile protests question official history of sculptures. *El País*, January 23, 2020.

El Mostrador, (2019), *Undersecretary Castillo Affirms That People Go Early to Consultorios Because It Is an Element of "social Gathering"* July 11.

Mostrador, E. (2020). Shutting up the street: Centro GAM and Arte Alameda Condemn the 'Erasure' of their facades that recorded the history of the social outburst. *El Mostrador*, February 19.

National Institute of Statistics (2020). *Statistical Bulletin: Labor Informality*. Instituto Nacional de Estadística (INE): Santiago https://www.ine.gob.cl/docs/default-source/informalidad-y-condiciones-laborales/boletines/2019/bolet%C3%ADn-informalidad-laboral-trimestre-octubre-diciembre-2019.pdf?sfvrsn=10ec75a_4.

Nuñez, A.G. (2021). Estructuración Del Espacio Público Entre Política y Fiesta: El Caso de Plaza Italia En Santiago, Chile. *Revista de Urbanismo* 44: June 2021), http://orcid.org/0000-0002-1884-643X.

Ojeda, J. (2021). Two years after the revolt: The key role of the territorial assemblies. *Radio JGM* October 4, https://radiojgm.uchile.cl/rol-asambleas-territoriales-revuelta-social/.

José Antonio Kast (2020). Twitter, March 2, https://twitter.com/joseantoniokast/status/1234577702125998081.

Fernando Pairican, (2019). *The Mapuche Flag and the Battle for Symbols*. December 6, https://www.ciperchile.cl/.

Ana Pais, (2019). Las Tesis on 'A Rapist on Your Way'. December 6, 2019. https://www.bbc.com/mundo/noticias-america-latina-50690475.

El Periscopio, (2020). *'Estamos En Guerra': Piñera's Most Controversial Phrases After the Social Outburst*. February. https://www.elperiscopio.cl/noticias/pinera-frases-polemicas-estallido-social/.

Roman, J.A.E. (n.d.). Two American experiences: Occupy Wall Street and Baltimore. *Aposta. Revista de Ciencias Sociales* 80: 129–147. http://apostadigital.com/revistav3/hemeroteca/jenrique.pdf.

Senate (2023). *Constituent Process: Expert Commission Is Installed and Elects Board of Directors*. March 6, https://www.senado.cl/noticias/proceso-constituyente/proceso-constituyente-se-instala-comision-experta-y-elige-mesa-directiva.

Serrano, C.H. (n.d.). De Plaza Italia a Plaza de La Dignidad, de Memorial de Guerra a Lugar de Memoria. *C´ Revista Común* https://revistacomun.com/blog/de-plaza-italia-a-plaza-de-la-dignidad-de-memorial-de-guerra-a-lugar-de-memoria/.

Serrano, S. and Vázquez, D. (2013). Principios de Aplicación. Núcleo Básico, Progresividad, No Regresión y Máximo Uso de Recursos Disponibles. In: *Los Derechos Humanos En Acción: Operacionalización de Los Estándares Internacionales de Los Derechos Humanos*. Ciudad de México, México: FLACSO.

Social, E. (2019). Former Metro Director, Clemente Perez, Challenges Students: 'Cabros, Esto No Prendió'. *Estallido Social* October 16.

de Sousa Santos, B. (2009). Beyond abysmal thinking: From global lines to an ecology of knowledge. In: *Epistemological Pluralism* (ed. L. Olave et al.), 31–84. La Paz, Bolivia: Muela del diablo Editores, Comuna, CLACSO, CIDES-UMSA.

de Sousa Santos, B. (2010). *Decolonizar El Saber, Reinventar El Poder*. Ediciones Tricle: Montevideo.

The Clinic, (2019). *For Romantics, the Price of Flowers Has Fallen*. October 18, https://www.theclinic.cl/2019/10/08/video-para-los-romanticos-ha-caido-el-precio-de-las-flores-ministro-felipe-larrain-y-su-particular-analisis-economico/.

César Tudela, (2020). *When the Flag Was Dyed Black: History of a Symbol of Resistance*. La Voz de Los Que Sobran,October18.https://lavozdelosquesobran.cl/cultura-b/cuando-la-bandera-se-tino-de-negro-historia-de-un-simbolo-de-resistencia/18102020.

Ukamau Chile Administrator (2019). 2 Years after the massive takeover of SERVIU RM by Ukamau, June 20, 2019. Anticipation of the Popular Revolt. *UKAMAU* (June 20): https://ukamau.cl/2021/06/21/a-2-anos-de-la-masiva-toma-del-serviu-rm-por-ukamau-20-de-junio-2019-anticipo-de-la-revuelta-popular/.

Variuos Artists, (2022). *Wall 18-O*. https://gam.cl/conocenos/edificio-gam/coleccion-de-arte/muro-18-octubre/.

11

Migration Justice in Times of Pandemics in the Borderland of Ciudad Juárez/El Paso

LUIS RUBÉN DÍAZ CEPEDA

Refugees driven from country to country represent the vanguard of their people.

Hannah Arendt

Latinx philosophy literature is abundant in how immigrants have fought for their rights once they are established in their new places. However, I believe there is a need to elaborate on the questions of migrants becoming or not politized while they are in transit, and, if they do so, should they be considered as legitimate active political actors? In this chapter, I will argue that the answers to both questions are positive.

I start my argument by pointing out that there is a record number of people in mobility in search of refuge. However, despite the adverse circumstances that migrants face in the countries they are escaping from and the threats they face in their transit, destination countries have increased the security of their borders in an attempt to prevent poor and racialized migrants from colonized countries to arrive in their territories. For the most part, they are deemed as not necessary to the market, in consequence, they are considered a null population whose lives are disposable to the modern-capitalistic system.[1] Yet, in a token of the liberal paradox, in order to keep the narrative that the capitalist system is the only way to improve the living conditions of humanity, metropolitan countries accept a very small percentage of documented migrants, proving they meet the criteria established by the former. Usually, these criteria are set according to the interests of the metropolitan countries without listening to migrants themselves. The colonial powers take as "good migrants" those that accept and play this representation of the submissive migrant grateful to them and willing to do as told, as Ariel. On the other hand, they characterize as "bad migrants" those that, as Caliban, challenge the system and offer some resistance to the commands of the powerful. I propose then, that by openly protesting the system, the "disobedient migrants" become political actors.

Struggles for Liberation in Abya Yala, First Edition. Edited by Luis Rubén Díaz Cepeda and Ernesto Rosen Velásquez.

I am using migrants as a comprehensive term that encapsulates economic migrants, returned migrants, displaced people, and asylum seekers. The common factor they have is that, for the most part, push not pull factors take them to set out their way. They leave their communities because harsh economic, criminal, and political violence makes their lives unfeasible. I am defining a political actor as a person that becomes aware that the ill conditions where they live are not due to a personal circumstance, but to the colonial matrix of power that oppresses them. Because of this awareness, they look for people in the same circumstance and level of consciousness and organize to fight back against the system that oppresses them. They do so as *people* with full capacity of agency, who are willing and able to make decisions. In order to show this, I will talk about the collective actions that migrants have self-organized such as caravans, camps, and protests. These actions can be conceived as acts of civil disobedience, which some may say are unlawful, for in-transit migrants are not citizens of the countries where they are passing by. However, Dussel's politics of liberation provides a response to this objection: when a law is detrimental to life, it is legitimate to break it.

To summarize, the current modern capitalistic system has created a null population, whose lives are disposable to the metropolitan countries. However, in order to maintain a good image of humanitarian countries and capitalist modernity as the only path to reach the well-being of societies, metropolitan countries offer refuge to some of the people that ask for protection in the North. Migrants are divided by the colonial countries as the "good" and the "bad" migrant, where the first is submissive and the latter is the one that becomes aware that their scarce living conditions are not due to a personal failure, but rather the consequence of a world system based on class, race, gender, and sexuality classification of people designed to favor the powerful and keep other people oppressed. When they become aware of this, they reclaim their dignity and demand their rights. I argue then that when they make that movement, they transition from being passive people in disgrace to active political actors, capable of challenging the system.

Historical Context

Through his concept of coloniality of power, Anibal Quijano (2020) has shown that the current modern/capitalist system, which has caused an exponential increase in economic inequalities worldwide, has its origins at the beginning of the sixteenth century with the conquest and colonization of America and the subsequent expansion of capitalism. This world system was, and still is, based on the classification of people based on their class, race, and gender where non-European-white-Christian males are deemed inferior.[2] Elaborating on this concept, Maria Lugones (2010), among other decolonial feminists, have added the classification of people based on their sexuality. This classification of people is the basis of the colonial matrix of power that elites from the colonizer countries and their allies in the colonized countries have implemented to appropriate labor and the resources of the planet, which have caused natural disasters, violence, and poverty all around the world.

Because of these changes, inhabitants of the peripheric countries are more vulnerable and are now increasingly being forced to migrate to the North looking for the material conditions that would allow them to live. It is estimated that nearly 90 million people worldwide have been forcibly displaced.[3] Most of them are rejected by the colonizer countries when asking for admittance, and even more, the few that are admitted suffer discrimination in the receiving countries. As argued by

Grosfoguel (2003), colonial immigrants—defined as those immigrants from peripherical locations that come to metropolitan countries—are racialized and discriminated against, which encumbers them to reach the same level of social and economic conditions as migrants from the North. While European/white/Christian migrants are welcome to relocate into the metropolitan countries, migrants from the Global South are rejected and discriminated against through an impeding legal migratory system.

Historically, migration to North America has occurred across the border between the United States and Mexico, especially through Texas where immigrants sought to enter the United States surreptitiously. The number and demographic composition of this migratory flow were stable. However, at the end of 2013, it had a notable increase in the number of people. The composition of this migratory flow also changed, with an increase in the number of family groups (mainly women with children) and unaccompanied infants who turned themselves in to be arrested by migration officials to later request political asylum.

The 45th President of the United States (2017–2021) was especially hard on immigrants as he promoted an incendiary discourse and actively attacked immigrants with aggressive measures such as allowing US border officials to refuse to allow people to pursue asylum claims, the criminal persecution of asylum seekers, and the separating of children from their families.[4] Forty-five also implemented the Migrant Protocol Protection (MPP), a program that made asylum-seekers wait in México—sometimes for even two years—for their hearing in an immigration court. Also, on March 20, 2020, he reinstalled Title 42, which allowed first-contact immigration officers to immediately return asylum-seekers without a chance to present an asylum petition under the excuse of them representing a health hazard to American citizens. It is also important to notice that during his administration, México's containment of Central Americans increased.[5]

While as a candidate, President Biden (2021–) promised a benevolent migratory agenda, this promise had been partially fulfilled. MPP was derogated and raids inside the United States have been reduced, but Title 42 continued being enforced up to 23:59 of Thursday, May 11, 2023, when the COVID emergency was officially declared ended and there was no longer a medical justification for the use of Title 42. At that time, Biden's administration reinforced the use of Title 8, which makes migrants crossing the border unlawfully subject to criminal penalties and a five years ban to come into the United States. Biden's administration also implemented CBP One as the legal way for asylum-seekers to apply for a petition from México without turning themselves physically in at the border ports of entry. This app has reduced the number of migrants on the borderline, but, as there are some problems with it (limited facial recognition, it is written in English, and there is a limited number of appointments available, among other issues) some migrants have returned to official and unofficial ports of entry in the border cities to turn themselves to the border officially asking for asylum or parole. Also, during the first days after the end of Title 42, it has been possible to see a change in México's migratory policy as it stopped granting humanitarian permits to transit for 45 days to migrants who want to reach the border with the United States in a safe way.

In the case of México, in major cities, such as Monterrey and Mexico City, as well as in border cities where there is a large concentration of migrants, local governments have created offices to manage the situation. Sometimes, they created councils where in some instances they invite international institutions such as the United Nations Office of the High Commissioner for Human Rights (OHCHR), and International Organization for Migration (IOM), and the United Nations Children's Fund (UNICEF), as well as local organizations, and academics. Despite the advice of humanitarian organizations, sometimes authorities reproduce the colonial discourse and take a xenophobic approach where migrants are portrayed as criminals or invaders that should be prevented from coming to the cities. In a better-case scenario, authorities have in mind the migrants´ interests and attempt to look for ways to protect and assist them. However, in both cases, for the most part, migrants themselves are not asked what they think. Arguably, this is so because they are not considered equals that should have a say in what is best for them and the receiving community, but as Ariel, gratefully must accept what the master has already decided. In a few words, they are not thought of as full beings with the capability to represent themselves.

Coloniality of being

The concept of the coloniality of being was initially developed by Walter Mignolo in 1995 and his ideas were taken up by Nelson Maldonado-Torres (2007) in the essay "On the Coloniality of Being" where—first through Emmanuel Levinas and later through the ideas of Enrique Dussel and Juan Carlos Scannone—he woke up "from what I would call my phenomenological and ontological dream." Maldonado-Torres explains that to the question, what is the Being? Heidegger answers that it is the Being of beings, the horizon on which beings are understood. Being and entities are separated by ontological differences. However, of all the beings in the world, there is one that is special, the *Dasein* (being-there), the human being, who is the only being capable of understanding the Being. But even in his singularity, the human being is thrown into a world already defined by history, laws, social relations, etc. . . . in such a way that a human being may get lost in the community, without a uniqueness. How then can a human being be authentically himself? Maldonado-Torres continues by explaining that "Heidegger's response is that authenticity can only be achieved by resoluteness, and that resoluteness can only emerge in an encounter with the possibility, which is inescapably one's own, that is, death."[6] No one else can die for you and it is also a unique and exceptional act. However, this exceptionality, Maldonado-Torres continues, is true only for the victors of the war, because for those of us who live in colonized countries, the possibility of death is something that happens to us daily.

The coloniality of being then refers above all to the living experience of the subject of coloniality, in the bodies of people whose own humanity is denied and/or questioned. Building from Quijano's theory of the coloniality of power and Enrique Dussel's *ego conquiro*, Maldonado-Torres argues that the concept of race that was established in the the sixteenth century was developed by an attitude characterized by a permanent suspicion of the humanity of the other. The Puerto Rican philosopher characterizes this attitude as racist/Manichaean imperial misanthropic skepticism. It could also be represented as an imperial attitude, which defines the modern imperial man. Misanthropic skepticism then subtly, but equally harmfully, changes the question asked in the colony to the conquered groups: do you have rights? To the question of coloniality, why do you think you have rights?[7]

This attitude of doubting the humanity of the other has configured capitalist modernity in such a way that a minority benefits from the oppression of the majority that was defeated in the conquest and later in the colonial enterprise. This ethics of war marks the colonial difference where the defeated enemy is seen as a servant, no longer circumstantial, but natural whose body is available for the master to satisfy his sexual desire or his need of labor exploitation. This intersubjective relationship of domination has been naturalized, ceasing to be an exceptional situation to become the code that guides conduct between the powerful and the non-powerful, creating a world where the people who inhabit the global South live in a clear situation of oppression and we are blamed for it.

When it comes to people in mobility, once again, the powerful embedded in the privileges of Western modernity repeats the colonial attitude and denies humanity to migrants. Migrants are not thought of as full human beings, but as creatures that can be defined by the powerful. Just as the colonizer thought of African and indigenous people as men-not, neo-colonialists portray migrants from the Global South as entities as not having the strong character and discipline that would bring them out of poverty or as short of moral qualities and courage to stand by themselves in their countries of origin against the corrupt governments that keep them oppressed. Once again, the colonizers hide their oppressing actions in the darker side of modernity and blame the colonized for its consequences.[8,9] The denial of the humanity of migrants can be perceived in the words that are used to refer to them as animals. They are called *pollos* and a human smuggler is referred to as a *pollero*,[10] as if the former were farm animals that can be controlled by the latter.

This entitlement over the bodies of the migrants is reflected in the way they are treated, as merchandise, as if they were mere objects that can be traded as the powerful decide. During their transit in México, it is common that women, but also men and children, to be sexually abused by the people controlling the migration routes. Their bodies are taken as a levy for allowing them to transit through a land where they are not welcome. Also, it is common that men to be kidnapped into slavery and put to work for the *carteles* or abandoned in the desert after they have paid to be smuggled into the central countries. Migrants' bodies are not only used to satisfy sexual and monetary desires but also the ego *conquiro* of the powerful and their need for power and control over other people by demanding absolute obedience to the oppressors and their institutions. That is the case of the documented migration systems when it classifies which asylum seeker has suffered enough and "deserves" to be protected by the metropolitan countries under "credible fear" claims. Those asylum-seekers who according to the central countries do not deserve their protection are sent back to the dangerous situations they were running from, and which were caused by those same countries that are now denying protection to asylum-seekers.

On their way to look for entry into the United States, migrants inhabit the cities of the peripheric countries adjacent to the center. But here, in colonized land among people that are also inhabitants of the Global South, they are discriminated against too.[11] Some local citizens look at migrants as if the latter were guilty of the circumstances that have forced them to leave their communities. They accuse them with questions such as: Why are you bringing your children? Why are you sleeping in the street? Why do you not work? This look pretends to command migrants to hide or to "stay in their place" by fitting in what a migrant should look and behave like.[12] In order to survive, asylum-seekers are supposed to make themselves fit into the narrative of the sad and obedient migrant that should be grateful for whatever aid he is given. They are forbidden to be happy or show a will, as they are supposed to obey the orders of everybody without asking questions, even less to refuse to do as told.

In a token of the rejection that asylum seekers may face, there is the case of Ciudad Juárez, México, which borders El Paso, TX, in the United States. As a response to the increasing flux of migrants, Mexico's government increased its asylum protection for migrants who decided to stay in the country and humanitarian temporary visas to migrants who were only in transit through the country.[13] These visas allow them to work and have free transit through México's territory. As in Ciudad Juárez, there is the need to fill thousands of labor positions, maquiladora's owners have offered asylum-seekers jobs. In fact, they pressured the government to expedite the issue of working visas and welcome them to the city. While some of them have taken that offer or have been employed in other businesses, some others are not looking for a job.

Migrants who do not look for a stable job and instead insist on their goal of entering the United States are portrayed as lazy people that are taking advantage of the citizens and as a danger to society. Some segments of the Businesspeople and citizenry stigmatized migrants without even listening to them. Should they have listened, they would have realized that some of the reasons they have for not taking those jobs are that they are low-paid positions that might be enough to cover their living needs, but not to send money back home, or that they have no place to shower before coming to work, and, since the app CBP One was set, that they need to spend endless hours searching for one of the limited appointments available a day, which does not allow them to take a regular job.

In this change of attitude, it is possible to see how when migrants were thought to be useful to the powerful businesspeople, the former were welcome to the city. However, when they disobeyed the command of the powerful there was a switch between thinking of migrants as people with problems to people that cause problems. Because of the stigmatization of migrants, people do not see that the obstacles are in fact created by a system designed to pretend to be rightful, but in fact, disregards the lives of those that are not needed by the market.

In a few words, for the colonial powers, the "good migrant" is the one that follows the directions of the system. It is treated as an object that can be molded to the will of the powerful. On the contrary, the "bad migrant" is one that fully displays their humanity and demands to be listened to. The "bad migrants" are segregated. Despite this harassment, migrants who disobey the orders of the powerful obtain in exchange for their unpopularity an inestimable advantage. In the words of Arendt (1943), "Those few refugees who insist upon telling the truth, even to the point of 'indecency,' get in exchange for their unpopularity one priceless advantage: history is no longer a closed book to them, and politics is no longer the privilege of Gentiles."

Political Agency

In the last years, Latin American and Latinx philosophy, Campos (2017), Mendoza (2017), Reed Sandoval and Díaz Cepeda (2021), Pereda (2008), and Rabinovich (2020) to name just a few have been amplifying the voice of the migrants advocating for their rights and emphasizing the contributions that immigrants make to the destination countries. While this chapter is inscribed in that demand for recognition and justice for migrants, I will emphasize not so much their national origin and destination, but their transit. I think this to be important because while both—resident and in-transit migrants—experience loss, sadness, and political resentment, the former are more likely to have a territory and a stable community that gives them some ground to persist, while the latter are not in that position which makes their struggle for their being even more amazing and admirable.[14]

Political actor

From authors of the Global South, such as Santiago Castro-Gómez (2015) we have learned that there is not a fixed political subject as some Marxism have proclaimed, but rather there are a diversity of them, such as women, indigenous people, among others. In the same sense, also Dussel

(2008) has a non-limited vision of who are the groups of people that are oppressed. He uses the term "victim" to refer to all the people who in one way or another are denied by the system. A political subject is then not a fixed group, but any person or community(ies) whose right to live is denied in a specific historical context. In this chapter, I am thinking of those migrants who have been forced to leave their countries because the patriarchal/capitalist/colonial system has brought extreme poverty, violence, and natural disasters to their communities of origin, but are not migrating quietly. Rather on their way to the North, they organize themselves and demand their right to be in the world.

Given the ill conditions of the asylum system worldwide, it is possible to think that admission policies are determined by politicians that are not concerned for their well-being, or for that purpose, for migrants from the Global South in general. This disdain for the lives of racialized strangers translates into a broken system and corruption that can be bought by a few. Some others, far from meeting the demands of the powerful, gain strength in their collective actions where they protect themselves, as it is harder for authorities or cartel members to extortionate them in the open, than doing it in the darkness of a solo trip. In the knowledge of the suffering that they will have to go through, migrants identify and find themselves in the face of the other. Sometimes, when they become aware of the power of collectivity, they organize to challenge the subordination they are asked for.

By organizing themselves, they emancipate from the image of the "good migrant," who must be submissive and come to the light only when they are required under the conditions of the powerful. On the contrary, for the now "disobedient migrant" when the roads are closed, they turn and see themselves, they recognize their own anguish in the face of the other suffering being and see themselves as a collectivity. They realize that their individual situation is in fact shared by many others, and they become aware that this was a political situation and hence requires a political solution. They leave the shadows and refuse to be denied their human dignity and their right to be treated ethically. They yell we are here! We have rights! By doing so, they empower themselves and become active collective agents in their liberation process. By standing for themselves, making themselves visible, attempting to establish a dialogue with other relevant actors, as well as attempting to control the narrative of their circumstances, migrants are to be considered political actors, who as such take political actions.

Caravans

Historically speaking, migrants that are rejected by the legal immigration system of the central countries have made their way to the North in a surreptitious way. They used to come to the United States hidden by a human smuggler or by themselves. As migratory policies became more impeding, migrants were pushed to even more dangerous routes. This was not an accident, but a planned consequence of a migratory policy designed to discourage undesired migrants to come. However, they cannot stop migrants as the living conditions have deteriorated in their countries of origin, so they are in an increasing need of refugee. In consequence, they started looking for other ways to migrate to the United States. Propelled by their "will-to-live" migrants went to the open and found other migrants under the same circumstances. They began to walk together in caravans, where they offer and find protection in the multitude.

In April 2014 what started in El Naranjo, Guatemala as a commemoration of the Way of the Cross in memory of all the migrants who have died on their way to the North, became a caravan that crossed the border to México. Migrants were self-organized and, in an assembly, made up entirely of them, they decide what they wanted to do. Migrants denounced the dangers they are exposed to on their way to the United States and demanded Mexico's government protection through the migratory routes, as well as free transit through México. The relative ease and support that the first caravans had to enter México, as well as the lesser exposure to attacks and extortion that migrants are normally imprisoned in their solo crossing through México, inspired other people to do the same.

Since the first one, several more caravans have been organized. In the last one before the end of Title 42 which started on April 23, 2023—despite their urgencies or because of them—migrants kept a minute of silence in memory of the 40 migrants and asylum seekers that died in a fire in a migratory detention center in Ciudad Juárez on March 27, 2023. They also made other acts in protest, such as sewing their lips. After several negotiations with officers of the National Migration Institute (*Instituto Nacional de Migración*, INM) members of the caravan were issued a humanitarian permit that allowed them 45 days of free transit through México on their way to the United States.

Protests

In the same token as not hiding anymore, migrants have attempted to follow the law, just for some of them to find the border closed anyway. As the Mexican government was pressured by the Biden administration, they implemented a contention migratory policy where migrants are stopped and detained under the ambiguous term of "rescued" However, the truth is that some of them are retained in migration stations where they are actually detained in precarious conditions. They may be detained because they do not have proper immigration documents. One of the reasons for migrants not having those documents is because they lack an I.D.—as they are stolen by cartel members or because, as in the case of Haiti, there is not a stable government to issue them. Another reason is that because of the increasing number of applicants, México´s immigration offices cannot meet the necessary numbers. Other times, when they have the documents, in the words of Ramón, a Venezuelan national I talked to "They [INM officers] tore the documents in my face because they wanted to blackmail me."

The conditions of the migration stations have taken migrants to protest. In May 2020, media reported several riots in migrants' detention centers in Mexico. They were protests made by migrants demanding epidemiologic actions to prevent the infection of COVID, as they were detained in overcrowded conditions lacking sanitary conditions. Also, because of the poor conditions of the detention facilities, there have been a couple of fire incidents. Arguably, the fire in a migration detention center in 2011 forced the creation of a new political migration in Mexico. Despite several protests made by migrants and human rights organizations, the disdain for the well-being and lives of the migrants has continued. On April 23, 2023, when protesting for the same reasons, a fire started in a migrant detention center in Ciudad Juárez. Because of authorities' failure of having minimal safety conditions such as not locking the cells and having fire extinguishers at reach, the fire expanded. Forty migrants died in the more inhumane conditions and 28 more were heavily injured.[15]

This fire brought meetings to decide the course of action about the migratory and humanitarian crisis, but once again migrants themselves were not invited to discuss what a possible solution may be. However, they organized and created spaces of resistance. The day after the fire, migrants summoned for a vigil where they called the names of the migrants that died in the fire. They set up a new camp in this place. This camp was tolerated by local authorities for several weeks, but they were removed to a temporary camp set a couple of blocks aside under the argument they will live in better conditions. However, this camp was also dismantled just a few weeks later. Migrants also have closed the international bridges in both a desperate attempt to cross the border and as a way to call the attention of the United States government. In the words of a protesting asylum-seeker "we want to tell Biden, to the Americans, that we are good, decent people. We just want to work."

Occupation of Spaces

As migrants walk together, their intersubjectivity is modified as they become part of a community, one that is an exodus but for that same reason the more they need each other. Trapped by the closed border and the no-return to home, they are here "pa´ pasar" (to go through). While asylum-seekers wait for their appointments to present their case or, in despair, to turn themselves to US migration officers or to attempt to cross the border undocumented, they inhabit non-places where they give a new significance to the territory. As nomads, they have the ability to build a home under harsh conditions.

Up to the Fall of 2022, government, but mostly religious organizations in Ciudad Juárez had been able to provide shelter to the increasing number of migrants arriving in the city.[16] There were an estimated number of 2500 people that were hosted in a network of about 30 shelters. However, as the United State government changed the rules unilaterally and retrieved the Title 42 exception for national Venezuelans, they were no longer able to enter the country and got stuck in the border city. However, they refused to go to the shelters and set a camp in the bed of the Rio Bravo. At first, they were a few people, but as more arrived the camp increased their number to the hundreds. They do this both to protect themselves by living in a community and to show the Biden administration that they come in peace and are just looking for a way to survive.

In Ciudad Juarez, this camp was dismantled under the argument that the living conditions were dangerous, and children were in unhealthy conditions. They were transported to the shelters. However, they did not stay there, for they want to be close to the borderline so they can react quickly in case there was a sudden change in the migratory policies. Anyhow, as the Spring of 2022 the number of migrants and asylum-seekers increased to about 10,000 people, shelters did not have the capacity to host them. Some migrants with limited economic resources set in abandoned houses where they protect themselves and share the little resources they have. As said before, others started a new camp outside of the INM facilities where 40 migrants and asylum-seekers died in a fire. Like the Okupa movements, migrants took some spaces and reconverted them from abandoned spaces to homes, where they found a sense of togetherness that provided them confront and safety, as they have learned not to trust authorities.

Counterarguments

A possible counterargument to my position is that migrants are not fighting for a cause but for their personal interests. To this, I reply that as Carol Hanisch has argued, the personal is political.[17] By every migrant standing for themselves, they are in fact challenging the *status quo* of the system that denies their very own being by not listening to them. Through their personal and collective struggles, they are advancing an agenda that benefits humanity by challenging the way the powerful treat the most vulnerable people. Is not this the goal of any liberation social movement?

Another possible counterargument is that international migrants are not citizens of the country they are passing by, so they do not have a right to protest, but they should be obeying the law and be quiet about the politics of the country they are going through. To answer this, I argue that nation states are a vital part of the unfair capitalist modernity that sets an arbitrary division between "them" and "us" that is detrimental to life. Under this system, for the colonizer the colonized do not have a voice. Contrary to this, from a decolonial approach, when the colonized desire to speak, they should be listened to. Usually, the only resource the oppressed have to be listened to is by raising their voice and protesting. Sometimes they do it through disruptive acts, but how Dussel argues this is not violence but legitime defense. The criterion then is life, not the rule of law. When a law is detrimental to life, it is not only legit to challenge it, but it is an ethical command.[18]

It is important to notice that recognizing migrants as political actors does not mean to say that they are flawless. Like any other group of people, they also make mistakes. Sometimes the very force that drives them—their will to live-may cause confusion that is detrimental to their goal. There are occasions where the solidarity they show by sharing useful information is taken for granted and asylum seekers believe in all the information received. On some occasions, this information has turned out to be wrong and has caused damage to them. One of these instances is when false rumors that the border will be open bring them to turn themselves expecting to gain legal entrance to the United States. Most of the asylum seekers doing so are returned to South México, so now they must make their way back to the borderline; a journey that is full of dangers.

Since knowledge is quite important, the way they gain it is also important. An ecology of knowledge, such as the one developed by Santos,[19] may help to facilitate the dialogue among the actors involved in the decision-making sessions. Asylum seekers could listen to allied organizations who could provide them with valuable information. At the same time, it could prevent these organizations from taking migrants as passive subjects with no agency. It may also help the receiving community to understand the needs and motivations of asylum seekers, and vice versa they may understand the mindset of the inhabitants of the cities they are staying or going through. It is important to clarify that I am not making this claim from the Discourse Ethics assumption that all people involved in a dialogue are in equal conditions. On the contrary, as Dussel (1994) argues, given that there is an evident disbalance of power, such dialogue must depart from the needs of the victim and be conducted in decolonial terms.

Conclusion

The increasing number of people in mobility shows, using W. Benjamin's (1999, p. 248) words, that "the state of emergency we live in is not the exception but the rule." The broken immigration system has caused a large number of migrants must follow dangerous routes crossing jungles, deserts, and cities where their lives are at risk. However, in order to protect themselves, some of them are now doing it in the open and demanding to be treated rightfully in their transit. I believe that it is the contribution that I can make to establish migrants not only as a group that requires protection but more importantly as an active political subject with agency capacity who can contribute to generate the political conditions to challenge the world order.

Notes

1   Giorgio Agamben (1998)
2   Immanuel Wallerstein (2004).
3   UNHCR (2022).
4   Josiah Heyman et al. (2018).
5   Ernesto Castañeda (2023).
6   p. 250.
7   Maldonado-Torres, p. 246.
8   For more on this topic see: Walter Mignolo (2011).
9   For discussion of immigration practices in relation to racist/sexist animalist talk (i.e. multiplying rats) and quasi-human-below animalist talk (i.e., anchor babies) (see Ernesto Rosen Velasquez 2019).
10   Shahram Khosravi (2010).
11   Howard Campell (2023).
12   See Iván Sandoval-Cervantes (2021).
13   Mexico's migratory policies have been erratic and changing. For more on the topic, see María Ines Barrios de la and Emilio Alberto López Reyes (2022).
14   For another approach on the topic, see Grant Silva (2019).
15   Josiah Heyman and Jeremy Slack (2023).
16   Oscar Armando Esparza del Villar and Marisela Gutiérrez Vega (2022).
17   *"The Personal Is Political"* (1969). https://www.carolhanisch.org/CHwritings/PIP.html.
18   Dussel, *Twenty Theses on Politics*.
19   Una Epistemología Del Sur (2009).

References

Agamben, G. (1998). *Homo Sacer: Sovereign Power and Bare Life*, (trans. Daniel Heller-Roazen). United States of America: Stanford University Press.

Arendt, H. (1943). We refugees. *Memorah Journal* 1943.

Barrios de la O, M.I and López Reyes, E.A. (2022). Análisis del Desplazamiento Interno Forzado en México: Avances y Retrocesos. In: *Contingencia Migratoria en Ciudad Juárez. Contexto de la Migración de Solicitantes de Protección Internacional (2018–2022)* (ed. O.A. Esparza del Villar and M. Gutiérrez Vega), 45–60. Ciudad Juárez, México: Universidad Autónoma de Ciudad Juárez.

Benjamin, W. (1999), *Illuminations*, 248. London: Random Houses.

Campell, H. (2023). Changing faces of immigrants crossing through Ciudad Juárez and into the United States: Reflections on migrants, culture, and crime. *Small Wars Journal* March 24. https://smallwarsjournal.com/jrnl/art/changing-faces-immigrants-crossing-through-ciudad-juarez-and-united-states-reflections.

Campos, D. (2017). *Loving Immigrants in America. An Experiential Philosophy of Personal Interaction*. United States of America: Lexington Books.

Castañeda, E. (2023). Expulsión de Migrantes como Oportunidad Perdida y Tarea para Sísifo. *Revista Mexicana de Sociología* 1 (1): 229–238. doi:10.22201/iis.01882503p.2023.1.

Castro-Gómez, S. (2015). *Revoluciones sin Sujeto. Slavoj Žižek y la Crítica del Historicismo Posmoderno*. Ciudad de México: Akal.

Dussel, E. (1994). *Debate en Torno a la Ética del Discurso de Apel. Diálogo Filosófico Norte-Sur desde América Latina*. México: Universidad Autónoma Metropolitana-Iztapalapa. Siglo veitiuno editores.

Dussel, E. (2008). *Twenty Theses on Politics* (trans. George Ciccariello-Maher). United States of America: Duke University Press.

Esparza Del Villar, O.A. and Gutiérrez Vega, M. (ed.) (2022). *Contingencia Migratoria en Ciudad Juárez. Contexto de la Migración de Solicitantes de Protección Internacional (2018–2022)*. Ciudad Juárez, México: Universidad Autónoma de Ciudad Juárez.

Grosfoguel, R. (2003). *Colonial Subjects: Puerto Ricans in a Global Perspective*. Berkeley: University of California Press.

Heyman, J. and Slack, J. (2023). *The Causes Behind the Ciudad Juárez Migrant Detention Center Fire*. Nacla, April 20, 2023, sec. Home, https://nacla.org/ciudad-juarez-migrant-shelter-fire.

Heyman, J., Slack, J., and Guerra, E. (2018). Bordering a 'Crisis': Central American asylum seekers and the reproduction of dominant border enforcement practices. *Journal of the Southwest* 60 (4 Winter): 754–786.

Khosravi, S. (2010). *'Illegal' Traveller: An Auto-Ethnography of Borders*. Basingstoke and New York: Palgrave MacMillan.

Lugones, M. (2010). Toward a decolonial feminism. *Hypatia* 25 (4): 742–759. https://www.jstor.org/stable/40928654.

Maldonado-Torres, N. (2007). On the coloniality of being. *Cultural Studies* 21 (2–3): 240. doi:10.1080/09502380601162548.

Mendoza, J.J. (2017). *The Moral and Political Philosophy of Immigration. Liberty, Security, and Equality*. United States of America, Lexington Books.

Mignolo, W. (2011). *The Darker Side of Western Modernity*. Durham and London: Duke University Press.

Pereda, C. (2008). *Los Aprendizajes del Exilio*. México, DF: Siglo XXI.

Quijano, A. (2020). Colonialidad del Poder, Eurocentrismo y América Latina. In: *La Colonialidad del Saber: Eurocentrismo y Ciencias Sociales*, 219–260. Buenos Aires: CLACSO, Ediciones CICUS, UNESCO.

Rabinovich, S. (2020). *Palabras Nómadas en Camino a una Justicia del Otro.México*. IIFL/UNAM.

Reed-Sandoval, A. and Díaz Cepeda, L.R. (2021). *Latin American Immigration Ethics*. Tucson: The University of Arizona Press.

Rosen Velasquez, E. (2019). Criminalization and undocumented migrante laborer identities in the zone of non being. *Critical Philosophy of Race* 7 (1): 144–159.

Sandoval-Cervantes, I. (2021). Ser un 'Migrante Verdadero': Temporalidad y Efemeridad al Atravesar México. In: *Ética, Política y Migración* (ed. L.R. Díaz Cepeda, A. Reed-Sandoval, and R. Sánchez Benítez), 103–124. Ciudad Juárez, México: Universidad Autónoma de Ciudad Juárez.

Santos, B.S. (2009). *Una Epistemología del Sur: La Reivención del Conocimiento y la Emancipación Social* (ed. J.G.G. Salgado). Argentina: Consejo Latinoamericano de Ciencias Sociales-CLACSO; Siglo XXI Editores.

Silva, G. (2019). Migratorial disobedience. The fetishization of immigration law. *RPA Magazine* https://www.rpamag.org/2019/01/migratorial-disobedience.

UNHCR (2022). *Figures at a Glance*. The United Nations Refugee Agency June 16, https://www.unhcr.org/about-unhcr/who-we-are/figures-glance.

Wallerstein, I. (2004). *World-Systems Analysis. An Introduction*. United States of America: Duke University Press.

12

Latin American Animal Ethics

IVÁN SANDOVAL-CERVANTES AND AMY REED-SANDOVAL

Introduction

The idea that nonhuman animals have rights and deserve to be treated humanely is widespread throughout the world. The specifics, however, are often still variable, and in constant negotiation and contestation depending on the geographical and historical contexts in question. Nevertheless, it is fair to say that since the movement for animal rights[1] started in the 1960s and 1970s, it has expanded considerably across the globe, often replicating ideas originally developed in the so-called Global North without taking into account local contextual factors and pre-existing models for existing with and treating nonhuman animals in so-called Global South regions.

This is no different in Latin America: a region that has recently seen an upsurge in terms of animal rights consciousness and activism. This trend toward animal ethics has taken many forms, including (1) new legislation seeking to protect individual animals from abuse and mistreatment; (2) the formal and informal organizations that have gotten involved, in different ways, in the protection of nonhuman animals; (3) the increasing popularization of vegan and vegetarian diets in Latin America; (4) the incorporation of nonhuman animals into formal party politics; and (5) in the development articulation of the so-called *animalista* movement in different countries of the subcontinent. This essay will mainly focus on point (5), emphasizing how it has played out in the context of Mexico (though, once again, the *animalista* movement exists throughout Latin America).

The term "movimiento animalista," as it used in Latin America, refers to a broad range of engagements with the animal rights movement. It is perhaps most accurate to define "movimiento animalista" as an extremely broad umbrella term that can include anyone who feels a special connection or empathy toward nonhuman animals. This means that on the ground, people can identify as *animalistas* if they are vegans and involved in the liberation of nonhuman animals, or if they feel a special connection toward dogs, have pets, and/or donate to animal shelters (even if they are not vegetarians or vegans). This term is used here in this broad way because, as we shall see, the umbrella definition helps us to understand the multiple ways in which nonhuman animals become political and politicized in Latin America not merely through the language of animal rights, but also through *animalistas'* emphasis on specific animals, specific territories, and specific political communities.

Indeed, the "movimiento animalista" in Latin America frequently responds to specific geographical and historical situations in which human and nonhuman animals are situated. In Latin America, *animalistas* have to take into account how violence and resistance have shaped local relationships between humans and animals, and how the current political situation of precarity and violence shapes *animalista* goals in relation to other social movements.[2] In this sense, understanding the *animalista* movement requires us also to understand the central ideals of the Animal Liberation Movement, which was initially developed in Anglo-American contexts. We can then contrast this to how *animalistas* have taken inspiration from the Philosophy of Liberation, as developed in Latin America, and generated a kind of Latin American animal ethics.

In the next section of this chapter, we further unpack what "animalista" means in the context of Latin America, again with considerable focus on the context of Mexico. We take into consideration how histories of colonial violence and the current context of generalized violence in Mexico and beyond have influenced the formation of this movement. Then, we analyze how the framework of animal rights that emerged in the so-called Global North has tended to be interpreted as individualizing nonhuman animals and thus conceptually removing them from their territories—territories shared with members of Indigenous communities and other marginalized groups. Such an animal rights framework is also seen by many *animalistas* as a top-down imposition from the Global North. Finally, drawing upon the work of Enrique Dussel, we explore how the *animalista* movement has successfully expanded upon the Philosophy of Liberation. Finally, we argue that the movement would benefit from even deeper engagement with this philosophical tradition.

Who Are the "Animalistas"?

Scholars of the *animalista* movement in Latin America, including Ávila Gaitán (2014) and Ponce León (2021), have argued for the need to simultaneously question how animal rights discourses from the Global North are reproduced in Latin America, on the one hand, and how to avoid the appropriation of Latin American experiences by Global North thinkers, on the other. In support of these objectives, they engage the work of decolonial and liberation philosophers theory such as Enrique Dussel (1977) and Walter Mignolo (2011), whose main objectives have been to theorize from the peripheries and avoid universalizing moral arguments that originate from colonial metropolises. Along these lines, Ávila Gaitán and Ponce León question how certain strains of animal rights and animal liberation have continued to promote what they call a problematic "new universalism" that fails to account for the diversity of experiences of human–animal interactions. They claim that universalist narratives, such as those of animal liberation, might continue to reproduce what Aníbal Quijano (2000) has called the "coloniality of power."

A first step, then, toward understanding the *animalista* movement in Latin America is to address the diversity of those who self-identify as *animalistas*, and to distinguish them, at least in certain respects, from the "animal rights activists" of the Global North. In the Global North (as a general rule), people who self-identify as "animal rights activists" generally adhere to a set of practices that seem to follow logically from the overarching general principles of "animal rights activism," such as following a vegetarian diet or vegan consumption practices. Global North animal rights activists are also less likely to consider cultural or political differences shaping human relationships to animals.[3] Although there is a growing number of "animal rights activists" in Latin America that also attempt to adhere to a universalist framework of practices associated with animal rights, many of the self-identified *animalistas* do not necessarily have universal moral norms in mind when they use the term *animalista*. Instead, *animalistas* see themselves as responding to specific class, political, and geographical circumstances in their activism. We might say, then, that the term *animalista* refers both to a descriptive relationship between humans and animals, and to a more context-sensitive ethical responses to animals. In this sense, the *animalista* movement does not emphasize a universal or universalist framework that should regulate human–animal relations, but a context-specific response to concrete animals in one's immediate surroundings and community.

For example, in many instances *animalistas* participate in the rescuing of abused animals and in the protection of street animals in their own neighborhoods. Indeed, in Mexico, numerous self-proclaimed *animalistas* dedicate most of their energy to rescuing and rehabilitating street dogs or abused dogs. Although there is a growing movement in Mexico, guided by large NGOs, to call attention to other forms of animal exploitation such as "big ag" and bullfighting, many of the "on the ground" *animalistas* are mostly concerned about animals in their immediate surroundings. This is also the case for animal protection organizations and dog shelters, that house injured and malnourished dogs.[4]

The size and the focus of these two different forms of involvement in animal protection might lead one to assume that the former—big NGOs fighting against Big Ag—have political agendas, while the latter—"on the ground" *animalistas*—worry only about animals in their proximity and lack political agendas. However, such an interpretation would be superficial and wrong, as both forms of engagement are political in different ways. "On the ground" *animalistas* use cases of animal abuse to make demands to local authorities, often asking officials to take direct action to solve specific cases. Their demands frequently exhibit the slow and uneven application of laws in Mexico, as well as the difficulty of attaining any form of justice in cases affecting animals. In this sense, even if sometimes indirectly, "on the ground" and context-sensitive *animalistas* highlight how an unjust system works. On this point, Ponce León (2021) explains that *animalistas* embody "plural, heterogeneous, and contradictory" politics that reflect the diversity of socio-political contexts that include class, race, gender, age, and ideologies.

We have seen, then, that the *animalista* movement has the following characteristics. First, it engages Global South and decolonial theories, such as those of Dussel and Mignolo, in support of its aims. Second, and relatedly, *animalistas* tend to eschew universalist and "top-down" approaches to animal ethics, which are often perceived as being imposed from above by Global North animal rights movements. Third, *animalistas* tend to respond to abuses against animals in their immediate surroundings—focusing, for instance, on helping abused street dogs as a salient "local" concern. Fourth, *animalistas*, in their contextualist approach to activism, tend also to engage intersecting social injustices in their work, such as those associated with inadequate criminal justice systems that undermine both human and nonhuman animals.

Finally, it is worth noting that the contextualist, "on the ground" nature of *animalista* activism—particularly inasmuch as that activism is politicized—poses challenges to *animalistas*. Often, the political parties they sometimes challenge, and with whom they sometimes seek to collaborate, sometimes exploit the "specifity" of their animal-focused work as they isolate *animalista* demands from other social movements, thus depoliticizing *animalista* struggles. This can be seen in the increasing attempts by politicians through Latin America—particularly in Brazil, Colombia, and Mexico—to incorporate issues of animal protection into their campaigns while pushing for a carceral state that targets working class and racialized minorities (see Marceau (2019) for the United States, and Ponce León 2021).

Animalistas and Adjacent Social Movements

Having explored some of the central features of the *animalista* movement in the previous section, we explore, in this section, the relationship between the *animalista* movement and what we may call "adjacent" social movements, particularly environmental movements.

Because of the heterogeneity of the *animalista* movement—especially of the "on the ground" *animalistas*, whose work focuses on rescuing and taking care of urban animals—it would be safe to say that many *animalistas* are not engaged in environmental activism. In broad strokes, we could say that the *animalista* "movement" has been developed on the basis of relationships between city dwellers and urban animals, while the environmental movement has adopted a broader approach that emphasizes not individual animal specimens, but the wider relationship between territories and environmental degradation.

It would also be fair to say that while the work of many "on the ground" *animalistas* is more disconnected from larger political movements than that of environmental activists, or *ambientalistas*. The work that *ambientalistas* do is often embedded in complex and violent political struggles that include both state and non-state actors, such as mining and logging companies, criminal organizations, and transnational soft drink companies. As a result, *ambientalistas* face increased personal dangers as they go about their lives. According to Global Witness, from 2012 to 2022, 68% of crimes against *ambientalistas* occurred in Latin America (with at least 1,733 *ambientalistas* murdered, that is one in every two days).[5] This alarming figure—and what it means in terms of impunity and loss of life—should sound alarms throughout Latin America, and *animalistas* ought to worry about what it might entail for humans and nonhuman animals.

Another difference between *animalista* movements and environmental activism is as follows: the individualization of animal rights that allows people to identify and empathize with specific animals is not necessarily present in environmental activism. This could be one of the reasons that people have more difficulty "connecting" to struggles to protect the environment, especially when such struggles are seen as happening in distant places and as dangerous. The main difference, as articulated by Zambrano et al. (2022), between the *animalista* and environmental activism is that while the former is worried about the life of each organism, the latter prioritizes habitat as the living environment. Thus, for many urban *animalistas*, who have associated the protection of animal life with individual animals, seeing pictures, or hearing stories about specific abused animals makes it easier to identify with this type of animal protection politics than with environmentalists who do not prioritize individual living creatures. This phenomenon is due, in part, to the use of social media and social media activism (a point we explore in further detail below).

However, in some cases *animalista* politics can align with environmentalism—though individual *animalistas* have not necessarily drawn out the connections—by linking specific species to a territory, and thus not only revealing concrete relationships between humans and nonhumans, but also highlighting the particular sociopolitical context of a territory. In most cases, this happens in Indigenous territories and with "charismatic" animals. For example, anthropologist Columba González-Duarte (2021) has extensively studied the monarch butterfly (Danaus plexipuss) and its complex role in Mexican and transnational conservation politics. In Mexico, González-Duarte (2021) addresses how transnational and neoliberal conservation efforts have eroded the political power of local communities that continue to resist by holding on to their autonomy. In addition, González-Duarte (2017) says it is through "the assembly of humans and butterflies" that resistance, at different levels, can occur, including "environmental cyber-resistance." In sum, while the *animalista* movement has traditionally not aligned itself with environmentalism, there is potential for the movement to do so.

Finally, there are important comparisons to be made between the *animalista* movement and that of anti-punitivist and anti-carceralist movements. Urban, "on the ground," *animalistas* have relied heavily on social media to activate the public and occasionally get immediate results, particularly in connection to animal abuse. In Mexico, *animalistas* have used platforms such as Facebook and twitter to denounce cases of animal abuse directly to local and state authorities—and in some cases they have managed to draw enough attention to specific animals that municipal presidents and even federal authorities have immediately intervened. However, regarding these interventions as *purely positive outcomes* is complicated.

One of the most common demands is to imprison the alleged perpetrator. Such demands are generally articulated in terms of punitivist narratives that stipulate that animal abuse will only end through prison and harsh punishments. This punitivist narrative not only focuses on individual and specific animals, it also feeds into a more generalized fantasy espoused by politicians who problematically maintain that the only valid solutions to most social problems are harsher criminal penalties. Thus, the punivist narratives of some *animalistas* fail to consider how animal abuse originates not in individual abusers but in a system that has continuously devalues both animal and human life.

Liberation Philosophy and the *Animalista* Movement

In engaging decolonial and liberation philosophies, *animalistas* have done important and creative philosophical work. Note that traditionally, the Philosophy of Liberation has not been known to be a doctrine of animal liberation. To illustrate this point: in his discussion of "cosa, ente y sentido" or "thing, entity, and meaning" in his pathbreaking book *Philosophy of Liberation*, Dussel wrote that "when we refer to a dog we refer to a thing, for example, that has an essence that can [engage in] proper canine operations; those of its concrete individuality." He adds that "if I cut off one of its legs, I can no longer say that this leg is a thing, because upon leaving the living being it shows that it is only part of a thing, the dog, as a totalizing constitutive unity."[6] In referring to dogs as mere "things," and using the idea of cutting of a dog's legs to illustrate a metaphysical point, we see that for Dussel (at least in this foundation text of the Philosophy of Liberation) is not considering nonhuman animals as the vulnerable "Others" whose liberation he fervently advocates.

Thus, in incorporating nonhuman animals into the ethics of liberation, *animalistas* are positioning themselves in a decades-long tradition of expanding upon, critiquing, and liberatingphilosophy. They have good reasons to do this; as mentioned previously, many *animalistas* turn to decolonial and liberatory critique and use it as a form of barrier between their activism and the top-down, universalist theorizing of many strands of Global North animal liberation movements. Furthermore, liberation philosophy—which emphasizes face-to-face, Levinasian moral encounters and attention to "the victims" or "Others" of an unjust world system—seems to support the kind of local, "hands on" activist work that characterizes the *animalista* movement. As Dussel explains, "prior to the world is the *pueblo*; prior to being is the reality of the other; prior to all that is prior is the responsibility for the weak, for that which still isn't . . ."[7] In sum, Dussel may not have included animal "Others" in his work, but *animalistas* are correct to extend liberation philosophy in precisely this way.

Of course, for *animalistas* (and liberation philosophers), this is not a mere intellectual exercise. We have already seen that *animalistas* not only theorize liberation for animals but also put their ideas into practice. Drawing upon previous discussion, we propose that part of the liberatory potential of many Latin American *animalistas* lies in their ability to link nonhuman animals with specific territories—thus escaping the individualist focus on animal rights activists, who are more focused on individual rights, and environmentalists who sometimes prioritize "the system" over the individuals of which it is comprised. This "linking" also emphasizes the role that animals play in political histories. In this respect, anthropologists have traced the material and symbolic connections between violence directed toward humans and toward animals. For example, María Elena García (n.d., 2021, pp. 20–21) draws our attention to how violence against animals is an important part of the ongoing violence rooted in colonialism in Peru both through its visual representation and in the politics of food. In this way, the analysis of nonhuman bodies, and how they are (mis)treated, and the relationship with specific territories and political histories needs to be understood within the context of settler colonialism.[8]

Another liberatory tendency on the part of *animalistas* is the reshaping of veganism by way of rethinking what popular veganism means when it takes into account the specific relationships and struggles of humans and animals in Latin America. One major obstacle that these struggles face, of course, is the ongoing de/politization of both animal rights and the environmental movement—often done by government officials and political parties that incorporate, in a cosmetic way, *animalistas* and environmentalist demands in their agendas but disconnecting them from other power structures. That is, government officials and politicians seek to individualize these efforts and turn them into campaign slogans to attract more voters without addressing structural issues.

One of the ongoing criticisms of veganism, as a result of an engagement with Global North conceptions of animal rights, is that it often only viable for middle/upper class people who are, in general, white or *mestizo* in the context of Latin America because of the history of colonialism and colorism. For the most part, this is true; even as vegetarian and vegan diets become more popular, they often require class privileges such as living in a city, having a car and an above average annual income, and being able to pay rent/mortgage in specific neighborhoods. However, scholars such as

Ponce León and Proaño (2020) have argued that a "popular veganism" can also be a decolonial practice if, and only if, it is rooted in the effort to "de-totalize" and "de-universalize" narratives surrounding the "humanization" of nonhuman animals. Instead, Ponce León and Proaño advocate for a liberatory re-animalization of the human as a way to counteract the discourses of modernity and Western civilization. In this sense, popular veganism can be directly linked to local foodstuffs, religious identity, food sovereignty, and feminist politics (e.g., Davidson 2021).

Still, we propose that even deeper engagement of liberation philosophy could benefit the animalist movement. First, we have seen that there are several instances where government officials and politicians have sought to incorporate animal rights into their platforms and campaigns. Although at first glance, this might seem like a step forward for the *animalistas*, it is often a way to absorb demands for justice into mainstream politics by individualizing accountability and decontextualizing violence. In most cases, government officials and politicians propose "easy, straightforward" solutions that rely on strengthening "tough-on-crime" measures by increasing jail time for alleged animal abusers. For example, Jair Bolsonaro, the right-wing president of Brazil from 2019 to 2022, increased jail sentences from one to five years for those who committed acts of animal cruelty to dogs and cats. Similar measures have been proposed in Mexico, with politicians seeking pre-trial detention for people accused of animal abuse. Given the imperative of liberation ethicists to consider the various ways in which the "totalizing system" oppressed marginalized others, a careful, liberatory rethinking of the criminal justice system and its relation to animal ethics is called for.

We also believe that the *animalista* movement would benefit from further engagement of the Philosophy of Liberation, because so doing could help the movement avoid the pitfalls of cultural relativism. While *animalistas* do well, we have argued, to focus on local concerns and eschew top-down, Global North moral frameworks, some clear ethical guidance is called for toward against unethical behaviors vis-à-vis animals. Across the globe, various types of nonhuman animal abuse are justified through nebulous appeals to "culture," or to claims that caring for animals is a Global North luxury (for example, claims that vegetarian diets are necessarily Global North impositions). Liberation philosophy's appeal to the imperative of caring for those oppressed and excluded by an unjust, hegemonic "system"—and appeal that, as we have seen, is successfully extended to nonhuman animals by *animalistas*—provides ethical guidance for prioritizing the needs of animals without falling back on colonialist moralizing tendencies.

Conclusion

The liberation potential of *animalistas* and environmentalists in Abya Yala lies in its the capacity of activists to keep the "pluriverses"[9] alive, which means rejecting the depolitization of the lives on nonhuman animals. As Ponce León (2021, p. 20) states, the narratives of some Global North animal rights scholars run the risk of ignoring the material conditions and the heterogeneity of the *animalista* movement, which could lead to a form of epistemic racism. *Animalistas*, who have successfully extended liberation ethics to the needs of nonhuman animals, should, we have argued, continue to engage decolonial and liberation philosophies as they conduct their important ethical work on behalf of nonhuman animals.

Notes

1 The reference here is directly for the movement of animal rights inscribed within the liberal regime of laws and subjects and not a reference to other movements that have also argued for the respect of non-human animals outside of the framework of rights.

2 For more on social movements and Latin American philosophy, see Luis Rubén Díaz Cepeda (2020).

3 For exceptions, see Karen Emmerman (2019).

4 It is important to point out that the *animalista* organizations, as well as the environmental activist (*ambientalistas*) organizations are diverse and that this chapter does not attempt to provide a typology or an exhaustive account of the genealogies or relationships of the wide array of organizations. For more information on this topic, specifically for Argentina, see Anahí Méndez (2016).

5 Lorena Arroyo (2022).

6 Dussel, *Filosofía de La Liberación*, 73 (our translation).

7 Dussel, 46.

8 See Billy-Ray Belcourt (2015).

9 Arturo Escobar (2014).

References

Arroyo, L. (2022). Bosques Manchados de Sangre: América Latina Registra Cerca de 1200 Ambientalistas Asesinados En Una Década. *El País* September 28. https://elpais.com/america-futura/2022-09-29/bosques-manchados-de-sangre-america-latina-registra-el-68-de-los-ambientalistas-asesinados-en-una-decada.html.

Ávila Gaitán, I.D. (2014). Especismo Antropocéntrico, Veganismo Moderno-Colonial y Configuración de Formas-de-Vida: Una Propuesta Política (Ya En Marcha). *Revista Desde Abajo* https://www.desdeabajo.info/ambiente/item/25149-especismo-antropocentrico-veganismo-moderno-colonial-y-configuracion-deformas-de-vida-una-propuesta-politica-ya-en-marcha.html.

Belcourt, B.-R. (2015). Animal bodies, colonial subjects: (Re)Locating animality in decolonial thought. *Societies* 5 (1): 1–11. doi:https://doi.org/10.3390/soc5010001.

Davidson, M. (2021). Feminismo e Projeto Decoloniais: Ferramentas Críticas Para Repensar o Veganismo. *Diversitates International Journal* 13 (1).

Díaz Cepeda, L.R. (2020). *Social Movements and Latin-American Philosophy: From Ciudad Juárez to Ayotzinapa*. United States of America: Lexington Books.

Dussel, E. (1977). *Filosofía de La Liberación*. México: Edicol.

Emmerman, K. (2019). What's love got to do with it? An ecofeminist approach to inter-animal and intra-cultural conflicts of interest. *Ethical Theory and Moral Practice* 22: 77–91.

Escobar, A. (2014). *Sentipensar Con La Tierra: Nuevas Lecturas Sobre Desarrollo, Territorio y Diferencia*. Medellín: Universidad Autónoma Latinoamericana UNAULA.

García, M.E. (2021). *Gastropolitics and the Specter of Race: Stories of Capital, Culture, and Coloniality in Peru*. United States of America: University of California Press.

García, M.E. (n.d.). *Landscapes of Death: Political Violence Beyond the Human in the Peruvian Andes*. Unpublished.

Gonzalez-Duarte, C. (2017). Resisting Monsanto: Monarch butterflies and cyber-actors. In: *Resistance to the Neoliberal Agri-Food Regime* (ed. A. Bonanno and S.A. Wolf), 176. London: Routledge.

Gonzalez-Duarte, C. (2021). Butterflies, organized crime, and 'Sad Trees': A critique of the Monarch Butterfly Biosphere Reserve Program in a context of rural violence. *World Development* 142: 105420.

Marceau, J. (2019). *Beyond Cages: Animal Law and Criminal Punishment.* Cambridge: Cambridge University Press.

Méndez, A. (2016). La emergencia de nuevos imaginarios socio-ambientales: Críticas y alternativas al especismo institucionalizado. Apuntes de Investigación del CECYP. Jun(27). http://www.scielo.org.ar/pdf/aicecyp/n27/n27a07.pdf

Mignolo, W. (2011). *The Darker Side of Western Modernity.* Durham and London: Duke University Press.

Ponce León, J.J. (2021). ¿Nuevo Abolicionismo o Veganismo Popular? El Problema de Las Políticas de La Liberación Total y Sus Vestigios Moderno-Coloniales. *Revista Latinoamericana de Estudios Críticos Animales* 8 (1): 20–21.

Ponce León, J.J. and Proaño, D. (2020). El Asunto Anti-Especista: Un Desafío Para La Izquierda. In: *Reflexiones Animalistas Desde El Sur,* 33–48. Ediciones Abya-Yala.

Quijano, A. (2000). Coloniality of power, eurocentrism, and Latin America. (trans. Michael Ennis), Nepantla:. *Views from the South* 1 (3): 533–580.

Zambrano, L., Ayala-Azcárraga, C., and Castelblanco-Martínez, N. (2022). ¡Ay Amor, Ya No Me Quieras Tanto! El Movimiento Animalista. *Este País,* January 3.

13

Zapata Revisited: Views on the Zapatista National Liberation Army

ERNESTO CASTAÑEDA

Introduction

On the New Year's Eve of 1994, an armed group the Ejercito Zapatista de Liberación Nacional (EZLN) took San Cristóbal de las Casas and various neighboring towns in Chiapas, the southernmost and poorest state in Mexico. Looking back years later this event can be correctly described as "historical," since it is one of the landmarks of recent Mexican history for all that it represents and all the paradigms it changed.

This chapter addresses the following questions: What is the brief history of the EZLN? Which is its importance? What is their purpose and agenda? The answer will vary depending on whom you ask. The Mexican major media companies showed one perspective, the Mexican government, the left, the EZLN itself, the people in Chiapas and different people outside of Mexico each have a different conception of what neo-Zapatismo represents depending on the paradigm through which the observer is looking. This polysemantic nature is part of its appeal. The EZLN is very self-reflexive and intentional. The EZLN refuses to give a concrete definition of who is a Zapatista. Many of the original militant Zapatistas have declared that whoever declares themself as Zapatista is Zapatista. Nominal membership is free, "entrada libre y gratuita," which is indeed an important way to build a movement by increasing numbers and perceptions of worth, unity, and commitment.[1] The abstract conception of Zapatismo is a tool that the EZLN has used to gain a broad civil base of supporters at home and abroad and to easily present what it opposes and what it supports. The Zapatista agenda is so broad it gained universal legitimation and so concrete as to create real pressure on the Mexican government on certain issues that would improve the conditions of the indigenous people.

The EZLN opposes the injustice, poverty, and discrimination suffered by the indigenous people of Chiapas, Mexico, and the Americas. From its beginning this was an anti-colonial movement, tracing many of the ailments of indigenous communities to European colonialism. All these abstract concepts generated widespread support among a wide national and international public. The EZLN protested unfair local, national, and international economic practices that severely exploited Chiapaneco labor through semi-feudal systems, and with prices for corn and coffee so low that it is hard for peasants to stay out of debt.[2]

The EZLN also called for real democracy and protested the PRI's electoral authoritarianism, what many Mexican scholars claim was an important push in the transition to democracy.[3] The EZLN called for justice, respect, land, and equality in 1994 even if through a failed armed revolution. Later they called for the approval of a specific bill (the San Andres Accords) and for the end of military and paramilitary intimidation, all these in hopes of affecting policy and therefore participating as and through interest groups in a maturing democracy. A big part of the success of the EZLN has been its flexibility, its ability to adapt to the changing circumstances in Mexico and the world, and its capability to change its approach while not its essence.

When did the Zapatistas come out of the jungle? The same day that the neoliberal paradigm chanted victory in Mexico City. The EZLN appeared on TV newscasts the same day that NAFTA went into effect: January 01, 1994. It was the day that then President Salinas had said would mark Mexico's entrance into the first world. But that day the EZLN challenged the neo-liberal paradigm reminding the world and to some Mexicans who had forgotten or wanted to forget that there were many poor people not only on the city streets but also in rural areas. Its de facto spokesman on its early years, Subcomandante Marcos also says that the EZLN took arms the day when symbolically Mexico disappeared as a nation and became part of the Global Market,[4] in what constituted a clear move against economic globalization and a nostalgic turn to nationalism. The EZLN also uses the symbol of Revolutionary General Emiliano Zapata and draws from the Mexican historic experience to appeal to the Mexicans. In the autonomous communities the Mexican hymn is sung, and the Mexican flag is honored before any "official" celebration. Contrary to what some of its detractors argued initially, the EZLN has never proposed making Chiapas an independent country and therefore they cannot be labeled as a secessionist group, nor do they target civilians. The EZLN asks for true federalism and their members proudly call themselves Mexicans even if they are poor, even if they are indigenous.

The EZLN has been especially important in bringing back into the discussion the themes of agrarian reform, racism, and the reality than in Mexico there is a marginalized fully indigenous minority. Thus, breaking the myth of the mestizaje of all the country which is such an integral part of the popular Mexican ideology. They also questioned the deep meanings of progress and democracy and questioned the liberal equation of economic liberalism = universal well-being.

To truly understand a social phenomenon, we need to know its history. First this chapter will present an historical synopsis of the evolution of the Ejército Zapatista de Liberación Nacional (EZLN) while discussing its challenges to the liberal paradigm through its rejection of the definition of Mexico as a homogenous monocultural capitalist liberal democracy. Then it will analyze how different observers and media have covered and reported on the movement through the years. To finish with an analysis of Marcos and the many challenges that he and the EZLN pose to the neoliberal paradigm.

Brief History of the Zapatista Liberation Army

"Within an hour we were in the plaza recording on film bright, young Indian men, women and even children, wearing clean and freshly pressed polyester khaki uniforms, sporting one-shot rifles, bayonets, home-made grenades, machetes, axes, and AK-47s. We talked with the masked leaders. The message was not new, not a surprise to anyone living here: we want land so we can grow food, access to health care, free schools, a decent wage, an end to racism. Our lives are not worth living if things do not change. We would rather die fighting than watch our children die of malnutrition or curable diseases."[5]

On New Year's Day 1994, when the North American Free Trade Agreement or NAFTA entered into effect, a voice from the Lacondon Jungle in Chiapas said "Ya Basta" or "It's enough." On the news we saw numerous armed individuals with ski masks who had started a revolt in the southern Mexican state of Chiapas. They took San Cristóbal de las Casas and other neighboring municipalities with little fighting. Some Mexicans saw with sympathy that a community finally defied the system successfully. They proved wrong all those people in power who thought that the poor would never revolt. At the same time, other Mexicans were fearful for their lives and their belongings. Overall, although many Mexicans agreed with the demands of the Zapatistas, few agreed with their armed methodology. The same was true for many poor Chiapanecos who did not join the EZLN. The Mexican society supported the indigenous and the poor but opposed an armed conflict. Fortunately, Zapatismo almost immediately turned more into a political and symbolic force than into an armed violent group. The EZLN called itself an army and was not afraid of donning arms, but they rarely fired or used violence, nonetheless they have been targets of military and paramilitary attacks. But they have survived them.

On January 1, 1994, NAFTA officially came into effect. The Mexican government as well as the middle and upper classes thought that by joining NAFTA, Mexico was finally part of the "first world." Salinas sold the dream that Mexico, with its sophisticated cities and educated elites, was modern and would enter the new millennium as a developed country. It was then when the EZLN appeared to remind the world of the many poor people in Mexico and the discrimination toward the indigenous people. January 1, 1994, was chosen as the day to start the revolution.

The first day was full of military successes for the EZLN, but the army soon regained terrain,

Over the next 10 days, in firefights, rocket attacks, and strafing runs, the Mexican army and air force regained control of Los Altos and sealed off the canyons. By the ceasefire on January 12th, the death counts were 13 Mexican army soldiers, 38 state police, more than 70 Zapatista soldiers and from 19 to 275 or more civilians. Meanwhile, whatever the FLN commander in chief's efforts, nothing military worth noting happened anywhere else [in Mexico].[6]

Neither the EZLN nor the army have talked much about what truly happened during the first days January of 1994 in their different armed confrontations. The EZLN has not talked about their history to the media probably for security purposes and the army and government have not released much information to keep things under control and not to seem incompetent or repressive.

César Romero Jacobo (1994), Eduardo Huchim (1994), and John Ross (1995) address some of the most important questions about the legitimacy of the EZLN. Including for example how could the Mexican government with its big intelligence and information networks ignore the existence of a guerrilla that according to Marcos had been training for more than 10 years? According to Ross,

Huchim, and Romero, the Mexican authorities were busy negotiating NAFTA and although they knew of the existence of an armed group in Chiapas, they refused to accept this publicly for fear that NAFTA could be canceled. There were articles published in 1993 in Proceso, El Tiempo, and La Jornada that suggested the existence of a guerrilla in Chiapas. The Mexican army had found training camps and had even confronted the rebels in combats where casualties occurred. In 1992 Patrocinio Gonzalez Garrido, governor of Chiapas, told the press; "My government, the Attorney General, and the Army will act swiftly to disarticulate the guerrilla."[7] In 1993, he was Salinas' Secretary of the Interior (Secretario de Gobernación), and after Proceso published a letter where he was informed of a guerilla in Chiapas, the former Chiapas governor said:

> Whoever circulates this false rumor will cause grave prejudice to development because the release can halt foreign and domestic investment in the agricultural sector. The Mexican government discounts the presence of a guerrilla movement in Chiapas.[8]

After the EZLN took the public by complete surprise on the New Year's Eve of 1994, the Mexican federal government first responded deploying the army, which had already been mobilized to Chiapas before then. After the EZLN public appearance in 1994, the government called the Zapatistas "transgressors of the law." The government wanted to control the situation and prevent a civil war without appearing like a human rights' violator. After internal and foreign pressure, the government showed conciliatory and sent Manuel Camacho Solis as the Peace Commissioner turning the issue very political. Later that year Mexico suffered many high-profile political assassinations[9] and the national atmosphere got even more politically charged. After Ernesto Zedillo won the July elections of 1994, in part thanks to *el voto del miedo* the "vote of fear" or "the vote for peace," Zedillo spoke of peace and his team signed the COCOPA or San Andres agreements, which he later refused to recognize.

Early in January of 1994, the EZLN and the government called for a cease-fire and negotiations started. The EZLN's (1994) demands were:

"We propose the following conditions for the initiation of dialogue:

A. Recognition of the EZLN as a belligerent force.
B. Cease fire on all sides in disputed territories.
C. Withdrawal of federal troops from all communities with full respect for the human rights of the rural population. Withdrawal of federal troops to their respective barracks in distinct parts of the country.
D. Stop the indiscriminate bombing of rural populations.
E. With the last three conditions as a base, the formation of an intermediary national commission."

After the cease-fire negotiations started, the most important agreement happened in the town of San Andres Larráinzar, Chiapas, in February 1996 where "government and the CCRI-EZLN delegates (still in arms, still masked) signed historic accords on Indian rights. This agreement, supposed to issue soon in federal legislation (never did)."[10] Although the accords were approved by the Subcomandante Marcos and the Mexican Secretary of the Interior, Zedillo did not allow the legislation to go to congress because the PRI was against the agreement, particularly because 1996 was a midterm election year. Zapatistas all over the world still ask for the respect of these agreements, which would give indigenous people in Mexico more cultural rights.

Vicente Fox's government presented the accord to Congress after he was elected in 2000. And in early 2001 the EZLN leaders and supporters organized a large peaceful march to Mexico City to defend these agreements in front of the Congress after a historical march through 12 states. This was a great strategic show of force and massive support at the national level. Indigenous congresses were held where ethnic groups from other states added their claims to those of the indigenous people of Chiapas.

When the EZLN addressed the National Congress, it was not Marcos who talked but indigenous men and women leaders something that challenged all the popular expectations and went beyond personalism into the fight for a just cause; the recognition of Mexican Indigenous people as human beings with legal rights including the right to be different. Unfortunately, despite the public support that Fox showed, the Congress diluted the agreements and politicians such as Manuel Bartlett, Diego Fernandez de Cevallos, and Felipe Calderon Hinojosa drafted a diluted law that did not satisfy the national indigenous demands. After this great intent to go through democratic channels, and not through Presidential favors, failed the EZLN and specially Marcos went into silence for years. At the same time, many civil organizations like the Frente Zapatista de Liberación Nacional (FZLN), a non-armed political arm inspired by the EZLN continued writing, working, and discussing these and other issues of discrimination and social justice. The EZLN proposed an expansion of national society to include marginalized groups.[11]

While the government talked of the stagnation of the peace process, it conducted what the Zapatistas call a "low-intensity war" that consisted in the harassment and intimidation of civilian populations in Zapatista regions. The Mexican government was operating under the old national paradigm and the international relations of sovereignty and nonintervention. Therefore, despite the large displays for solidarity from abroad and people from all over the world flying to Chiapas to show their support, the Mexican government framed the revolt as an internal national security issue.

The Mexican government showed a different discourse under the PRI than under the PAN national parties. Salinas first acknowledged the Zapatistas as transgressors of the law but was forced to negotiate with them because of international and national pressure. Zedillo wanted to appear conciliatory and wanting peace but without giving in to their demands. Later, Fox and his cabinet denied that there was even a problem in Chiapas.[12] Fox used a different approach talking much about his willingness for peace and called Marcos his partner in peace, but still, actions did not fully match his words. Nonetheless, it has been very important that despite the post 9/11 environment, the Mexican army and government have abstained from even suggesting that the EZLN is a terrorist group.

It was the desire to look politically stable and respecting of human rights to foreign investors and the demands of the national and international public opinion that saved the Zapatistas from being eliminated through force as happened some decades earlier to armed opposition groups during the so-called guerra sucia or dirty war period.[13] Transnational advocacy networks interested in Chiapas gave legitimization to the EZLN and thus saved it from been exterminated. Genocide was the word that the media used to describe the government military campaigns in January 1994. And it was also these international networks that created a channel to get their demands to the government as serious issues to solve. We saw that besides the use of arms and later mass demonstrations, the best way by which the EZLN had its demands listened to was because of the pressure that individuals abroad put on their governments which in turn pressed the Mexican government to address the Zapatista demands in what Keck and Sikkink (1998) call the boomerang effect.

The Mexican government was not counting on the EZLN's use of the media, especially the internet.[14] The Zapatista word is out there freely accessible on the web. The Zapatistas themselves often called to press conferences. Nonetheless, it is important to notice how most of Mexican and international media failed in 1994 to voice their words; only the progressive, left, and independent media reproduced their diagnoses and demands. Readers had to be proactive to find the Zapatista statements and version of the story before it was distorted by the non-sympathizers on mainstream Mexican media. Juana Ponce resumes very well the situation of the media regarding the rebellion.

> "With the media trained on him and on Chiapas, a stream of rebel communiqués—often penned by Marcos—start to appear in the press and run like wildfire through the Internet. Over time, through a campaign of misinformation and silence, the Mexican government struggles to control the situation and denies that there is a conflict. With the exception of coverage in La Jornada—the second largest newspaper in Mexico—and Proceso magazine—an important news and arts weekly—and Chiapas' own El Tiempo, the Zapatistas practically disappear from the national press. But not so on the Internet, where the lifeline for the movement reaches out, grows, and spreads."[15]

"La Jornada," regularly published the EZLN communiqués and followed the development of this movement, but the favorite media of the Zapatistas and their sympathizers is the Internet, which has allowed people throughout Mexico and the world know about the EZ struggle.

The Zapatista leaders through Marcos' pen have made sure that their demands are always clearly stated and justified. The person interested just needs to be subscribed to their mailing list, go to their homepage, or read "La Jornada" to know their reaction to the latest events affecting Mexican and their struggle for indigenous rights and decoloniality. This is just one of the things that differentiates the EZLN from other Latin American guerillas.

In 1994, the major Mexican press and TV only reported the government's version of the conflict. The media talked about foreign influences, about a conspiracy from the left (maybe Cárdenas) or from the right (maybe a PRI ex-president against the new the new PRI technocrats) to destabilize Mexico, thus robbing agency from indigenous people and EZLN activists. With Fox's openness to the conflict and the march to Mexico City in 2001, the two big Mexican TV networks Televisa and TV Azteca even united to bring "A Concert for Peace" a drastic change from their initial omission of the Zapatistas. The independent channels that have brought together civil society and the EZLN were the cause for this change. The media could not continue hiding information without losing credibility.

The EZLN is famous and well-respected outside of Mexico, thanks to its strong NGO-like organization and because the EZLN leaders are conscious of the importance of national civil and international support. The EZ knows that the best way to gain support is through intellectual and moral means, and by the fact that the indigenous people in México have many reasons to protest. That is why "[The EZLN on] its Second Declaration from the Lacandón Jungle" announced in effect a civil strategy for the formation of a nonpartisan popular front against the regime. The tactics were ingenious: "from websites on the Internet, globally, virtually, bring the outside inside, convoke a national concentration of "civil society" in the jungle."[16]

This worked and the Zapatistas had numerous sympathizers in Italy, the United States, Spain, and many other countries. For example, in November 2002 there was an Aguascalientes convention in Madrid discussing the importance of Zapatismo at an international level. The EZ had also done solidarity tours throughout the United States.

Although the supporters of the Zapatistas outside of Mexico are portrayed as been young people, there are also many educated adults, workers, Italian politicians, and intellectuals including Noam Chomsky and the Portuguese literature-Nobel Prize José Saramago as well as popular musicians who support them. Many people in developed countries may not have many things in common with the Zapatistas in their daily lives, but they agree with them on one thing: ideology. It is not that people go in caravans or support trips to Chiapas just to see the community as if it was a museum or to find the exotic and pure that they cannot find home, but the majority does it out of principle because they see it as a just cause. Neo-Zapatismo also became a rallying cry against economic neo-liberalism worldwide.

Zapatismo with its blaming on the NAFTA, open markets, international uneven trade, and US imperialism has also served as a source of inspiration to members of the so-called antiglobalization movement.[17] Many organizers and activists protesting in Seattle against the World Trade Organization in 1999 were inspired and supportive of the EZLN, so were those protesting the World Bank and the International Monetary Fund in Washington, DC, in April 2000.

After Mexico opened its frontiers to international trade, the importation of American corn and Argentinean meat made it hard for many small farmers, like rural people of Chiapas to make a living.[18] As in other parts of Latin America, indigenous people must chop down forests to make a living or burn them to farm the land; something that is bad for the environment. Globalization has not stopped this. On the other hand, the demand for meat that the IMF imposed on Mexico has depleted many areas to turn them into grazing land. Multinational and big local companies have lands rich in forests and jungles all throughout Latin America and exploit the natural resources whether they be oil, lumber, or biological diversity. The EZLN stood to remind the world that there is more to life than the market and that the price of corn set in the market should not have preference over the dignity of those who grow it. And the EZLN called on the word to this reality and similar realities happening in every country.

The Many Marcos Behind the Mask

For many Zapatismo and the EZLN are synonymous with *Marcos*. Juana Ponce de León describes Marcos as "... the most wanted man in Mexico, transgressor of the law, Internet guerrilla, catalyst for a new kind of revolution, poet."[19] Marcos became a well-known writer, an ideologist against economic globalization and in favor of indigenous rights, he openly declared war on the government and has challenged the governments of Salinas, Zedillo Fox, etc. Marcos has spoken in the national and international media since 1994 and his charisma has only grown.

The Zapatistas have stated many times that war is their last resort and that only when they started using ski masks, they started to be seen. The justification of war is the extreme poverty that the people of Chiapas must endure; even Salinas could not deny this reality. The Zapatista soldiers' reason to fight was that they had nothing to lose and a lot to win. At least fighting, they raised their voices and could die in dignity compared with the former ignominy. This is clearly stated in Marcos' letter "Dying in Order to Live" of January 6, 1994.

DURING THE PAST TEN years more than 150,000 indigenous have died of curable diseases. The federal, state, and municipal governments and their economic and social programs do not take into account any real solution to our problems; they limit themselves to giving us charity every time elections roll around. Charity resolves nothing but for the moment, and again death visits our homes. This is why we think no, no more; enough dying this useless death; it is better to fight for change. If we die now, it will not be with shame but with dignity, like our ancestors. We are ready to die, 150,000 more if necessary, so that our people awaken from this dream of deceit that holds us hostage, Subcomandante Marcos.[20]

To understand the conditions that the people in Chiapas live, there is no better text than the ironic tourist-guide-styled "A Storm and a Prophecy. Chiapas: The Southeast in Two Winds."[21] Written by Marcos in August 1992 but not released publicly until 1994. As written by Marcos himself, the "First Wind: The one from above, which narrates how the supreme government, touched by the poverty of the indigenous peoples of Chiapas lavished the area with hotels, prisons, barracks, and a military airport. It also tells how the beast feeds on the blood of the people, as well as other miserable and unfortunate happenings."[22] In this text, we can see Marcos literary ability and his literary influences, familiar to literate Mexicans.

The EZLN was only able to make its demands heard after taking up arms. As Subcomandante Marcos put it "We did not go to war on January 1st to kill or to have them kill us. We went to make ourselves heard."[23] The EZLN now uses weapons more as a means of defense than as a means of attack. The EZLN is a group that has fought more on the intellectual level than on the battlefield. The EZ has had more victories in the political and civilian fields than through military actions. The Zapatistas' most effective weapon is its representative, el "sub-comandante Marcos" and his communiqués.[24] Marcos represents the later figure of the Romanticism, an educated man fighting for the rights of those who have less. Many women confessed to have felt in love with him because of his courage, sexy eyes, and eloquent speeches. Marcos is a dark and anonymous figure behind a mask. His only contacts with the outside world are his eyes and his wise words. Marcos has turned out to be more of a warrior of the pen than a military commander. Zapatistas say that they wear masks, other than for personal security reasons, to represent the people who have no face; the marginalized, the forgotten and left behind. They represent the common people who are always left behind, the poor, the disposed not only of Chiapas but of Mexico and the world. In their call on people from all over the world, their use of electronic media and the written word, Zapatismo represents the warfare of the 21st century.

Marcos is the undeniable leader and the public figure of this movement, but there are many enigmas surrounding him. He insists on calling himself *subcomandante* and he says that he is only the spokesperson of the group, not the chief. Proof of this was the fact that there were other commandants who addressed the Mexican Congress in 2001, especially when Comandante Esther referred to him as the chief of the army but not the highest chief of the EZLN.

At the beginning, some people thought that Marcos was just the person who happened to be in front of the cameras. Marcos himself has said that he was not in charge of the taking of San Cristóbal, but it was a woman who oversaw taking the town in 1994. Many journalists have testified that he was reading the communiqués, giving speeches, and talking to the people of San Cristóbal and to the tourists in the town's center plaza or "zócalo." Later Marcos would say that he was the one chosen to address people and the media because he was familiar with "Castilla" or Spanish. Many witnesses testified that Marcos speaks four languages; indeed, one can see in his communiqués that he often uses words in English and sometimes even some in French. Juana Ponce has testified to his mastery of English.[25] Marcos has a distinctive feature; while most Zapatistas are indigenous, Marcos is not. The fact that he has light skin invited a lot of criticism some people said he was using the Chiapas indigenous to carry *his own* revolution.

Maybe the fact that Marcos has a white appearance and that he speaks like a middle class, educated person with an accent from Mexico City makes him appealing to other middle class, educated people with a social consciousness both in Mexico and in the world. Many foreigners have been allowed to participate in this struggle and feel identified with the leadership, ideology, and methodology of this movement, which many have redirected against unbridled economic globalization and big international economic interests.

Many call him crazy and opportunist. During the march to Mexico City fighting for the recognition of the COCOPA agreement as federal law, many criticized him for talking in name of indigenous people. But the EZLN proved them wrong when throughout the march many other EZLN leaders, indeed Comandantes and not *subcomandantes*, among them many women, gave public speeches. The most important tactic was that Marcos did not speak in the Congress; it was various indigenous representatives who did. Critics did not falter—a Spanish member of the government called him a coward and said that he suffered "pánico escénico" for not talking in front of the Mexican Congress. But this was an intentional act to avoid individual protagonism and show the horizontal nature of the Zapatista movement.

The style of Marcos' writings is now familiar to many people around the globe. Marcos uses sarcasm and irony when possible. He is irreverent while addressing authority (just ask the Governor or Queretaro, who Marcos now calls "firulais," a familiar way to refer to a common dog in Mexico). He even has literary characters such as Don Durito de la Lacandona a beetle, or Don Juan an old Mayan Shaman. In letters and speeches, the Zapatistas frequently start with the words "Brothers and sisters ..." Marcos signs as Subcomandante Insurgente Marcos, which by itself expresses his rebellious state and his dependence on a higher body, one which often is the signatory of the communiqués "The Clandestine Indigenous Revolutionary Committee-General Command of the Zapatista National Liberation Army."

In his writings, Marcos makes reference to women, to the indigenous, to the poor and the oppressed. He questions the Mexican government, an unequal international trade. In his "First Declaration of the Lacandon Jungle," the EZLN through Marcos calls for the end of 500 hundred years of oppression that started with the arrival of the Spanish colonizers. The EZLN members ask for true democracy and following all the formalities they declare Salinas' government an illegitimate dictatorship. The EZLN also declares war on the Mexican army and asks for the unconditioned surrender of the Mexican army and at the same time calls for the protection of the civil society and asset the EZLN recognition of the Geneva War conventions. This document states that after taking a region, the Zapatistas would call for democratic elections and respect the natural resources of that region.

As the Subcomandante Insurgente Marcos said in his communiqué to Fernando Yáñez Muñoz regarding the launching of the self-denominated Zapatista magazine *Rebeldía*, "In present-day Mexico, the practice of politics and culture are full of myths. Ergo, the critique by the left should combat those myths. And there are not a few myths which inhabit the culture."[26] Marcos is not only an iconoclast, but he is also a paradigm shifter. Revolutions are paradigm changes in themselves, and Marcos is a full revolutionary in both senses of the word though rising in arms and changing the way in which people see issues. As a leader, as a public figure, and as an intellectual writer, he also defies paradigms.[27]

According to the dictionary, a paradigm is "a set of assumptions, concepts, values, and practices that constitutes a way of viewing reality for the community that shares them, especially in an intellectual discipline."[28] Thomas Kuhn "used the term to refer to a collection of procedures or ideas that instruct scientists, *implicitly*, what to believe and how to work."[29] Pubic sociologists and organic intellectuals have set to themselves as a task to challenge the paradigms in the sense of the prevailing or dominant ways of viewing the world.[30] In this sense, Marcos is a public intellectual. He has been able to identify many of the ills that affect Mexico. He has targeted some of the causes and some of the solutions only to be blocked by those in power. But in the process, changing the ways those in power are seen locally and abroad.

Marcos even defies not only the system but also the concept of early revolutionary movements which saw as the ultimate prize the acquisition of "Power." The neo-Zapatistas want structural and policy changes, but they do not want power in itself or for themselves. Like the indigenous people they represent, the Zapatistas want self-governance not to govern others. In this last point they keep loyal to Emiliano Zapata who along with Pancho Villa left Mexico City after having taken control of it and sitting on the "silla presidencial" for a photo session. Like a throne, the chair represents the Mexican central power. The Mexican Imperial Presidency. After helping oust Huerta, Emiliano Zapata let Pancho Villa be the one sitting in the presidential seat "for the photo."[31] They soon left the capital keeping their demands for lands for agricultural and cattle workers in the north and south of the country, but they did not see themselves as fit or interested in governing.

Photo of Francisco Villa, Emiliana Zapata, and their close associates. Taken by Agustín Víctor Casasola in 1914 in Palacio Nacional, Mexico City. Now in the public domain. Source: The Granger Collection.

There are many other historical paragons between Marcos and Emiliano Zapata. "Though a leader of peons, Zapata was not a peon himself. His father, Gabriel, was a small property owner and Emiliano grew up not in a *choza* (hut) but in a comfortable abode-and-stone house. Neither he nor his brother, Eufemio, ever had to work as day laborers on one of the big haciendas."[32] Marcos is by all accounts an urban, middle class, educated, intellectual but like Zapata, he decided to give up for good any privileges he had to join the disenfranchised.[33] Youth as always is moved by those romantic Che-like Quixotic figures who show heroism in daring to challenge the system even though they know their victory is almost impossible. Recalling the Greek tragedy of the self-immolated hero, who faces its fate although he knows his destiny.

First through arms, later through the pen, and then through silence and self-effacement, Marcos is trying to bring down the system because he knew it is not fair for the majority. Otilio Montaño was the rural school leader who was the intellectual advisor of Zapata. Moreover, Marcos seems to be a fusion of Zapata and Otilio Montaño. As he underlines in the EZLN communiqués, he is not the leader, he is not the head of the EZLN. Marcos does not want to be like Zapata. Emiliano Zapata was killed and when he died the first Zapatismo practically also died with me. The memory and the myth remain, but the political program and lobbying ending. An agrarian reform probably did not go as far as needed. It was also something dismantled by Salinas de Gortari with his neoliberal reforms. Marcos is aware of history and ready to learn its lessons. Maybe that is why he correctly did not support Fox as the opposition pro-Democracy candidate in the 2000 elections, because Marcos knew that Vicente Fox could be another Gustavo Madero in the sense that there could be no major structural changes even after he took power. Fox is just another opposition leader who once in the government adopted many of the same "realist" perspective as the former inhabitants of Los Pinos (former Presidential House).

In Mexico and abroad the intellectuals from the left started supporting the original Zapatismo after the publication of the Plan de Ayala, the arrival of General Huerta, and the closure of La Casa del Obrero Mundial. In the case of the EZLN, intellectuals followed the movement and spoke favorably only after the cease-fire since many criticized the use of force.

Marcos is an intellectual inspired by classic and contemporary intellectuals and he is also inspiring to present-day intellectuals by his rhetoric ability as a rebel leader who never became mainstream or part of the power elite.

The EZLN is post-modern because it does not claim to have the answer. As Marcos said, the EZLN asks the question knowing that the answer will be plural.[34] He and the EZLN are experimenting with the "autonomous communities," but he does not claim he has realized the final utopia or a Heaven on Earth. He knows that only time can tell but that it may be worth trying.

Marcos does not aspire to hold political power through an official position but this carries a contradiction in itself since through a cosmopolitan paradigm the success that Marcos has had establishing networks and gaining recognition for home and abroad has brought power to the EZLN, the indigenous peoples, and his own person.[35] As James Petras (2002) remarks, the only way that the EZLN can keep legitimation as an armed force (even in a defensive way) is as long as it is attacked by paramilitaries and harassed by the army, which largely has been the case to this day. But if this was to change the only way for the EZLN to keep the support of the urban and international groups would be to get integrated into civil society and to work through conventional political routes.

On January 1st, 1996 in the Fourth Declaration from the Lacandon Jungle, the Zapatistas' high command called for the formation of the Zapatista Front of National Liberation, the FZLN, a civil and non-violent organization, independent and democratic, Mexican and international, to struggle for democracy, liberty and justice in Mexico. The new front would certainly be out of the ordinary in Mexico, "a political force whose members will not hold or aspire to take power, a force that would not be a political party."[36] Just as Villa and Zapata did, the FZLN would fight to bring political change in Mexico but not to substitute the people in power.

In the summer of 2000, Vicente Fox from the PAN won the Mexican Presidency and Pablo Salazar Mendiguchía, candidate from the alliance of eight opposition parties, was elected as the new governor of Chiapas. Did the Zapatistas let the genie of political inconformity in Mexico out of the bottle? Many Mexicans were tired of the PRI and the system after many years, but they didn't do anything. It seems that after the EZ stroke, civil society woke up and made sure to participate more in politics and improve the electoral system. First, Cardenas from the PRD won Mexico City, then Vicente Fox from the PAN won the presidential election in Mexico. Pablo Salazar Mendiguchía from the coalition of all opposition parties won in Chiapas. But the change has just begun, and many things needed to be changed. The fact that the opposition won many important positions does not disappear *la raison d'être* of the Zapatistas. As Salazar said, "the causes of the EZLN revolt are still with us and they will continue with us for a long time," because the lag of Chiapas is enormous. Decades will be necessary to bring Chiapas to the standards that Northern Mexican states enjoy today.[37]

The big question Mexico faces is how its people should be helped. It will be hard to incorporate a better standard of living for the indigenous communities, especially with limited economic resources and bad services, while respecting nature and their indigenous traditions. Mexico became and early adopter of economic globalization, and Fox nor AMLO are going back despite the latter's rhetoric. Nevertheless, the EZ made sure that the system cannot continue ignoring indigenous people.

The Zapatista image, both national and international, is susceptible to many distortions. The EZLN communiqués and official resources show us one view, the media shows a different one, and the government tries to minimize the issues as much as possible. The researcher, the reader, and the public in general have a great task trying to find what lies behind the Zapatista masks. To recognize our own paradigm is the first way to understand others because as Marcos says, "The intellectual work of the left should, above all else, be a critical and self-critical exercise."[38]

So, despite its name, the EZLN became more of a social movement than an army. Its tactics were those of contentious politics where violence was used to conduct politics through other means beyond the electoral process, lobbying, or marching by themselves.[39] Zapatismo is both deeply local, based on the highlands and Lacandon jungle in Chiapas, as well as a transnational social movement.[40] It is simultaneously an anti-colonial movement asking for indigenous rights, as well as a movement for radical democracy where the power is truly based in civil society, and an open defiance and opposition to neoliberal globalization where international exchange and cooperation do not mean putting the interest of transnational corporations first.[41] The Zapatista movement was a training ground for alter-globalization activists, which in turn later influence the May 15 movement in Spain which in turn propelled the Occupy movement.[42] In not strictly winning nor loosing, in not becoming a martyr nor staying continuously in the public eye, the Zapatista movement has succeeded in reminding people not to put all their faith in a charismatic leader but rather in the people as a collective.[43] The EZLN social movement became the paradigm for issues to address in the twentieth-first century: indigenous rights, environmental stewardship, civil rights, asking for liberal equality while respecting minority rights and cultures, international solidarity among activists and civil society, a horizontal organization, and a true collective democratic practice.

Notes

1   Charles Tilly (2020).
2   Marco Estrada Saavedra (2016).
3   Andreas Schedler (2002)
4   *Zapatista*, Documentary (Big Noise Films, 1999).
5   Peter Rosset and Shea Cunningham (1994).
6   John Womack (1999).
7   Ross, p. 32.
8   Ross, p. 32.
9   Huchim, *México* (1994).
10 Womack, Rebellion in Chiapas, 50.
11 Carlos Monsiváis et al. (2001).
12 Elio Enriquez (2001).
13 Carlos Montemayor (2008).
14 Fiona Jeffries (2001).
15 Subcomandante Marcos (2011).
16 Womack, Rebellion in Chiapas, 48.
17 "Sin importar cuánto intento se ha hecho para reducir el asunto de Chiapas al de solo un conflicto local, cuya solución debería ser encontrada dentro de los límites estrictos de una aplicación de una ley nacional... lo que se está llevando a cabo en las montañas de Chiapas y en la selva Lacandona alcanza más allá de las fronteras de México al corazón de esa parte de la humanidad que no ha renunciado, y jamás renunciará, a los sueños y las esperanzas, el simple imperativo de una justicia igual para todos," Jose Saramago.
18 Tom Barry (1995).
19 Marcos, Our Word Is Our Weapon, XXV.
20 Marcos, 17.
21 Subcomandante Marcos (1994).
22 Marcos, Our Word Is Our Weapon, 22.
23 Womack, Rebellion in Chiapas, 44.
24 Subcomandante Marcos (1995).
25 Marcos, Our Word Is Our Weapon.
26 Subcomandante Marcos (2002).
27 Rubén Dri (2002).
28 Dictionary.com (2000).
29 John Horgan (1996).
30 Dri, "Debate Sobre El Poder En El Movimiento Popular."
31 Infobae (2021).
32 Jim Tuck (2008).
33 "Marcos es un serio desafío que la intelligentsia mundial tiene que medir: ha integrado valores democráti-cos revolucionarios en su vida cotidiana. Lleva la misma vida austera de sus camaradas indios. Discute y "gobierna obedeciendo". Soporta una difícil situación existencial, reflejada en las profundas consecuen-cias de un giro hacia la política civil o la continuación de la lucha armada ... Trata de adecuarse a reali-dades que plantean decisiones difíciles. Se toma en serio las ideas." James Petras. La Izquierda Devuelve El Golpe, Rebeldia. November 2002.
34 Zapatista.

35 "El poder es una realidad propia del ámbito de las relaciones humanas que, de una u otra manera, siempre son sociales y políticas. No existe, no es, igual que los sujetos. Se hace, se construye de la misma manera en que se construyen los sujetos. Éstos, para crearse, empeñan una lucha a muerte por el reconocimiento. Esta lucha genera poder. Generarse como sujeto es generar poder." Rubén Dri (2002).

36 Womack, Rebellion in Chiapas, 50.

37 Pablo Salazar Mendiguchía (2000).

38 Marcos, "Letter from the Subcomandante Insurgente Marcos EZLN to Architect Fernando Yáñez Muñoz."

39 Ernesto Castañeda and Cathy Lisa Schneider (2017).

40 Guiomar Rovira Sancho (2009).

41 Ernesto Castañeda and Amber Shemesh (2020).

42 Ernesto Castañeda (2012).

43 BBC (2018).

References

Barry, T. (1995). *Zapata's Revenge: Free Trade and the Farm Crisis in Mexico*. Boston, MA: South End Press.

BBC (2018). El día que el subcomandante Marcos 'se quitó la capucha' en una entrevista con BBC Mundo. *BBC News Mundo* December 30, https://www.bbc.com/mundo/noticias-america-latina-46317955.

Castañeda, E. (2012). The indignados of Spain: A precedent to occupy Wall Street. *Social Movement Studies* 11 (3–4) August 1: 309–319. https://doi.org/10.1080/14742837.2012.708830.

Castañeda, E. and Schneider, C.L. (2017). *Collective Violence, Contentious Politics, and Social Change: A Charles Tilly Reader*. New York: Routledge.

Castañeda, E. and Shemesh, A. (2020). Overselling globalization: The misleading conflation of economic globalization and immigration, and the subsequent Backlash. *Social Sciences* 9 (5) (2020): 61.

Dictionary.com, (2000). *The American Heritage Dictionary of the English Language. Fourth Edition*. New York: Houghton Mifflin Company. www.dictionary.com.

Dri, R. (2002). Debate Sobre El Poder En El Movimiento Popular. *Rebeldia* (November edition).

Enriquez, E. (2001). Culpa Marcos a Castañeda de Haber Bloqueado La Participación Del CICR En La Marcha Zapatista. *La Jornada* February 23, https://www.jornada.com.mx/2001/02/23/012n1pol.html.

EZLN (1994). *Zapatistas! Documents of the New Mexican Revolution*, 68–69. Brooklyn, New York: Autonomedia http://lanic.utexas.edu/project/Zapatistas/index.html.

Horgan, J. (1996). *The End of Science*, 43. New York: Broadway Books.

Huchim, E. (1994). *México 1994: la rebelión y el magnicidio*. Nueva Imagen.

Infobae (2021). Villa y Zapata: la historia detrás de la icónica fotografía en la silla presidencial. *Infobae* December 7, https://www.infobae.com/america/mexico/2021/12/07/villa-y-zapata-la-historia-detras-de-la-iconica-fotografia-en-la-silla-presidencial/.

Jacobo, C.R. (1994). *Los altos de Chiapas: la voz de las armas*. Grupo Editorial Planeta.

Jeffries, F. (2001). Zapatismo and the intergalactic age. In: *Globalization and Postmodern Politics: From Zapatistas to High-Tech Robber Barons* (ed. R. Burbach, F. Jeffries, and W.I. Robinson), 129–144. Sterling, VA: Pluto Press.

Keck, M.E. and Sikkink, K. (1998). *Activists Beyond Borders: Advocacy Networks in International Politics*. Cornell University Press.

Marcos, S. (1994). *Chiapas: The Southeast in Two Winds*. Zapatistas! LANIC: http://lanic.utexas.edu/project/Zapatistas/chiapas.html.

Marcos, S. (1995). *Shadows of Tender Fury: The Letters and Communiqués of Subcomandante Marcos and the Zapatista Army of National Liberation.* Watsonville, CA: Human Rights Committee https://www.si.edu/object/siris_sil_1011354.

Marcos, S. (2002). Letter from the Subcomandante Insurgente Marcos EZLN to Architect Fernando Yáñez Muñoz. *La Jornada.*

Marcos, S. (2011). *Our Word Is Our Weapon: Selected Writings,* XXV–XXVI. New York: Seven Stories Press.

Mendiguchía, P.S. (2000). *Talk About the Situation in Chiapas at the University of California Berkeley.* UC Berkeley, Berkeley, CA: Center for Latin American Studies October.

Monsiváis, C., Bellinghausen, H., and Marcos, S. (2001). Subcomandante Marcos, entrevista con Carlos Monsiváis y Hermann Bellinghausen. *Enlace Zapatista* (blog), January 8, https://enlacezapatista.ezln.org.mx/2001/01/08/subcomandante-marcos-entrevista-con-carlos-monsivais-y-hermann-bellinghausen/.

Montemayor, C. (2008). *Guerra En El Paraíso.* Editorial Seix Barral: Mexico City.

Petras, J. (2002). La Izquierda Devuelve El Golpe. *Rebeldia* November.

Ross, J. (1995). *Rebellion from the Roots: Indian Uprising in Chiapas.* Monroe, ME: Common Courage Press.

Rosset, P. and Cunningham, S. (1994). *Understanding Chiapas.* Institute for Food & Development Policy.

Saavedra, M.E. (2016). *La Comunidad Armada Rebelde y El EZLN: Un Estudio Histórico y Sociológico Sobre Las Bases de Apoyo Zapatistas En Las Cañadas Tojolabales de La Selva Lacandona (1930-2005), Segunda edición corregida y aumentada.* El Colegio de México: México, D.F.

Sancho, G.R. (2009). *Zapatistas Sin Fronteras: Las Redes de Solidaridad Con Chiapas y El Altermundismo, 1., Biblioteca Era.* Ediciones Era: México, D.F.

Schedler, A. (2002). Elections without democracy: The menu of manipulation. *Journal of Democracy* 13 (2): 36–50.

Tilly, C., Castañeda, E., and Wood, L.J. (2020). *Social Movements, 1768–2018.* New York: Routledge http://www.loc.gov/catdir/toc/ecip0411/2003025659.html.

Tuck, J. (2008). Zapata and the intellectuals. *MexConnect* October 9, https://www.mexconnect.com/articles/302-zapata-and-the-intellectuals/.

Womack, J. (1999). *Rebellion in Chiapas: An Historical Reader,* 43. New York: New Press http://archive.org/details/rebellioninchiap00woma.

14

Decolonizing Peyote Politics in Mexico and Southwest U.S.

OSIRIS SINUHÉ GONZÁLEZ ROMERO

Introduction

This analysis thoroughly examines how colonialism has greatly influenced the creation and implementation of prohibition policies, ultimately denying several fundamental rights. This chapter aims to analyze the significant impact of these policies on critical areas such as the right to health, the rights of indigenous peoples, and the right to cognitive liberty. "Historically, the first Indian tribes who use peyote religiously and medicinally were the Indian tribes of Mexico and southern Texas, including the Aztecs, Huichol, Tarahumara, Lipan Apaches and Mescalero Apaches. Eventually, the peyote religion disseminated from Mexico to tribes throughout North America".[1] It is crucial to comprehend colonialism's extensive and far-reaching effects on diverse aspects of society and culture. One of the first objectives is to explain how the paradox of criminalizing nature, but also the knowledge and spirituality of native peoples, was generated by considering the ritual and ceremonial uses of psychoactive substances such as idolatry and superstition.

This study employs *critical historiography* to scrutinize historical sources, particularly from the early colonial period, to comprehend the emergence of colonialism as a political and ideological system in the latter half of the sixteenth century. The pertinence of decolonial theory lies in recognizing that the repercussions of colonialism persist to this day.[2] Therefore, it is imperative to investigate how colonialism has influenced the formulation and implementation of public policies and the ethical and cultural practices that endorse prohibition policies.[3]

Three significant historical moments have influenced drug policies in Latin America. The first occurred during colonization in the sixteenth century, when the trade of endemic plants like cacao and tobacco became globalized. A prevailing Puritanism persisted for around four centuries.[4] The second turning point emerged in the mid-twentieth century after the discovery of Mescaline, LSD, and the spreading of knowledge about ceremonies with psilocybin mushrooms in Mexico. This sparked international interest in studying and potentially using psychoactive substances for therapeutic, commercial, or military purposes. The counterculture and social movements against the Vietnam War resulted in implementation of the "War on Drugs." The third point of emergence occurred in the second decade of the twenty-first century, known as the Psychedelic Renaissance.[5] Scientific research resumed after several decades of interruption due to the therapeutic efficacy of certain psychedelic substances against mental illnesses and the emergence of a new and broad market.

The Criminalization of Nature (1620–1820)

The criminalization of nature during the colonial era was colonialism's stark and contradictory effect. Native plants, ceremonies, and rituals were unjustly condemned by the evangelization enterprise initiated by the friars. Psychoactive plants were unfairly labeled as idolatrous or superstitious practices rather than being recognized for their therapeutic properties. This colonial approach is evident in various historical works, such as the *Florentine Codex* by Friar Bernardino de Sahagún[6] and the *Natural History of New Spain* by physician Francisco Hernández (2015),[7] all of which were written prior to the Inquisition's edicts in 1620. It is worth noting that *the Geographical Reports of New Spain* and other notable documents do mention the therapeutic uses of psychoactive plants.

The therapeutic effects of psilocybin mushrooms, peyote (*Lophophora williamsii*), and some species of daturas (*Datura stramonium* and *Datura inoxia*) are recognized in these works. However, their sacred and ceremonial uses were condemned, as they are linked to elements of ancient indigenous spirituality. During pre-colonial times, plants, fungi, or animals were considered deities or sacred entities in themselves or as a way of communicating with ancestors or other non-human or supernatural entities. These works show how, before the legal prohibition was implemented, a moral condemnation was developed; sacred and ceremonial uses were stigmatized, which can be explained in the context of the religious evangelization enterprise associated with establishing the colonial regime.[8]

The point of emergence of this criminalization of Nature is found in the edict of the Inquisition of 1620, in which the consumption of peyote and other herbs is prohibited under penalty of ex-communication and trial. It is no longer just a moral condemnation but a legal order. It is, therefore, the origin of the first prohibitionist policy developed on the American continent. Infringement of this order resulted in the possibility of being brought to trial and punished with imprisonment, public humiliation, and physical torture. This is not a theological debate or a metaphysical abstraction; the politics of prohibition has been installed in the body and outlined how behavior and morals are modeled concerning the cultural uses of psychoactive plants and mushrooms.

The paradox is twofold because peyote, mushrooms, and other plants are criminalized because their psychoactive effects were related to ancient cults. However, the users have also been criminalized, and their bodies have been punished. There is a double criminalization of Nature; firstly, plants, fungi, and animals, and secondly, human behavior. Unfortunately, this criminalization continues today, as we intend to explain in this research. In summary, the edict of the Inquisition in 1620 represents the emergence of the politics of punishment.[9]

Despite the stigmatization in the following decades, the consumption of plants and substances for various purposes did not completely vanish. Several documents reference trials and inquisitorial processes on the consumption of peyote during the colonial period, representing a valuable source for understanding the cultural uses of psychoactive substances during that time. However, these documents are still awaiting systematic study.

The documents reveal that peyote consumption and rituals, and trade persisted. They offer valuable insights into the study of issues such as consumption based on race, gender roles, and divination practices. The inquisitorial peyote archives are a valuable resource for comprehending the impact of colonialism on the cultural usage of this cactus, both by mestizo people and native communities.

To understand the effects of colonialism and acculturation during the colonial era, it is crucial to consider Dr. Gonzálo Aguirre Beltrán's (1963) work and decolonial theory. While there are numerous accounts of peyote use, there is limited documentation on the consumption of mushrooms in archives. Although some trials were recorded in central Mexico in the early sixteenth century, information on mushroom use in the seventeenth and eighteenth centuries is scarce. Despite this, specialists have discovered that the knowledge of psilocybin mushrooms remained clandestine and was passed down through generations by word of mouth. This kept it hidden from outsiders and friars.

A valuable historical source is the *Treatise of the Heathen Superstitions That Today Live Among the Indians Native to This New Spain*, written by Hernando Ruiz de Alarcón (1984). As a zealous priest, he documented and initiated inquisitorial processes against individuals in Morelos and Guerrero. This colonial source sheds light on the cultural uses of *ololiuhqui* but also reveals the prohibitionist mentality of the Holy Inquisition's edict and the criminalization of the spirituality of indigenous peoples and Nature.

The criminalization of Nature and demonization of the cultural uses of psychoactive substances are some of the most notorious effects of colonialism. By developing clandestinely, many rituals had to be moved to secluded and silent places, performed late at night, and changed the names of sacred plants and mushrooms to those corresponding to the saints of the Catholic Church. The mushrooms were called "holy children," the peyote: "Santa Rosa," and the *ololiuhqui*: "Seeds of the Virgin." This change in the nomenclature and the incorporation of symbols and characters of the Catholic religion has led researchers to speak of a religious syncretism or spiritual synergy.

Antidrug Crusades and Internal Colonialism (1820–1950)

The situation in Latin America remained unchanged after the Independence movements and the establishment of national states. In Mexico, there was a legislative debate on the rights of native peoples. The liberal historian José María Luis Mora believed it was unnecessary to legislate on "indigenous rights" because all citizens were now equal according to the law, regardless of ethnicity or race. However, Nahua lawyer Juan de Dios Rodriguez Puebla argued that historical, economic, and cultural injustices faced by native peoples during the colonial period could not simply be erased by decree.[10] Rodriguez Puebla believed that true equality could only be achieved by creating a legal framework that recognized certain specific rights, such as the right to communal property and educational support for talented young people from different communities.

The recent political reconfiguration has transformed the old Indian Republics into town councils. The country distanced itself from its past, including the cultural heritage of the native peoples and the Spanish Monarchy, after gaining independence. Liberalism was embraced and put into practice through Enlightenment ideals. However, the religiosity of the native peoples was considered a hindrance to the country's "modernization" by liberal ideology. Political alliances with the Catholic Church were formed with some communities to protect the communal or collective ownership of land, contested by liberal ideology.

During this period, internal colonialism started to emerge. This was not just because people adopted the theoretical framework and values of colonial thought but also because of economic and social factors that persisted even after political independence. Unfortunately, the adverse effects of colonial thought, such as discrimination, stigmatization, and racism, continued to affect various aspects of culture.[11] One major mistake was denying the cultural heritage of native peoples, which hindered the colonization of thought and imagination.

> The use of peyote became a marker that separated the civilized, from the savage and with the advent of racial science a symptom of hereditary degeneration and inferiority. In response, the cactus became even more tightly bound into Indian identity and sacred practices. By the time anti-peyote campaigns emerged in the United States in the late nineteenth century government policy was largely conducted in the modern language of public health and social progress, but it was still shaped by missionaries for whom the suppression of peyote had long being a crucial aspect of the war for souls.[12]

The language and semantics around prohibition policies shifted in the nineteenth century. Rather than focusing on religious condemnation, the emphasis shifted to social condemnation. This resulted in less emphasis on superstitions and idolatrous customs and more on the dangers of diseases, madness, and primitive behavior. The hybrid language blurred the lines between medical, religious, and moral arguments. Peyote, for example, was described as a plague, pagan cult, and threat to civilization.[13] These antidrug crusades were incorporated into international treaties of the twentieth century, and their influence continues to be felt today. The rise of the Native American Church (NAC) was a response to overcoming the ban on ghost songs rituals, which became very popular among indigenous peoples in U.S., and an issue of concern for settlers and conservative groups. In 1883, U.S. Congress passed the "Indian Religious Crime Code of 1883" that impose ninety-days imprisonment and the withholding of government rations upon Indians found possessing peyote. Furthermore, this law specifically targeted the Lakota Sioux Sun Dance and Ghost Dance ceremonies, including any other religious and cultural practices of American Indians.[14]

In the late 1800s, interest in peyote arose after mescaline was discovered as the active substance that impacts the central nervous system. Anthropologist Carl Lumholtz studied the Sierra Tarahumara region and documented peyote's cultural and therapeutic uses in his book *Unknown México*. "So pleasing to the Tarahumaras is the effect of the plant that they attribute to it the power to give health and long life and to purify body and soul. They grind these cacti on a fresh or dried metate to put them in water. This liquid is the usual form in which they consume the jiculi."[15]

The Smithsonian Institution funded Lumholtz's expeditions through the National Museum of Natural History. However, despite its academic value, some scholars criticized Lumholtz's work for reproducing colonial values and practices in his theoretical framework and methodologies.[16] This demonstrates the paradox of colonialism, where even scientific or humanistic research can contribute to reproducing colonialism's values and practices, whether intentional or not.

During the last decades of the nineteenth century, various conservative social movements were organized that promoted the consolidation of the prohibition policy through the organization of "antidrug crusades." These crusades provoked significant changes in language and discourse. However, they strengthened the activism of organizations such as the "tea party" that would promote initiatives such as the "Prohibition Law."[17] These conservative groups would continue to push prohibition policies, but now in the context of implementing internal colonialism. On the one hand, due to the efforts of the emerging bourgeois elite, in their efforts to dissociate themselves from the past, and on the other hand, due to the estrangement between the cultural heritage bequeathed by indigenous peoples in U.S., and political institutions. In 1890, the Federal government classified peyote as an intoxicant and ordered Indian agents to destroy any peyote confiscated. The Oklahoma anti-peyote law subjected violators to a two-hundred dollar fine and six-month imprisionment and resulted on the incarceration of several Comanche and Kiowa Indians for the possession of peyote in 1907.[18]

During the antidrug movement, the Native American Church emerged, intending to protect the religious freedoms of its members. However, since the beginning, NAC members have been harassed, prosecuted, and incarcerated. The church's rituals involve the sacramental use of peyote, known for its therapeutic properties in treating mental and spiritual health issues. This interpretation of the peyote cult helped to restore connections between various Native American groups in the southern United States that were broken due to colonization. In 1918, the right of the Native American Church to use peyote for sacramental purposes was officially acknowledged.

Native American Church

Historically, Native American religious activities were disrespected and even outlawed by the federal government, frequently resulting in Native Americans being prosecuted and incarcerated for practicing their indigenous religious beliefs.[19] Nowadays, ritual and spiritual uses of psychedelics are central to the so-called psychedelic renaissance, particularly in anthropology and religious history. Both disciplines have contributed to a greater understanding of ritual applications in ancient cultures, indigenous peoples' spirituality, and new-age reinterpretations. Religious freedom is one of the critical elements of the so-called psychedelic research rebirth, primarily due to the implementation of the Religious Freedom Restoration Act (RFRA) in the United States. This modification has had a significant impact since it provides for some exceptions to the general norm, and, more importantly, it constitutes a crack in the armor of prohibition policies. The Native American Church of Jesus Christ (NAC) and some ayahuasca churches such as *Santo Daime* and *Uniâo do Vegetal* are well-known examples in the U.S. All of them are syncretic cults which embrace indigenous spirituality and Christian cultural features. This syncretism could explain their acceptance in the U.S.

The foundation of NAC was a response to overcome the ban of the ghost songs ritual and the harassment, discrimination, and lack of recognition of indigenous peoples within the United States. The peyote ritual comes from Mexico, especially due to the influence of Guillermo Chevato a Lipan Apache from Coahuila, who fled from his hometown, due to the harrasment of Mexican Army. He crossed the border and became a relative of Quanah Parker, a roadman, and founder of the Half-Moon ritual. The peyote cult grew rapidly among the native peoples of Oklahoma. A significant cultural feature was that Native peoples considered peyote as a medicine, in spite of the fact of the anti-peyote crusades of the late nineteenth century. Furthermore, the peyote cult was considered a counter balance against colonialism: "Bodies healed by peyote recovered a kind of truth, the truth of their indigeneity. Peyote was a means of expressing that truth because it allowed them to claim a space beyond the colonizers's gaze, in which their bodies gain a degree of distance from the marginalization and exploitation they face in everyday life."[20]

Establishing and recognizing NAC was challenging. Even within Native American peoples, there is a history of hostility and anti-peyotist activities. "Among the Navajos, the main barrier was not the Bureau of Indian Affairs, but the Navajo Tribal Council and anti-Peyotist Navajos acting independently. After the arrests of Peyotist priests in 1938, the Tribal Council met to discuss peyote in 1940." Furthermore, the media significantly influenced the stigmatization and criminalization of NAC. Many legal efforts were made to make it illegal, and many states introduced anti-peyote legislation throughout the first half of the twentieth century. However, because of its organization as a church (which began in Oklahoma in 1918), NAC has survived and thrived. Peyotism continued to spread throughout the twentieth century, providing a degree of spiritual and cultural autonomy to its members. It also developed variations in its nightlong service such as the Big Moon, half-Moon and Cross-Fire versions, the last incorporating elements of Christianity. As a defense against legal assaults peyotists sough constitutional protection.[21]

Nonetheless, the Employment Division of Oregon v. Smith trial, 494 US 872 (1990), prompted a profound shift in the cultural paradigm disputes. Alfred Smith, a Klamath Tribe member who was taken from his family and placed in a boarding school when he was eight years old, was hired by a substance abuse treatment facility in Roseburg, Oregon. The facility's director fired him even though Alfred Smith was a member of the NAC and had attended a peyote ceremony. Alfred Smith and Galen Black, who were both dismissed for attending the event, filed for unemployment benefits. The case reached the United States Supreme Court, which made a judgment about Native Americans without considering the First Amendment. If peyote is prohibited, and Oregon could send Smith and Black to prison for using it, it could surely refuse to pay them unemployment compensation.[22]

Antonin Scalia declared in 1990 that enjoying First Amendment religious freedom should allow police enforcement since religious pluralism was a "luxury" that should not be permitted. For example, religious convictions did not prevent somebody from complying with a statute barring state-regulated behavior. The NAC lost the privilege to use peyote due to that verdict. This trial sparked significant debate and revealed a paradox, given that religious freedom was one of the primary motivations for settlers' entrance into the United States. It is, paradoxically, one of the country's cornerstones, yet that ruling deprived Native Americans of their religious freedom. As leaders of other religious organizations recognized a threat to their religious freedom, the Supreme Court verdict sparked a movement to safeguard this civil right. This movement led to implementation of the Religious Freedom Restoration Act (RFRA). However, nowadays, peyote is considered Schedule I within the UN Convention on Psychotropic Substances (1971), i.e., without any therapeutic value. However, on the other hand, NAC considers it to have therapeutic properties. Both sides of the coin clearly show one of the core traits concerning the cultural paradigm clash mentioned above. Furthermore, peyotism is not an escape from reality as the general audience and many intellectuals and researchers believe, perhaps it is shocking, but it could be understood as a way to overcome colonialism: "Peyotism is an attempt by American Indians not only to cope with contemporary social and economic conditions but also to master and ultimately to transform them."[23]

During the last two decades NAC membership increased and placed a great demand for more peyote in Texas. At the present time an estimated of 400,000 or more NAC members purchase peyote from Texas dealers. This rapid increase in the number of its members has caused some concerns regarding sustainability. Scientists researching peyote reduction have concluded that a major cause is habitat destruction and overharvesting of the plant for ceremonial use. Currently, the annual peyote harvest in the United States has reached around 2,000,000 buttons and the federally-licensed Texas peyote dealers sell them to NAC members.

Nowadays, NAC embraces many regional chapters, and there is not a unified single cult. Different approaches coexist, especially regarding recent efforts to decriminalize peyote. Some leaders considers that only the members of the churchhave the right to consume peyote. Meanwhile, other leaders agree to decriminalize for everyone. There is no consensus on this issue, and this divergence position is at the core of the so-called peyote crisis. For example, the peyote growing in Texas is not enough to satisfy the requirements of the NAC, and due to this, some regions in Mexico face an over-expliotation. To face this issue, indigenous peiples condemn the exportation of Mexican peyote by foreigners, including NAC members, and strongly recommend that the U.S. government enciurage management plans for the collection of peyote that are appropiate for the Texas region.

In the Global South, a legal exemption in Mexico enables indigenous peoples to consume psychedelics (mostly psilocybin mushrooms and peyote) for ritual and spiritual purposes. The Mexican government decriminalized all narcotics in early 1940, right in the heart of World War II, by publishing the Reglamento Federal de Toxicomanas (Federal Drug Addiction Regulations). However, this attempt was short-lived due to international treaties signed and the pressure of Harry J. Anslinger (1892–1975), the first Commissioner of the Federal Bureau of Narcotics. The legal structure of Mexico is not based primarily on the right to religious freedom; instead, the legal framework is more akin to the Customary Law System, a mild form of legal pluralism. Nonetheless, there is considerable legal ambiguity, for psychedelics prevailed in Mexican society. For example, "even though signing of the Vienna Convention on Psychotropic Substances in 1971, the Mexican government agreed to tolerate the ritual use of these substances by indigenous peoples."[24] However, the Mexican government never passed legislation to this effect, and Mexican police regularly persecuted indigenous Peyotists during these years.

Wixárika Regional Council

The Wixárika (or Huichol) people have been making an annual pilgrimage to the sacred desert of Wirikuta for several centuries. During this pilgrimage, they perform their religious ceremonies and rituals, which involve the ingestion of peyote or *hikuri*. These practices have a long history, dating back to pre-colonial times,[25] and were initially developed by the native peoples of the North of Mexico and the South of the United States, where peyote grows. The Raramuris (Tarahumaras), Wixárika (Huicholes), Coras, and Lipan Apaches in Mexico have all documented the use of this cactus.

Archaeological evidence suggests that peyote buttons have been used for ceremonial purposes in southern Texas for 8500 years and 8900 years in Mexico. Soil, seeds, pollen samples, and rock art have been studied recently.[26,27] Some ceramics from Colima and Jalisco in western Mexico also display iconographic motifs that indirectly suggest the presence of peyote use from 300 BC. Based on its extensive use, it can be assumed that a market enabled the trade of this cactus from its origin in the Arid American deserts to other cities, particularly in central and southern Mexico.

In the worldview of the Wixárika people, the sacred desert of Wirikuta has a preponderant place because it is not only the place where peyote or *hikuri* grows but the place where the spirits of their ancestors dwell. There is the *Cerro Quemado*, which is the place where the sun was born in the cosmogony of the Wixárika and the desert inhabited by Tatewari, the fire grandfather who was the first *marakame* or "shaman" who led a pilgrimage to the sacred desert of Wirikuta.[28]

For centuries or even millennia, the Wixárika people have maintained their calendarical system, sacred geography, language, and knowledge about the therapeutic properties and ceremonial uses of a sacred cactus.[29] Despite Spanish colonization, the establishment of the modern State, and the "War on Drugs," the ceremonial and ritual uses of native peoples in Northern Mexico and Southern United States have persisted.

Anthropologist Fernándo Benítez documented the first pilgrimage to the Wirikuta desert in a small book called: *En la tierra mágica del peyote*. To deepen our understanding of specific aspects such as the corn-deer-peyote triad, the Nierika concept, and the festivals of the annual calendar system, we can refer to the works of Peter Furst (1976), Mariana Fresán Jiménez (2002), Johannes Neurath (2005), and Diana Negrín (2020). These works are also helpful in exploring the position of the Wixaritari people regarding the prohibition and decriminalization of peyote. It is worth noting that Article 195 bis of the penal code permits the Wixaritari people to use peyote for ceremonial purposes. However, this legal framework was not disseminated among the indigenous communities during the early years of its approval.

The current conflict began when the Mexican government granted 79 mining concessions to various companies, which covers a large portion of Wirikuta, roughly 70% of the total area, which is 140,212 ha. One of the companies, Revolution Resources, was granted a concession of 59,000 ha for its "Universo" project without considering the environmental impact that mining activity would have on the area.[30] This is a protected natural area, not just because of the endangered peyote species but also due to the value of the ecosystem. Additionally, the government should have recognized Wirikuta as a place of cultural significance for the Wixaritari people, making it a part of the nation's cultural heritage. The Wixárika opposes the large-scale mining operations and development of their ancestral land because rhese activities are destroying theor sacred religious sites at Wirikuta, where land development activities such as mining and agriculture have caused massive damage and destruction to the peyote habitat. Some foreign corporations remain in control of the indigenous lands. In Real de Catorce, México mountain silver mining operations have disposed of toxic metals like lead, mercury and arsenic on the soil where peyote cacti grow.[31]

Mining concessions were granted at the same time that Mexico's "War on Drugs" began. This served a dual purpose of taking away the Wixárika people's land and endangering the cultural and biological heritage connected to the cactus used for ceremonies and therapeutic purposes. These mining concessions involve a cultural genocide. Following the attack, various responses surfaced, including establishing the Wirikuta Defense Front and the participation of the Consejo Regional Wixárika (CRW). These organizations united leaders from different Wixárika communities and civil society groups, which previously worked with the communities such as the Wixárika Research Center. The conflict became more intricate due to the involvement of tomato farm owners who had started expanding their businesses on the outskirts of the desert. The mining industry and tomato farming require substantial amounts of water, which has a more significant impact on the region because it is a desert area.

Regarding this issue, a large greenhouse tomato industry deposits saline soilon the peyote habitat, which causes the peyote cactus perish. These greenhouse agricultural companies have planted hundreds of acres in the past five years, a dramatic increase for the fragile desert ecosystem. Scientists in Mexico studyng the declining peyote problem conclude that most significant threats are in ascending order: the induction of cattle pastures, conventional farming, and modern agriculture greenhouses, also population growth and development that entails, such as roads, dams, levees, mining and exploitation materials such as sand quarries, lime kilns, and quarries.

Several social movements have responded to the mining company's aggressive actions. Their goal is to revoke the mining concession, but they have been unsuccessful so far. The conflict is ongoing, and members of Wixaritari communities who oppose the company have been persecuted and imprisoned. Meanwhile, the mining company is promoting its project to bring economic benefits to the region and reduce migration, particularly among young people seeking better employment opportunities elsewhere.

The conflict in Wirikuta is of great significance to the National Indigenous Council. Exploiting antimony, uranium, gold, and silver in the San José de Coronados communities and the Santa Gertrudis dam, located in the municipalities of Catorce and Charcas, is unacceptable. This conflict must be resolved immediately. Failure to do so will result in the territory where the sacred cactus is currently growing being granted to Silver Majestic, a Canadian mining company.

According to the CRW, the land conflict os not only located in the Witikuta region. In 2007, the community filled 47 lawsuits to recover around 10,500 hectares; on September 22, 2016, the first restitution of the territory was forcebly executed without warranty of the rule of law nor the neccesary security, putting at risk the integrity of the people and the exact execution of the territory. As of 2017, the irregular possesors began to impede the executions violently, closing roads and threatening various people, which is why is not been possible to execute the other judgments won. Currently, there are 54 lawsuits filed, 35 won, and only fout were restituted. In 2022, a Wixárika caravan demanded an audience with Mexico´s president to resolce the agrarian conflict.

Mexican Legal Framework

As previously mentioned, the shift in the language during the nineteenth century did not change the colonial approach regarding the ritual uses of peyote among indigenous peoples: "The language that resulted was a hybrid that blurred the medical, the religious and the moral: peyote was a plague, a heathen cult and a ménage to civilization. Texts of these era's anti-drug campaigns were incorporated into the international treatises of the twentieth century and still underpin them today. The 1961 United Nations Single Convention on Drugs, the foundation of the global drug control system, is unique among UN documents in its use of the word evil to describe the dangers that drugs pose, a term not deployed in its official definition of child abuse, terrorism or genocide."[32]

Under Article 245 of the General Health Law, entheogens and psychedelic substances are categorized as Schedule 1 in Mexico. This results in a strict prohibition on using, distributing, and researching psilocybin or mushroom species and mescaline or *Lophophora williamsii*. However, after the signature, there are exceptions for religious and ceremonial purposes for indigenous groups with ancestral ties to these mushrooms or cacti, as specified in Article 195 bis of the Penal Code.

In spite the fact of this strict prohibition, the decline of peyote due to overexpliotation for ceremonial purposes, illegal terade to the U.S., psychedelic tourism, mining and climate change caused indigenous peoples to request special protection. In response the Mexican government promulgated a legal framwork entitled NOM-059-SEMARNAT-2010, which classified peyote as a threatened and protected species within Mexico. This measure was a palliative resource to face the decline of peyote and the damage to the ecosystem. This norm prohibits the exportation of peyote to foreign countries while permitting Mexican indigenous peoples an exemption for the ceremonial use of peyote. The NOM-059-SEMARNAT-2010 is the official norm issued by the national authorities in matters of biodiversity conservation. It establishes a methodology to evaluate the risk of extiction of native species and presents a list of species that must be considered for conservation; this norm establishes four categories of protection that, in order of lesser to greater importance, are: Subject to Special Protection, Threatened, Endangered, and Probably Extinct in the Wild. Since the begining of the first NOM (1994) peyote species have been included in their lists and only have been corrected the taxonomy and included nrw synonims regarding the protection of peyote.

Several factors, including land development, poaching, psychedelic tourism and incirrected harvesting techniques have causes Mexico´s declining peyote population. Like the effects on other plant and animal species, global warming also contributes to the decline of peyote. According to journalism research up to 5,000 tourists, a year visit north Mexico to take peyote cactus. Many of these foreign tourists and their tour guides lack knowledge about peyote conservation. They are not concerned about harvesting peyote correctly so the plant can rejuvenate; instead they dig up the entire cactus to terminate the plant completely. Due to this number of factors, the implementation of cross-cultural policies is required. The market and trade will not dissapear with prohibitionist policies and palliative exemptions, so a broader regulation focused on ecological sustainability must be developed. Indigenous knowlege and scientific research could help overcome the peyote population´s decline. Educational programs with culturally appropriate frameworks and a collaborative approach with indigenous communities and researchers could be applied.

In Mexico, proposals have been made to change the legal framework governing natural resources.[33] Armando Contreras Castillo presented one proposal to the Chamber of Deputies. Although it was published in the Legislative Gazette (March 3, 2021), it never reached the plenary for voting and remained unresolved. The proposal notes that out of 4,500 potential plants, only 5% have therapeutic uses, and no sustainable management plans are in place. The proposal questions whether the *Lophophora williamsii* cactus and psilocybin mushrooms should be classified as Schedule I drugs with little or no therapeutic value under Article 245 of the General Health Law. Instead, the proposal suggests reclassifying them as Schedule 4 drugs under the 1971 Convention on Psychotropic Substances.

The reclassification aims to eliminate the structural barriers that impede the development of scientific research programs, promote the recognition of ancestral knowledge, and investigate its potential therapeutic uses. It also suggests considering the knowledge and ceremonies linked to *Lophophora williamssii* and psilocybin mushrooms as part of the nation's biocultural heritage. The initiative highlights the historical use of peyote and mushrooms for ceremonial and therapeutic purposes and the Inquisition's first decree that made their consumption a criminal offense. The criminalization of these natural substances is what led to prohibiting policies. Furthermore, their classification under Schedule 1 of Article 245 of the General Health Law has impeded scientific research.

This proposed bill aims to reevaluate the classification of peyote and mushrooms as substances with little to no therapeutic value, considering the extent of their misuse and determining whether they pose a public health concern. However, it fails to mention the amount of funding allocated by the Mexican State for mental health, particularly for treatments targeting resistant depression. It neglects to highlight the potential cost savings. Additionally, the proposal falls short of emphasizing the significance of these treatments in palliative medicine.[34]

The second proposal was presented by attorney Jorge Mario Pardo Rebolledo, an activist of the organization *Latinoamérica por una Política Sensata de Drogas*.[35] He presented a request for legal protection 374/2020, arguing his self-ascription as indigenous. However, the proposal was rejected by the first chamber of the Suprema Corte de Justicia de la Nación (SCJN), which determined that this attorney did not accredit his self-ascription. In that sense, it determined that his rights were not being violated, since the Penal Code in force (article 195 bis) mentions that mainly indigenous peoples have the right to the ritual and ceremonial uses of psilocybin mushrooms and peyote.

The SCJN ruled that the complainant's right to self-ascription was not violated. The complaint was based on the request to use psilocybin and mescaline for personal, cultural, and therapeutic purposes. However, the court found that consuming these substances based on ideological affinity or identity alone cannot be recognized as self-ascription. The SCJN also stated that their decision did not go against Article 2 of the Mexican Constitution and that the alleged violation of the complainant's rights was invalid. Concerning the criteria to determine which identity expressions are compatible with the values and the right to participate in cultural life. Since the self-ascription with an ethnoreligious group was not accredited, there were no elements to analyze, particularly a custom or tradition associated with peyote and mushrooms.

Conclusion

In conclusion, prohibition policies significantly impact three fundamental rights: the right to health, the rights of indigenous peoples, the right to cognitive freedom. To protect these rights, creating a legal framework that ensures their safeguarding is essential. Prohibition policies fail to guarantee the right to health when citizens cannot choose the treatment that best suits their physiological and mental conditions. Decolonizing peyote politics involves decriminalizing its cultural uses, such as medical, ceremonial, scientific, philosophical, and ludic, to achieve a better regulation.

Decolonization is attached to decriminalization; for instance, indigenous rights face lack of acknowledgement due to the absence of legal frameworks that recognizes the significance of their ancestral knowledge, despite some palliative exceptions in the U.S. and Mexico. Regarding indigenous rights, a decolonial approach has to take into account two significant issues: a) Wixárika people urge the Mexican government to create a federal protection area for its sacred territory and cultural-historical routes where peyote grows and b) Mexican indigenous peoples have demanded that the U.S. government legalize peyote cultivation for NAC members. Indigenous peoples condemn the exportation of peyote by mestizos and foreigners including NAC members, and strongly recommend that the U.S. government encourage management plants for the preservation and collection of peyote that are appropriate to the Texas region. As a result, it is possible to outline six proposals to achieve a decolonial approach to peyote politics in Mexico. For instance, it will be helpful:

1. Recognition of Wirikuta as a protected area and applying growing and preservation programs to preserve the ecosystem and natural habitat of the cactus.
2. Recognition of indigenous knowledge and rituals as cultural heritage according to UNESCO standards.
3. Legalize peyote cultivation in the U.S. for the NAC members to stop the overexploitation of Mexican peyote areas.
4. Establish a temporary closure 10-15 years before any attempt to decriminalize or reschedule it to guarantee the growing and preservation of the cactus in its natural habitat.
5. Reschedule synthetic mescaline for therapeutic, scientific, and philosophical research.
6. Decriminalize the homegrowing, collective gardens and green-houses cultivation to reduce the impact of psychedelic tourism and the spiritual market.

This chapter demonstrated how the current legal framework and prohibitionists policies are attached to colonialism. Another significant featureis recognizing that peyote among indigenous peoples is not a way of alienation; conversely, it is a way to cope with economic and social conditions to transform it, as the two examples analyzed demosntrated. Decolonizing peyote politics requires a paradigm shift, not only in the legal or political arena but also within cultural and philosophical spheres. However, it is crucial to highlight that any decriminalization or rescheduling attempt must be sure not to reproduce neo-colonial mechanisms.

Cross-cultural preservation and educational programs must be developed, and land conflicts must be solved in order to reach an integral solution to the cultural genocide caused by the lack of recognition of indigenous knowledge and extractivist endeavors. Indigenous peoples face higher rates of suicide than the average population in the U.S. and Mexico; also, racism, discrimination and lack of services such as pipeline water, schools and hospitals are issues of concern, so a decolonial approach has to move forward from a naive idealization or spiritual exoticism, to develop a reciprocal dialogue ro share the benefits from Western culture, but also to learn from the wisdom and experience of indigenous knowledge. Applying better public policies is closely related to the democratization of knowledge and the rise of an ecological consciousness. The challenge for the following years is to encourage peyote preservation while taking to account indigenous rights, the right to health of non-indigenous populations, and the right to science and cognitive liberty of scholars and research institutions.

Notes

1   J. Muneta (2020, p. 148).
2   A. Quijano (2007).
3   Ch. Hauskeller et al. (2022).
4   A. Escohotado (1999).
5   D. Negrín (2020).
6   B. de Sahagún (1975).

7   F. Hernández (2015).
8   A. Morales-Sarabia (2014).
9   M. Jay (2019).
10 O. González Romero (2021).
11 P. González Casanova (2006).
12 M. Jay (2019, p. 39).
13 A. Escohotado (1999).
14 J. Muneta (2020, p. 140).
15 C. Lumholtz (2006).
16 A. Moszowski (2010).
17 A. Escohotado (1999, pp. 603–608).
18 J. Muneta (2020, p. 141).
19 J. Muneta (2020, p. 145).
20 A. Dawson (2018, 58).
21 T. Maroukis (2013, p. 162).
22 J. D. Calabrese (2013, p. 91).
23 R. Wagner (1975, p. 204).
24 A. Dawson (2015, p. 127).
25 M. de la Garza (2012).
26 G. Samorini (2019).
27 R. Narváez Elizondo (2018, p. 189).
28 F. Benítez (1968).
29 M. Fresán Jiménez (2002).
30 I. Álvarez (2014).
31 J. Muneta (2020, p. 162).
32 M. Jay (2019, p. 39).
33 J. Anaya (2021).
34 Cámara de Diputados (2021).
35 J. Anaya (2021).

References

Aguirre Beltrán, G. (1963). *Magia y medicina. Los procesos de aculturación en la estructura colonial*. Instituto Nacional Indigenista.

Álvarez, I. (2014). *El Frente en Defensa de Wirikuta: la construcción de lo sagrado*. Pacarina del Sur. Revista de pensamiento Crítico Latinoamericano. http://pacarinadelsur.com/dossier-12/977-el-frente-en-defensa-de-wirikuta-la-construccion-de-lo-sagrado.

Anaya, J. (2021). *Dos proyectos quisieron cambiar el estatus legal del peyote y los hongos en México*. Chacruna Institute for Psychedelic Plant Medicines. https://chacrunala.org/decriminalizacion_hongos_peyote_mexico/

Benítez, F. (1968). *En la tierra mágica del peyote*. Ediciones Era.

Calabrese, J.D. (2013). *A Different Medicine. Postcolonial Healing in the Native American Church*. Oxford University Press.

Cámara de Diputados (2021). *Gaceta Parlamentaria, XXVI, 5731-V*, 3 de marzo de. http://gaceta.diputados.gob.mx/Gaceta/64/2021/mar/20210303-V.html#Iniciativa6.

Dawson, A. (2015). Salvador Roquet, María Sabina, and the trouble with Jipies. *Hispanic American Historical Review* 95 (1): 103–133.

Dawson, A. (2018). *The Peyote Effect. From the Inquisition to the War on Drugs*. University of California Press.

De la Garza, M. (2012). *Sueño y éxtasis. Visión chamánica de los nahuas y los Mayas*. UNAM-Fondo de Cultura Económica.

Escohotado, A. (1999). *Historia general de las drogas*. Espasa Calpe.

Fresán Jiménez, M. (2002). *Nierika. Una ventana al mundo de los antepasados*. Consejo Nacional para la Cultura y las Artes.

Furst, P. (1976). *Hallucinogens and Culture*. Chandler and Sharp Publishers.

González Casanova, P. (2006). Colonialismo interno (una redefinición). In *La teoría marxista hoy*. In A. Borón, J. Amadeo y S. González (Eds). CLACSO.

González Romero, O. (2021). *Tlamatiliztli: la sabiduría del pueblo nahua. Filosofía intercultural y derecho a la tierra*. Leiden University Press.

Hauskeller, Ch., Artinian, T., Fiske, A., et al. (2023). Decolonization is a metaphor towards a different ethic. The case from psychedelic studies. *Interdisciplinary Science Reviews* 48: 5: 732–751. https://doi.org/10.108 0/03080188.2022.212278.

Hernández, F. (2015). *Historia Natural de la Nueva España*. Universidad Nacional Autónoma de México. http:// www.franciscohernandez.unam.mx/home.html.

Jay, M. (2019). *Mescaline a Global History of the First Psychedelic*. Yale University Press.

Lumholtz, C. (2006 [1902]). *Unknown Mexico*. Vol. 1. Nueva York: Scribner.

Maroukis, T.C. (2013). The Peyote Controversy and the Demise of the Society of American Indians. *The American Indian Quarterly* 37 (3): 159–180.

Morales-Sarabia, A. (2014). The culture of peyote: between divination and decease in early modern New Spain. In Slater, J. (Ed.), *Medical Cultures of the Early Modern Spanish Empire*, pp. 21–29. Taylor & Francis.

Moszowski, A. (2010). *Los ojos imperiales de un coleccionista mercenario: Carl Sofus Lumholtz y El México Desconocido*. M.A.Thesis. UNAM. https://ru.atheneadigital.filos.unam.mx/jspui/handle/FFYL_UNAM/5505.

Muneta, J.D. (2020). Peyote Crisis Confronting Modern Indigenous Peoples. The Declining Peyote Population and a Demand for Conservation. *American Indian Law Journal* 9 (1): 134–181.

Nájera, P. (n.d.). Peyote de Querétaro es declarado en peligro de extinción. *Peyote News* 1 (1). https://hable mosdehikuri.com/2021/08/21/peyote-noticias-volume-1-no-1/ (accessed 15 January 2024).

Narváez Elizondo, R., Silva Martínez, L.E., and Breen Murray, W. (2018). El brebaje del desierto: usos del peyote (*Lophophora Williamsii, Cactaceae*) entre los cazadores recolectores de Nuevo León. *Desde el herbario CICY* 10: 186–196.

Negrín, D. (June 9, 2020). *Colonial Shadows in the Psychedelic Renaissance*. Chacruna Institute for Psychedelic Plant Medicines. https://chacruna.net/colonial-shadows-in-the-psychedelic-renaissance/

Neurath, J. (2005). *Materiales del arte huichol. Artes de México*, 75: 26–30.

Quijano, A. (2007). Coloniality and modernity/rationality. *Cultural Studies* 21 (2–3): 168–178. https://doi. org/10.1080/09502380601164353.

Ruiz de Alarcón, H. (1984). *The Treatise of the Heathen Superstitions That Today Live Among the Indians Native to This New Spain*. University of Oklahoma Press.

de Sahagún, B. 1499–1590. (1950–1982). *Florentine Codex: General History of the Things of New Spain* (trans C.E. Dibble and A.J.O. Anderson). University of Utah Press.

Samorini, G. (2019). The oldest archeological data evidencing the relationship of Homo sapiens with psycho-active plants: a worldwide overview. *Journal of Psychedelic Studies* 3 (2): 63–80.

Tuck, E. and Yang, K.W. (2012). Decolonization is not a metaphor. *Decolonization: Indigeneity, Education and Society* 1 (1): 1–40.

Tuhiwai, L. (2007). *Decolonizing methodologies. research and Indigenous Peoples*. Zed Books.

Wagner, R. (1975). *Some Pragmatic Aspects of Navajo Peyotism. Plains anthropol*. Vol. 20, 197–205.

Index

Abya Yala, 2–3, 21, 66–67, 179
Abysmal invisible line, Abysmal thought, 150
Adorno, 39
Aesthetic object, 152–153
Aesthetics, 30, 33–6, 38–39, 133, 146–147, 150–153
Africana philosophy, 3, 92–93
Aguilar, M., 143
Ahmed, S., 80
Alexander, M. J., 78
Algerian National Liberation Front, 15
Alienation, 14, 19, 66–67, 106, 118, 152, 206
Alighieri, Dante, 120
Alterity, 5, 56, 61, 64–67, 69, 112, 118, 130–134
   anthropological alterity, 131
Al-Yabri, 55
Amadiume, I., 79
Amaru II, T., 18
AMLO, 293
Analectic method, 68–69
Analogical pluriverse, 130
Ancalao, L., 124–125
Áñez, J., 120
Animal liberation, 174, 177–178
Animal rights, *animalistas*, 4, 7, 173–179
Anslinger, H. J., 202
Anthropocene, 57, 70, 131
Anti-black police violence, 1, 2, 91
Anti-combative, 4, 12, 23
Antidrug crusades, 199–201
Anti-modern, 56
Anti-phenomena, 36–39
Anti-punitivism, anti-carcelism, 177
Anti-racism documents, 87, 89–92, 103
Antoinette, M., 145
Anzaldúa, G., 66, 112–113
Apple, M., 123
Arendt, H., 161, 166

Arguedas, J. M., 40
Assimilation stage, 12, 43
Assistance networks, 151
Auge, M., 147, 148
Ausgang, 146
Authenticity, 12–13, 16–17, 20–23, 52, 71, 164
Autonomous communities, 183, 192
Autopoiesis, 65, 79–80
Awakening, Reconquest, 146–150, 154, 156

Bambara, T. C., 79
Baquedano, General, statue, 150, 152–153
Barthes, R., 93
Bartlett, M., 186
Bastidas, M., 18, 21
Beauvoir, S., 66
Beltrán, Dr. G. A., 149, 199
Benítez, F., 203
Benjamin, W., 39, 170
Bernal, 48
Biden, President J., 2, 163, 168–169
Big Ag, 175
Binary, 31, 33, 40, 53, 67, 69–70, 73–74, 76–77, 79
Biological, 63, 73–75, 77–80
Black, G., 201
Blackhouse Kollective, 23
Black Indigenous People of Color (BIPOC), 87, 94–95, 99, 103
Black legend, 47, 54
Black Lives Matter, 2, 5, 87, 89–91, 93, 97, 107
Blackness, 14–15, 18, 21, 107, 121
Blake, J., 91
Blanquemiento, 52
Bolívar, S., 2, 51
Bolsonaro, J., 179
Bondy, A. S., 4, 12, 14–23
Boomerang effect, 186
Boric, G., 6, 145

INDEX

Bourdieu, P., 136
Braudel, 54
Brecht, 39
Breonna Taylor Day, 5, 96–103
Brown, E., 79
Bureau of Indian Affairs, 201
Butler, J., 66, 80

Calderon Hinojosa, F., 186
Caliban, 76, 80, 161
Camacho Solis, M., 185
Campos, 166
Cannabis, 205
Capetillo, L., 113
Carabineros, 144, 155
Caravans, 7, 162, 167–168, 188
Cardenas, 193
Carlos V, 49
Cartels, 165, 167, 168
Casalla, M., 14
Castillo, A. C., 204
Castillo, L., 151
Castro-Gomez, S., 166
Categorical imperative, 130
CBP One, 163, 166
Center-periphery tension, 116
Centro de Estudios Públicos (CEP), 145
Ceremonial uses of psychoactive substances, 7, 197–198, 201,
    203–206
Cerro Quemado, 203
Chevato, G., 201
Chilean Constitution, 6, 154–156
Chomsky, N., 188
Christendom, 44, 47, 55
Claim to goodness, 130, 132
Clarke, C., 79
Class struggle, 64
COCOPA, San Andres agreements, 185, 190
Cohen, 80
Cold War, 51–52
Coloniality of being, 7, 74, 164
Coloniality of gender, 15, 36
Coloniality of knowledge, 30
Coloniality of power, 3, 4, 29–40, 162, 164, 174
Colonization as global catastrophe, 14, 15
Colonized intellectuals, 4, 12, 14, 89
Columbus, C., Colon, C., 2, 18, 51, 101
Combative decoloniality, 4, 12, 15–16, 20, 22
Combat stage, 12
Cometa, P., 149
Communiqués, 128, 187, 189, 190, 192, 193
Communist party, 156
Compassion, 132
Conquest, 3, 17, 44, 47, 50, 51, 53, 55, 118–119, 146–156
Conquest of the desert, 124
Consciousness, 17, 19, 21–23, 33–35, 37–40, 45, 51, 55–56, 66,
    108–109, 111, 128, 162, 173, 190
Continental philosophy, 33
Contingency, 63, 67, 79
Coordinadora de Asembleas Territoriales (CAT), Coordinating
    Committee of Territorial Assemblies, 148

Coordinadora Feminista 8M, 143
Copernican Revolution, 75
COVID-19, 91–92, 144, 163, 168, 206
Credible fear, 165
Criollismo, 51
Crisis of Marxism, 136
Critical consciousness, 33, 108–109, 111
Critical race theory, 3, 103
Critical Social Sciences, 6, 130
Critical theory, 11, 108
Crusade, 56, 199–201
Cuadra, P. A., 52
Cultural affirmation, 45–46, 53, 57
Culture of poverty, 91
Curiel, O., 66

Darwin, 63, 75, 77
Dasein, 164
Daturas, 198
Death drive, 128
de Ayala, F. G. P., 20, 92
Decolonial reason, 4
Decolonial turn, 3, 4, 11, 13–15, 17, 20, 30, 35
Decolonization of consciousness, 17
Decolonize This Place, 4, 23
de Dios Rodriguez Puebla, J., 199
Defund the pólice, 2, 89
de Las Casas, B., 17–20, 23, 47, 51, 54, 75, 92
de Quiroga, V., 92
Descartes, 38, 53
de Sepúlveda, J. G., 17, 19, 51, 92
de Sousa Santos, B., 146, 150–151
Díaz Cepeda, 166
Diego Fernandez de Cevallos, 186
Discovery, 2, 17, 20–21, 113
Disposable, 161, 162
Diversity hires, 93
Divine transcendence, 20
Dogs, 174–175, 177–178
Don Diego, 18
Drive for alterity, 65
Drug policy, 7, 197
Dussel, E., 5, 6, 20–22, 54–55, 61, 116–120, 122, 124–125,
    129–130, 136, 147, 150, 154, 162, 164, 166, 170,
    174–175, 177–178

Ecology of knowledge, 160
Edict of the Inquisition of 1620, 198–199
Education, 3–6, 32–33, 38, 52, 89, 92, 99, 101, 103, 106, 108,
    109, 111, 116–117, 119, 134, 142–144, 199
Ego cogito, 5, 31, 61
Ego conquiro, 164–165
Ejército Zapatista de Liberación Nacional (EZLN), Zapatista Army of
    National Liberation, 7, 21, 127–128, 182–193
Eliso de Medinilla, B., 69
El Tiempo, 185, 187
Employment Division of Oregon v. Smith, 201–202
Encounter with the face of the other, face-to-face, 69, 134,
    146–147, 167, 178
Engels, F., 63
English Industrial Revolution, 48, 50

"En la lucha," 15
Enlightenment, 46–47, 55, 75, 200
Environmental activism, environmentalism, *ambientalistas*, 176–178
Environmental cyber-resistance, 177
Epistemic catastrophe, 92
Epistemic racism, 179
Epistemological resistance, 6, 116, 127, 132
Equity, 94, 110, 122–123
Erotic, eros, familiar, 5, 36, 61–71, 117–118, 120, 132, 135
  of liberation, 61–71
Espinoza, Y., 66
Estar-siendo, 37
Ethical criteria, 69
Ethics, 3, 6, 7, 70, 92, 111, 118–119, 129–130, 136–137, 164,
    170, 173–179
  animal ethics, 173–179
  discourse ethics, 170
  of neoliberalism, 129
  of war, 164
Ethnic studies, 94–95, 102–103
Eurocentrism, 4, 11, 44, 46–57, 91–95, 108, 119, 124
Evil, 204
Existentialism, 16
Exteriority, 20–21, 54, 56, 65–71, 119, 131

Fanon, F., 3, 4, 11–23
Federal Bureau of Narcotics, 202
Federal Education Law in Argentina, No. 24,195, 121
Feminism, feminist, 5, 61–64, 66, 68–71, 73, 75, 77–81, 92, 93,
    107, 112, 113, 143–144, 148–150, 155, 162, 179
Fernández Retamar, R., 2
Fetishization, 45, 63, 65, 147
Field work, 132
First Line, 150–151
Flags, 149, 151, 153, 183
Floyd, G., 5, 87, 91, 107, 112
Fox, V., 186–188, 192–193
Freire, P., 109, 120, 131, 142
French famine, 145
French Revolution, 145
Frente Zapatista de Liberación Nacional (FZLN), 186
Freud, S., 77, 78
Friar Bernardino de Sahagún, 198
Fuentes, C., 117
Furst, P., 203

Gaitán, Á., 174
Galindo, A. F., 40
Galindo, M., 68
Gaos, J., 16, 17
Garcia-Marquez, G., 39
García, M. E., 178
García Peña, L., 3
Gargallo, F., 66
General Health Law, 204–205
Geneva War conventions, 190
Genocide, extermination, epistemicide, 45, 53, 75, 99, 119,
    124–125, 152, 186, 204
Geopolitical analysis, 131
Gilio-Whitaker, D., 111
Glissant, 111

Globalization, 4, 7, 11, 21, 35, 38, 43, 56, 74, 131, 183, 188, 190,
    193, 197
Globalized trade of endemic plants, 7, 197
Gonzalez-Duarte, C., 177
Gonzalez Garrido, P., 185
Gordon, L., 91
Gracia, J. J. E., 93
Grandy, J., 97
Grosfoguel, R., 119–120, 163
Guerilla, 185, 187
Guerra sucia, 186
Guevara, E. "Che," 15, 17, 19

Habermas, 53
Haitian revolution, 3, 51
Halberstam, J., 80
Hale, J., 80
Half-Moon ritual, 201
Hanisch, C., 169
Hatuey, 17–23
Haynes, T., 74–79, 81
Hegel, 31, 46, 48, 49, 66
Hegelian dialectic, 66
Hegemonic radical, 108
Heidegger, 25, 92, 137, 164
Hellenocentrism, 48–49
Heritage months, 99
Hermeneutics, 4, 29, 66, 80, 91
Heteronormativity, 67, 79
Hikuri, 202–203
Historical linearity (diffusionism), 46, 48, 49, 54
Hodge, M., 79
Holy children, 199
Homophobia, 78
Hong Bao, 50
Hoplites, 18
Horizon of liberation, 5, 61
Horizontal spaces, 5, 61
Housing and Urbanization Service (SERVIU), 143
Huchim, E., 184–185
Huerta, General, 191–192

Iberian culture, 44, 92, 93
ICE, 103
Ideology, 47, 51, 53, 67, 119, 183, 188, 190, 200
Idolatry, superstition, 151, 197
Imaginaries, imago, 30, 33–40, 109, 118, 146–147, 150, 154
IMF, 188
Individualism, 14, 18, 147, 149
Inoculation, 90, 93, 95, 99
Insurgency, 5, 91, 101, 128–129
Intercultural exchange, 131, 134
Interiority, 34, 35, 129, 130, 134
International Organization for Migration (IOM), 163
Intersubjective community, 33, 36, 127, 131, 133, 164
Irigaray, L., 78, 80
Islamophobia, 49, 53
Itihāsa, 49

Jacobo, C. R., 184
January 1st, 1994, 184, 186, 189

INDEX

Jara, V., 149
Jímenez, M. F., 203
Judeo-Christian religions, 33, 38, 49

Kant, 55, 136, 146
Kast, J. A., 145–146
Kelley, V., 97
Kierkegaard, 130
Kimmerer, R. W., 111
Kinship technologies, 105
Kuhn, T., 191
Kuna, 45

La Colectiva Feminista en Construcción, 4, 23
Lagarde, M., 127
Lagunes, A., 205
La Jornada, 185, 187
Land, 3, 20, 36, 52, 97, 106–108, 111, 133, 142, 165, 183–184, 188, 191, 200, 203
la paperson, 106–109, 111
Larraín, F., 145
Las Tesis, 149
León, P., 174–176, 179
Lerner, G., 62–64
Levinas, E., 20–21, 62, 164, 178
Liberal Academy, 11, 13
Liberating philosophy, 15
Limpieza de sangre, 92
Logging, 176
Lorde, A., 64, 66
Louis XVI, 145
LSD, 7, 197
Lugones, M., 36, 37, 66, 162
Lukacs, 39
Lumholz, C., 200

Machismo, 64
Macri, M., 120
Madero, G., 192
Madonado-Torres, N., 164
Manicheanism, 14–15, 164
Man 1, homo politicus, 75–77
Man 2, homo economicus, 75–77
Mapuche, Mapuce, Rarámuri, 45, 124, 142, 151, 152
Maquilas, maquiladora, 7, 165
Marakame, shaman, 203
Marcos, Subcommondante, 7, 183–193
Martínez, J., 152–153
Marxism, 55, 134, 136, 145, 166
Marx, K., 67, 134
Masculine hegemony, 65
Material death, 44
Maturana, H., Verela, F., 65
Mayol, A., 145
Mendoza, J. J., 166
Men-not, 165
Mental illness, 8, 198
Menzies, G., 50
Mescaline, 7, 197, 200, 204–206
Mestizaje, 20–23, 51, 183

Mestizo-filia, 20
Metaphorization of decolonization, 111
Metropolis, 47, 108
Mexican Press, 187
Mignolo, W., 3, 16, 164, 174–175
Migrant Protocol Protection (MPP), 163
Migrants, 4, 6, 7, 144, 161–170
  bad, 161, 166
  disobedient, 161, 167
  good, 161, 166–167
Ming dynasty, 50
Mining, 176, 203–204
Miranda, 76, 81
Moctezuma, 20–21
Modern scientism, 131
Modern secularism, 75
Modern/western homo academicus, 11
Montafio, O., 192
Moraga, C., 66
Mora, J. M. L., 199
Morel, C., 146
Mother-wife, 67
Mujeres Creando en Bolivia, 66
Muñoz, F. Y., 190
Murena, H., 52
Myth, 31, 34, 37–40, 49, 63, 65, 124–125, 147, 149, 150, 152–154, 183, 190, 192

NAFTA, 183–185, 188
National Indigenous Council, 204
National Institute of Human Rights (INDH), 150
National Migration Institute, Instituto Nacional de Migración, (INM), 168–169
Native American Church (NAC), 201–202
Nazism, 53
Needham, 50
Negrín, D., 203
Neo-colonialist, 165
Neoconservatism, 120
Neoliberal paradigm, 7, 183
Neoliberal turn, 106
Neo-Zapatismo, 182, 188, 191
Neurath, J., 203
Nietzche, 53
Noncombative, 4, 12–13, 22–23
Non-places, 147–150, 153, 154, 169
Nos-otros, 38
Null population, 161–162
Nzegwu, N., 79

Object of study, 6, 127, 130
Occupy Movement, 193
Okupa, 169
Ollas Comunes, 148
Ololiuhqui, 198–199
Oniric, oneiros, dream, 35
Orientalism, 49
Ornamental multiculturalism, 3, 89, 93
Ortega, M., 109–110
"the other side of the line." 146, 150–151, 154

Overmodernity, 147
Oyĕwùmí, O., 79

Pachamama, 130
Pacification, 44, 124
Pagan, 75–76, 200
PAN, 193
"Pa' Pasar," 169
Pappas, G., F., 109–110
Paradigm of war, 20
Paradox of colonialism, 200
Paradox of criminalizing nature, 197
Parka, 141–142, 153
Parker, Q., 201
Participatory proto-diagnosis, 133
Patriarchal epistemology, 68
Patriarchal hegemony, 63
Patriarchy, 62–71, 79
Patrón, 30–36, 39
Paz, O., 52
Pedagogy, 13, 51, 52, 108, 117–120, 122, 124
Pereda, 166
Pérez, C., 145
Pervasiveness of death, 12
Petras, J., 192
Peyote, peyotism, peyote cult, 7, 197–206
Phallocentrism, phallocracy, 67, 69, 118
Phenomenology, 16, 92, 164
Piñera, S., 144–146
Plan de Ayala, 192
Plaza de la Dignidad, Dignity Square, 148, 150, 153–155
Pluriverse, pluriversalism, pluriversalist, pluriversality, 6, 45–46, 48, 56, 130–131, 134, 149, 154, 179
Political actor, 136, 161–162, 166–167, 170
Political assassinations, 185
Political feasibility, 45
Political philosophy, 3, 54
Politics of punishment, 198
Pollos, pollero, 165
Polychromy, 144, 154–155
Ponce, J., 187–189
Popular veganism, 178–179
Post-continental philosophy, 13
Post-modern, 45, 48, 53–54, 56, 136, 192
Posturing, 109–110
Praxis of liberation, 128, 134, 136
PRD, 193
Precombat stage, 12
Pre-trial detention, 179
PRI, 185–187, 193
Primitive accumulation, 49, 54, 200
Privatization of education, 116
PRO, 122
Proceso magazine, 185, 187
Prohibition law, prohibition policy, 197, 200–201, 206
Province, 47
Psilocybin mushrooms, 7, 197–199, 202, 204–205
Psychedelic-assisted therapy, 205–206
Psychedelic renaissance, 8, 198, 201
Public Education network, 121

Puebla-Panama Plan, Mérida Initiative, 128, 199
Pueblo originario, 44, 51, 52, 55

Quijano, A., 3, 4, 29–40

Rabinovich, 166
Racial illiteracy, 95
Ramose, 13, M.
Ramos, R., 17
Rarámuri, 45
Rational point zero, 39
Rebeldía magazine, 190
Reclassification, 204–206
Reed Sandoval, A., 166
Re-education, 32, 34, 38
Reglamento Federal de Toxicomanas (Federal Drug Addiction Regulations), 202
Re-identification, 32, 34–37
Reinaga, F., 21–22
Religious evangelization enterprise, 198
Religious Freedom Restoration Act (RFRA), 201–202
Religious syncretism, spiritual synergy, 199
Reoccupation, 109
Re-patriation of Indigenous life and land, 111
Resettlement, 109
Reverse empiricism, 90–91, 94–95
Rights of indigenous peoples, 197, 204, 206
Right to cognitive liberty, 197, 206
Right to health, 197, 206
Rivera Cusicanqui, S., 5
Rivera, O., 29, 30, 33
Ross, J., 184
Rubin, G., 62–63
Ruíz de Alarcón, H. R., 199
Rushdie, 49

Saberes, 13
Sacrifice zones, 144
Sanctuary, 149
Sandoval, C., 93
Santa Rosa, 199
Saramago, J., 188
Sartre, J.P., 17
Scalia, A., 202
Scannone, J. C., 164
Schutte, O., 112
Scyborg, 111
Second World War, World War II, 39, 53, 202
Seeds of the Virgin, 199
Self-diagnosis, 134
Senghor, L., 17
Settler-native-slave triad, 106–107, 109, 112
Sex-gender systems, 62–63, 69
Sexual control of bodies, 36, 63–64
Shakespeare, 76
Sharpe, C., 11
Silver Majestic, 204
Silvestri, L., 71
Simulacra, 33
Simultaneous temporality, 35, 38–39

Sinocentrism, 51
Smith, Ad., 51
Smith, Al., 201–202
Snorton, C. R., 79
Social discredit, 121
Social Outburst, estallido social, 143–145
Social Unity Union Block, Social Unity, Unidad Social, 148, 155
Solidarity, 3, 23, 80, 111, 132–133, 136, 170, 186–187, 193
Somatic mode of difference, 77
Soto Paillalef, M., 152–153
Space of non-being, 147
Specialists, 14, 62, 90–94
State-issued identification, 168
State of emergency, 3, 91, 170
State of well-being, 122
Stone, S., 79
Subalterity, 45
Subsumption, 66–67
Suicide, 45, 128, 130
Sullivan, S., 99
Suprema Corte de Justicia de la Nación (SCJN), 205
Symbolic death, 44

Teacher's College strike, 143–144
Tea party, 200
Teillier, G., 156
Televisa, 187
Territorial Councils, Territorial Assemblies, 148
Theologies of liberation, 11
Third World Liberation Front, 94
Thomas, G., 79
Title 8, 163
Title 42, 163, 168–169
Token representation, Tokenization, 5, 90–104
Totality, 4, 20, 39, 43, 45, 56–57, 62, 67–71, 80, 118–120
Training-action, 133
Training of local organizers, 133, 135
Trans, 5, 68, 69, 73, 78–81
Trans-Atlantic slave trade, 75
Trans Exclusionary Radical Feminists (TERFS), 78
Transgenerational wounds, 113
Transmodernity, 4, 43, 46, 53–57
Transparency, 112
Trap of critique, 5, 111, 112
Tuck and Yang, 108–112
Turāt, 55
TV Azteca, 187

Ukamau, 143, 155
Unintended consequences, 129–130
Union, 70, 121, 144

United Nations Children's Fund (UNICEF), 163
United Nations Office of the High Commissioner for Human Rights
    (OHCHR), 163
United States-Mexico border, 6–7, 38, 161, 163, 165, 168–169
Universalism, 16, 45–48, 55, 63, 74, 75, 77–78, 80, 118–119,
    129–131, 174–175, 178–179, 182, 183
Un-knowing, 109–110
Urban animals, 176

Valladolid debate of 1550, 51, 75
Varela, 65
Vegans, vegan diet, vegetarians, vegetarian diet, 173–175,
    178, 179
Vespucci, A., 2
Vidal, M. E., 122
Vienna/UN Convention on Psychotropic Substances (1971), 202,
    204–205
Villa, P., 191, 193
Villoro, L., 110
Visibility, invisibility, hypervisibility, 90–96, 106
Vitalism, 16
Vitoria, F., 92
Vrai, 80

Walcott, R., 80, 81
War on drugs, 7, 198, 203
Way of the Cross, 167
Weltanschauung, 13, 14
Westernized university, 3–5, 89–103
White supremacy, 70, 91, 95
White vanguard, 101
Whyte, K., 111
Will to live, life drive, 69–71, 128, 131, 170
Will to power, 131
Wiredu, K., 13
Wirikuta Defense Front, 202–203
Wong, N., 66
Wynter, S., 5, 73–81

Xenophobia, 164

Yang Qing, 50

Zamba, 18, 21
Zapata, General E., 183, 191–193
Zapatista, 7, 21, 110, 127–128, 182–193
Zea, L., 4, 16–17, 22
Zedillo, 185–186, 188
Zheng He, 50
Zhou Man, 50
Zhou Wen, 50